G000243138

NICHOLAS
MEETS
BARRINGTON

NICHOLAS BARRINGTON

NICHOLAS
MEETS
BARRINGTON

The Personal Journey of a Former Diplomat

The Radcliffe Press
LONDON • NEW YORK

An imprint of I.B.Tauris

Published in 2014 by The Radcliffe Press
An imprint of I.B.Tauris & Co Ltd
6 Salem Road, London W2 4BU
175 Fifth Avenue, New York NY 10010
www.ibtauris.com

Distributed in the United States and Canada
Exclusively by Palgrave Macmillan
175 Fifth Avenue, New York NY 10010

Copyright © 2014 Nicholas Barrington

The right of Nicholas Barrington to be identified as the author of this work has
been asserted by him in accordance with the Copyright, Designs and Patents Act
1988.

All rights reserved. Except for brief quotations in a review, this book, or any part
thereof, may not be reproduced, stored in or introduced into a retrieval system, or
transmitted, in any form or by any means, electronic, mechanical, photocopying,
recording or otherwise, without the prior written permission of the publisher.

ISBN: 978 1 78076 800 7

A full CIP record for this book is available from the British Library
A full CIP record is available from the Library of Congress

Library of Congress Catalog Card Number: available

Typeset by Data Standards Ltd, Frome, Somerset, BA11 2RY, UK
Printed and bound by CPI Group (UK) Ltd, Croydon, CR0 4YY

CONTENTS

LIST OF PLATES

ACKNOWLEDGEMENTS AND DEDICATION

I am deeply grateful to Jenny Colling for the time and effort she has taken over a longish period to type this text and prepare it for publication. Sharon Cairns has also helped me greatly. My sister was kind enough to read through the material, but the result is of course entirely my own responsibility. I dedicate this volume to my nephews, godchildren and honorary godchildren who should have their own contribution to make in the world.

Most of the photographs are from private sources. Otherwise I have made acknowledgements where I can. If there are originators I have failed to trace I hope that they will contact me and forgive me.

Any profits the author may derive from these books will be consigned to the Ancient India and Iran Trust in Cambridge.

PREFACE

This book is a strange animal. It is a companion to the more serious account of my life in the Diplomatic Service to be found in *Envoy: A Diplomatic Journey*, by the same publishers. As the preface to that volume explains, I set out originally to write an autobiography which went beyond the story of my Foreign Office postings, relying not only on my memory but on the letters that I had regularly sent home to my parents, which they had kept – the sort of archive that is becoming increasingly rare. I thought that personal material would put my diplomatic life into context. The result would have been, however, a book of excessive girth, and cost.

The account of my childhood and family background, my time at school, in the army and at university has thus been consigned to this volume, along with an account of my main activities since retirement. Recorded here also are incidents and experiences during my career that were peripheral to my work, sometimes matters only briefly hinted at in the main book. There are more indications here of what it was actually like living as a diplomat in different environments around the world, and in London. Some passages may be considered self-indulgent or frivolous. The narrative will inevitably be somewhat disconnected. I am afraid that a comprehensive understanding of my life and views will require perusal of both volumes, which I recognise is an imposition.

The title of this book may be puzzling. I always tried to cooperate with journalists, whose jobs had many similarities with mine. Some inaccuracies by them were inevitable, especially, for instance, when I was travelling to the more remote parts of Pakistan. There would be small items in the local press headed 'Barrington meets Governor', 'The British

High Commissioner calls on the Chief Justice' or 'Sir Nicholas visits University'. One classic headline was 'Nicholas meets Barrington' which suggested to me profound insight about my identity, when I came to think about it! I felt it would be a fitting title for this work.

PART I

1

STARTING AT THE BEGINNING

What memories of early days? The first tableau is from inside a big old-fashioned pram in a small front garden. A marmalade-coloured cat slips through the straggling hedge into the road. There is sunlight (I have always liked ginger cats).

At 'Whitegates', the small house on the west side of Brentwood where I lived until I was about four, I had a small bedroom under the steep roof. There was a corner of the garden that I was told was mine to arrange – I didn't enjoy the responsibility. I played with big Alma Mary from down the road. One day I remember running away (I did it again later in Norfolk), up the road to the house of the lady who kept goldfish. She was very astonished to see me.

'Mollands' was the house that my parents then built in a field the other side of Brentwood. Lots of light came through the big Georgian windows. The garden was virgin rough meadow when we arrived, but it became silky and elegant and full of charm and colour by the time my parents sold the house in 1964. Everyone loved Mollands. It was my home.

At first there was a living-in maid, Kathleen. I wouldn't allow her to bath me – what a little prude! The morning-room with gas fire and bay window was my place downstairs. There I set out my extensive zoo and animal sets, or on the terrace, turning the blocks of Portland stone into fields. I am embarrassed that I still have hanging in my London basement three of my oldest dolls: Pinda the panda, a sad little beast,

Roger, a sort of 'Disneyesque' dog whose clothes I had embroidered, and a wise-looking monkey glove puppet, of some antiquity.

Dear Mary Burns with the brittle metallic laugh was always there washing and ironing in the long kitchen. Her husband Dan was a thin, weedy fellow and her two adopted sons appeared to show little gratitude for the loving affection that Mary had poured out to them for years. But she went on in her cheery indomitable way. She was a Catholic. When she was babysitting, my parents would come home and find me playing cards with her in the bedroom. She used to give us better Christmas presents than we gave her.

The gardener to end all gardeners was Onwin, with his beautiful, grizzled face. He had a way with plants and used to tell me long stories about them and about the insects and the moles. His only fault: he used to leave my father's precious gardens tools all over the place in the damp dew. His wife was crippled with arthritis and was my first acquaintance with suffering. My sister remembers that whenever Onwin didn't want to do something, his excuse was that he had 'a bone in his leg'.

I never liked the later gardeners so much: Polly the tough railway porter; old Nicholas who whistled and spat so much when he talked that you couldn't grasp a word he said. People thought well of him because he came from a good local farmer's family and had come down in the world. He was so pathetically anxious to talk that he bothered me, particularly as I couldn't understand him. And he was such an appalling non-worker. The only thing he could really do, and liked doing, was making bonfires. Each time he borrowed a new box of matches. I used to think that he sold them afterwards. But he could burn up an old root and a heap of damp cuttings without any difficulty.

In later days at Mollands we all depended on Fred, a widower who ought to have married again. He was pleasant, reliable, competent both inside the house (painting rooms with mother) and out, especially with the motor mower and other machines.

* * *

The above was written many years ago when I first had the idea to write about my life (I wish that I had had a 'Fred' character around in later places). But I got no further, and what follows both here and in my diplomatic book is based on my 75-year-old plus memory, helped by letters and other hoarded material, of the main events in my varied life. It is sliced, like a multiple sandwich, into a series of episodes. Essentially it is my own story, the events and personalities that impressed me and seemed worth recording. This volume covers mainly the non-diplomatic stories. I am afraid it will inevitably seem egocentric. I found an appropriate quote in the preface to the third volume of memoirs of my distant relation Sir Jonah Barrington, judge in Ireland in the early nineteenth century: 'It would be a task somewhat difficult for the wisest author that ever put pen to paper, to separate egotism from autobiography.'

I never had the advantage of an unhappy childhood, which I could then blame for my character defects. I was the first child and only son of attractive young parents, whom I judge remained in love with each other until they died. After my father's death my mother found a note addressed to her in his deed box. It said 'My darling wife, this note is just to tell you that my mind is full of the greatness of God's gift to me when he put you at my side. If I should not be here when you read this, please keep this thought of mine in your generous heart. Your Eric.'

Eric and Mildred Barrington came from different families and backgrounds. What brought them together was tennis. My mother was the ninth child and second daughter of a large family. Her grandfather had come from south Wales to establish a woollen retail and wholesale business in London. They bore the unusual surname of Bill. My grandfather, whom I never met, was William Bill, but I doubt that he was ever teased about it since he was something of a Victorian martinet, ruling his gentle diminutive wife, and all his children, with a rod of iron. It was only when I later got access to some of his letters that I discovered that he had been a thoughtful father. William and his brother married two sisters. There were 13 in the other family. I did meet my great-uncle Hubert when I was tiny. He was bearded and upright and opinionated. I never forgot an incident on the terrace of Mollands when uncle Hubert told my mother that he didn't approve of make-up. My mother responded that she didn't much care for beards. It was a dramatic blow for emancipation! I was told later by one of his descendants that fierce old uncle Hubert was terrified of frogs. When some of his children saw toads they had to go and lie down.

My mother's six eldest brothers all fought in World War I. Two of them were killed – or rather one died in France in the terrible flu epidemic immediately after the war. Another, uncle Jack, lost a leg.

My mother was a dark-haired beauty whose confidence didn't come from her education. She only went to art school, where her undoubted skill never got beyond life drawings, etchings and watercolours. But she was cherished by her brothers and was a good athlete. On occasion she would dance for joy in the Mollands' garden and I would try to emulate her. She was particularly close to her next eldest brother, uncle Geoff, who had a strong artistic bent and was a great influence on me in later life. He had clear-cut features and a sallow, almost Spanish complexion. He and my fair-haired father, who had only one, younger, sister, met and became close friends playing tennis at a local club in Gidea Park, east of London commuter territory. That was how my father met my mother. I have a silver cup in my possession inscribed 'Manor Lawn Tennis Club Ladies Single Championships'. It tells the story, because among the names listed are '1928 Miss M A Bill, 1929 Miss M A Bill, 1930 Mrs A R Muir, 1931 Mrs S G Mitchell, 1932 Mrs E A Barrington, 1933 Mrs E A Barrington.' The last entry was 1934, after which perhaps they thought mother deserved to keep the cup. I was born in July of that year.

My father would have loved to have gone to university (I was the first in my family to have that honour) but after City of London School, and training as an accountant, he felt obliged to start earning money straight away. Buying a plot in the Hutton Mount Estate and building Mollands (a name found in a book of old English) must have been a brave step to take. It served the family well, providing the setting for my childhood and that of my sister. A group of local children in the area remain friends to this day. All the Hutton Mount houses had big gardens, some of them with tennis courts. No swimming pools. There are now three other houses on what used to be our garden. The main attraction was a short walk down to Shenfield Station, which had an excellent train service into Liverpool Street. Apart from some local solicitors and estate agents most of the husbands worked in the City, many of them at Lloyds (insurance).

My father's employer was Henry Gardner, a company trading in non-ferrous metals and other commodities around the world. Shortly after World War II started he was whisked off to the Midlands to play a role in the distribution of metals throughout the UK, for defence and other purposes. No one ever talked about such war experiences, but I wish I had probed my father further on precisely what he had been doing. I do remember that in those early days father usually worked on Saturday mornings.

I have become interested in numbers, for example how all our lives around the world are divided into packages of seven (the week), because the Jewish Old Testament said that God had decreed resting on the seventh day. They may have been influenced by the Babylonian respect for seven as the number of main stars identified in the sky. When the Emperor Constantine adopted the Christian religion, the week of seven days was formally instituted and has been internationally accepted over the years. Revolutionary France's attempt to institute a ten-day week proved very unpopular and didn't last long. Most workers in the Western world now, of course, have two days clear holiday out of seven, whereas within living memory many only had one, or one and a half: a tremendous improvement in standards of living and opportunity for leisure.

A key institution in Hutton Mount was Mrs Hall's kindergarten school at the bottom of the hill near the station. All my friends went there at one time or another. Mrs Hall ran a tight ship. I remember her as tall, and dressed in brown, with a large protruding bosom, which was not only a repository for fallen monocles, but under which small children could sometimes get lost out of her line of sight. It was there that I learnt to read and write. There were gangs in the playground. A friend of my mother's from art school, Joan Muriel, had two daughters, one of whom was a bit older, and a gang leader. So I was protected. She was boss of the 'Robins' as opposed to the 'Nightingales'.

One thing I clearly recall is poetry. My mother loved poetry. She used to recite it to me while ironing in the kitchen. At one special event at Mrs Hall's the other children were reciting, with difficulty, little verses about birds sitting on bushes, and I came out with that grand passage from Julius Caesar: 'Friends, Romans, countrymen...'. I can remember the surprise on the faces of teachers and other parents! Later I used to recite passages from the Lays of Ancient Rome, about Horatius who kept the bridge. I made a speciality of the passage that begins 'Meanwhile the Tuscan army, right glorious to behold, came flashing back the noonday light, rank behind rank like surges bright of a broad sea of gold ...'. I was so familiar with Macauley that I joked about it with my aunt Freda, father's sister. When I came to the passage 'For how can man die better than facing fearful odds, for the ashes of his fathers and the temples of his gods', I would say: 'the ashes of his Aunty!' Ever after, Freda's letters to me were signed 'ashes'. Our private joke.

My mother and her women friends in Hutton Mount did their best to educate themselves. There was a group where papers were presented.

When mother gave a talk on poetry I hid myself in the next room, so that when she spoke of Milton, for example, I declaimed the beginning of *Paradise Lost*: 'Of man's first disobedience...' in sonorous voice. It gave them all a start, and I was told a thrill! It was quite early on that I began to keep a commonplace book of poems that appealed to me, that I still maintain. Conventional taste, starting with *Jabberwocky* and bits of Shakespeare and the Bible, becoming more adventurous over the years. Prufock came in early on. But there was much less after Dylan Thomas.

I shall always remember my parents' drawn faces as they listened in my presence to Chamberlain's declaration on the radio that Britain was at war with Germany. It is easy to forget how uncertain the whole future was for people like my parents at that time. My mother told me that they were not sure if they wanted to bring any more children into that world. In the beginning, however, war was exciting for me. At night searchlights dramatically criss-crossed the sky, occasionally picking out some invading aircraft. The doodlebugs, pilotless bombs, made a menacing grinding noise on their way via Essex to London. It was only a little frightening when the noise shut out and one knew they were drifting down to end up in an explosion not too far away. I can still remember the swoop of the warning sirens and the delight of the level all clear. We would go for safety to a tiny lavatory under the stairs.

Eventually, with my father mostly away, we moved from the line of fire, staying first of all on a farm in Devonshire where we had holidayed before. We were there with my mother's sister, and her daughters. I loved the farm and learned a lot: finding free range eggs in the bushes and nettles, scratching with sticks the backs of pigs, watching the milking and trying it myself. Also, the processing of curds and butter. Thick Devonshire cream was often on the menu. There were two groups of chickens on either side of the farm, each with a dominant rooster. I used to be able to imitate the roosters' calls, so that I would set them off competing with each other. This became something of a tour de force at dinner parties in later life. There were several beaches where we could bathe. On one occasion when I was going into the sea I saw with astonishment people rushing out of the water looking scared. Then I noticed a cloud of smoke where a bomb had been dropped on the far side of Salcombe estuary. Our mothers hurried us inside protectively. We were told it had only been a German aircraft pursued – we caught a glimpse of it – and lightening its load.

My uncle Geoff, in America during the war, kept a lot of my mother's letters. They might be checked by censors. Things like bombs couldn't be mentioned. But she did write of the difficulty of finding food and clothes. I had not realised how many parcels of such items, as well as comics and toys, my uncle sent to us, most of which seem to have arrived safely. In one letter my mother mentioned that the family was in Devonshire when they heard on the radio Churchill's famous 'We will fight them on the beaches' speech.

After Devonshire we moved up to stay with eccentric distant relations in Ruthin (pronounced Rithin), north Wales, where life was spartan and frugal. Only five inches of water in the bath, and jam or butter on bread, but not both. All strictly observed by our hosts, two spinster sisters, Audrey and church-going Carol. Their mother, who we were not allowed to see, was in pain and dying upstairs. For many years after, a warm and deep hot bath was a guilty luxury for me. We were taken to see a series of weird and sometimes grim-looking Welsh farmers, who all seemed to be interbred relations. My mother warned me not to drink any milk offered by aunt Margaret, because she had noticed that this lady used the same bucket for milk and for slops! I have visions of aunt Margaret with streaked yellow and green hair.

Our final family resting place at the height of the war was in the Buckinghamshire beechwoods, not too far from Chequers. Little Hampden was a remote village up a dead-end lane that no one would have ever tried to bomb on purpose. We lived in a few rooms in Yew Tree Cottage, owned by a Muriel relation, enclosed by greenery. Down the road was the Rising Sun pub, where one of the owner's boys lost a finger in a chain saw (a thought to make one wince). There was a little church, a lady artist who lived nearby, and a rather batty house-help who wore funny hats. At the end of the road was the longish drive to the local squire's house. The Trevor Batties, a Catholic family, had two daughters, Mary and Theresa, about my own age. We had endless fun exploring the bracken and extensive beechwoods; and ourselves, noticing the differences. Up at the big house, their governess, Miss Donat, taught a kindergarten class. I could appreciate that she was an attractive woman. By an extraordinary chance, years later, a colleague in the High Commission in Rawalpindi, Stephen Burbridge, seconded from the Department of Trade, reminded me that he had resided in the same cottage with us and after us. He has written eloquently about life in that village where everyone knew everyone. One set-back at the Trevor Batties' classroom was when I was told by another child that Father Christmas did not really exist. It was a shock. But it didn't stop me pretending that I did believe, for many years, because I didn't want to risk interrupting the flow of presents on the bed on Christmas morning. I still cherish waking up, moving my feet, and hearing the reassuring rustle of the Christmas stocking. I was certainly a loved and probably spoilt child. 'Here's to the happiest days of lives' I used to quote later in speeches to wake people up, 'spent in the arms of other men's wives.' Pause. Some consternation. 'Our mother's arms!' Ah yes.

My parents went back to Essex and Mollands in 1942, presumably because bombardment had diminished, although the V2 rockets still occasionally fell in our area. We had to have sandbags at the windows of one room and our bedding under a reinforced steel dining table that was designed to protect us if the house fell in. On rare trips to London I saw evidence of the Blitz – plenty of ruined buildings. But there was also a feeling of good fellowship in hard times among all the people that one met, which I sensed as a small boy. Londoners' grit was epitomised in the cartoon of the old woman emerging from the ruins of her bombed house saying 'That Adolf Hitler, one day he'll go too far!' Dorothy Sayers' little-known poem *Praise God Now for an English War* captures the spirit of British defiance, which still has power to move me. Also Alice Duer Miller's collection of poems *The White Cliffs of Dover*. I discovered a very early letter of mine, kept by the family, with a p.s.: 'I don't like Hitler'! My mother told me that on one occasion travelling with her in a train a lady was sitting opposite in the compartment with a preposterous hat covered in flowers. 'Mummy look at that hat,' I said. 'Hush, keep quiet,' said my mother, fearing dreadful embarrassment. 'Isn't it beautiful,' I went on. The lady was wreathed in smiles. Very early signs of diplomatic skills?

I went back to Mrs Hall's school, carrying my gas mask as I walked down the hill. Nobody thought it was unsafe for an eight year old to walk to school alone. Soon I was introduced to the bicycle (such an efficient machine) by which I travelled three or four miles to Brentwood Grammar School, for a year or so. I remember one tense occasion on my way back from school when I had to cycle through a whole swarm of schoolgirls. I kept my head down and was horrified when someone shouted 'You've dropped something!' Fortunately, as I began to turn round, another added 'It's your manners, boy!' They all giggled. Blushing madly, I pedalled on.

Several of the masters at Brentwood were so long-serving that they had also taught my father, before he had gone away to school in London, also my Bill uncles. This was true of the rather desiccated headmaster in my time, James Hough. I recently found a beautiful bound book of Ruskin lectures signed by Hough as headmaster and given to my father as a form prize in 1916. (Father never spoke about his school achievements.) I also have a manuscript letter which he wrote to my father that year, when my father was 14 and probably leaving to attend the City of London School. Hough related poignant news of other pupils in the Great War, some good and some bad. He was headmaster from 1914 to 1945 – quite a stretch. There was also the austere Mr Higgs (Latin), and the jokey Mr Cockles (French), who used to make boys who fell asleep stand on their chairs: 'Now, if you fall asleep, you will drop off!' I thought it very funny at the time. One of our Masters was rightly proud that he was doing part-time service during the war on top of St Paul's with a water-hose, trying to make sure that German incendiary bombs didn't stick on the surface of the dome, which of course survived.

The size of Brentwood School could be intimidating. It was all right in the form, where the roll-call stays in my mind: 'Allen, Arrondale, Bates, Buckland, Barrington, Church, Craig, Coull...'. But the houses where we went for lunch used to battle against each other. They lanced conkers as weapons. Sometimes small boys were taken as hostages. I learned to keep out of trouble. Also to avoid getting debagged in the changing room. For a time I was a Cub, mastered knots and chanted 'Akela'. I never graduated to Scout. I also learned to swim, but not very well. We were discouraged from going to public swimming pools because of the real threat of polio, and when I stayed with my Barrington grandparents at Worthing in Sussex the sea always seemed to be too rough to swim in any comfort. I wish I had been taught properly. I have never ceased to marvel at how good crawl swimmers avoid gulping in great quantities of water. A sort of swimming achievement came later when I was driving down to my uncle's villa in southern Spain and stopped for a night in Benidorm, then little more than a fine beach backed by olive trees. There were lots of people on the beach, however, and in the water. I was swimming and floating, not too far out, when I noticed a spluttering hand of a young man not far from me, and saw his head going under the water once or twice. He was trying to call out but in that crowded place no one noticed him. I went over, took hold of him and pulled him up onto the shore. He was still choking. People gathered round. Eventually he coughed up a mass of sea water. Help was being sought. I think that I saved him from drowning, on a crowded beach. It was at a rare visit to a swimming pool in Brentwood that the younger Muriel girl, Judith, told me that she had heard how people made babies: a man and woman would lie down together. 'How absolutely ridiculous,' I said!

This explains why one day in 1942 when I came back from school and some friends in the house said 'She's arrived!', I couldn't think what they were talking about. Taken upstairs I saw to my great surprise my mother in bed with a baby girl, my sister Sara. My first reaction was curiosity and jealously, rather than affection. That came later. My sister took over my bedroom so that I was consigned to the little former maid's room. She damaged some of my toys and could attract everyone's sympathy and attention better than I could. In fact, I think I was pretty beastly to her, and I don't know how she forgave me. I used deliberately to spook her out by playing the role of a sinister 'limp man'. I would hobble into her room, walk into the cupboard and stay there. This was a technique I used when staying with friends in Japanese ryokans years later, when I was posted to Tokyo – men together in one room, women in the other. I would get inside a cupboard, sit in the lotus posture (another of my party pieces) and close the doors, waiting for someone to come in and get a shock when opening them! Quite a perverted sense of humour. The panelled headmaster's study at Repton School had a cupboard door that precisely matched the door of entry. Several boys, making a hurried exit after a ticking off, would find themselves in the cupboard.

Mention of jealousy reminds me of one of the most remarkable episodes of my childhood. I must have been about eight years old in the summer of 1942–43. On a beach in Sheringham, Norfolk, a regular holiday destination, my parents and I were with a group of their friends, including some slightly older children, by the sea. I felt neglected, and thought I would teach them a lesson. I set off, with my spade and pail, up behind the beach and into the town. I expected them to come running after me with an apology, but they didn't. So I went on, through the town and out onto the road towards Holt, several miles away, where I knew my aunt Freda lived (she and her husband, Tom, an engineer, had recently come home from Jamaica where he had been working). I was a mile or two out of town, patiently plodding along the road beside the sunlight-speckled trees, when a man in a car stopped and asked me what I was doing and where I was going. I said that I was going to see my aunt, pretending as if it was something perfectly normal. I must have been able to show him the way, as this was before mobile or car phones. Today, of course, a man would be extremely reluctant to give a lift to a child in that way. Anyway, he delivered me to my aunt, whose look of shock and concern I remember clearly. She eventually got in touch with my parents, who must have been distraught at my disappearance. When I had explained why I had left they never showed anger or criticism, perhaps feeling unnecessarily guilty. I had been thoughtless. But I had also shown determination.

Life was tough in wartime and rationing continued for some time after, but since I had never known anything better it hardly affected me. I do remember that powdered egg and potato were unpleasant. I was conscious of my parents making sacrifices, for instance, giving up their weekly egg rations to me. Once we made a car journey to friends and returned with a whole tray of black-market eggs, which I was carefully coached not to discuss. I enjoyed the conspiracy, suggesting that we should use the word 'tickets' as the code for eggs, i.e. how are the 'tickets'? Strange fruits like peaches were sometimes so much admired that they rotted in the dish. Bananas were amazing. As a result certain things have always been luxuries for me: two eggs, foreign fruits, good steaks, as well as deep baths. I was trained never to leave anything on my plate, bearing in mind those who had greater need of food, so that waste was shameful. I still persist in scraping the last bits of marmalade out of a bottle, for example. In latter years the habit of not leaving things has damaged my waistline, because I cannot bear to throw things away.

The garden at Mollands was a full acre. At the top and under a line of trees where cuckoos called in spring, was a swing hanging from a great branch of an oak tree. There was a shed, clumps of rhubarb, raspberries and English artichokes (a vegetable that I enjoy but can rarely now find). In a ditch at the end of the garden I discovered a flint which turned out to be a prehistoric human artefact dating back perhaps 10,000 years, according to experts. My parents didn't seem to know much about it and let me keep it. It has great patina and fits easily into the grasp of a right hand. I still treasure it. Further down towards the house there were herbaceous beds, and healthy roses and rhododendrons flourishing in clay soil. I remember one summer watching humming-bird hawk moths nosing at the flowers. Plenty of butterflies. There was a field below the house where goats were allowed to graze since it was discovered that at one time I was more tolerant of goats' milk than cows' milk. I used to hold the horns of the old billy goat and have a pushing match.

My father had planted apple trees in the garden, which produced a lot of fruit, with one exception. The biggest and most prominent tree, well shaped, was barren. One year my father decided that the next year it would have to be cut down and make way for something more fecund. It must have heard, because the following year it was covered in blossom and then huge Bramley apples. If the Prince of Wales does talk to plants I think it is a perfectly reasonable thing to do. So much we don't know, like the truth of what my uncle Tom told us when he was water-divining. We often saw him holding a twig which bent sharply and appeared to identify subterranean running water. It was said that he had done it as an engineer overseas. He was a sober sort of man, not a practical joker. He also claimed to be able to detect metals. My cousin Susan, his daughter, is confident that she also has the gift of dowsing. Since there appears to be no identifiable explanation, scientists are sceptical. Is it an example of a phenomenon that science has not yet mastered, or is it an illusion? I am still unsure.

My father picked and carefully stored his apples, while my mother filled the pantry with stewed fruits, jams, chutneys and marmalades. We didn't go hungry, though I noticed that my mother had to use her charm to make sure she got decent cuts from the butcher and fishmonger. Shop keepers were in control. I used to hate buying fruit and not being allowed to pick items myself. You had to take what you were given and sometimes this included fruit that was damaged. So I have welcomed the European Union's rules on unblemished fruit.

My parents never objected when I came and listened to their adult conversation with friends, and sometimes joined in. No amount of social mobility measures can take the place of being exposed to discussion with educated parents. They also encouraged me to read. I still keep a faded damaged copy of my mother's childhood *Alice Through the Looking Glass* illustrated by Tenniel. I loved the paradoxes and convolutions in the story. I was devoted to the Mowgli tales with easy relationship between man and beasts. I read the Hornblower stories and Rider Haggard avidly. It didn't take me long to graduate to Dickens. I remember, for some reason, reading *Barnaby Rudge* with a torch under the sheets, after my parents had told me to switch the bedroom light off. *David Copperfield* was my favourite.

For sport, I was lucky enough to have an eye for a ball. I enjoyed tennis and watching my parents play. For practice I used to be quite happy knocking up against the house with tennis ball and racket. Once when I was doing this my ball went through an open sash window and broke a pot on the mantel-piece. My mother was nearby on the telephone. I saw her eyes open wide but she wasn't angry. We played tennis with Hutton Mount friends, including the Herman Taylors over the road. Herman, a distinguished rough-hewn surgeon (who absolutely did not believe in water-divining), and Mearie, his elegant wife, were good friends of my parents. Their children straddled the ages of me and my sister. The latter distinguished herself when we were all about to play tennis one day by saying 'Nicholas says that whenever we come here to play tennis he always has to work beforehand to prepare and mark out the court'! I glared at her, but there was nothing to do but cringe in embarrassment.

The five Taylor children were attractive and talented. They all took part with Sara and me in a nativity play I organised and directed, reserving for myself the best part of Herod. It was the start of my amateur theatrical career. Life goes in circles. In succeeding years I took the part of Herod on two other occasions, and began to feel an affinity for the old reprobate! On that first occasion I must have confused the two Herods because my sister remembers playing the part of Salome!

At Hutton Mount parties we all enjoyed dancing. At one stage some parents had the foresight to organise lessons, including for the boys, so that we could keep our end up for waltz, quickstep, samba and the eightsome. New Year's Eve balls were special because, when the clock struck, you could kiss all the girls. Years later, after retirement, I helped arrange a reunion of Hutton Mount friends at my London club. We tracked down about 100 people with their spouses. There were several local marriages. Perhaps the most distinguished of our contemporaries, in some ways, though she couldn't come on that particular occasion, was the effervescent Mary O'Sullivan, whose daughter is now the Countess of Wessex. (Mary's name is inscribed on the large card in the form of a silver key, along with names of other family and friends who came to the 21st birthday party that my parents organised for me at Mollands.) To organise that reunion party over 40 years later I worked with three other

male friends with whom I have kept in touch annually since: Sir Jeffrey
Bowman, former senior partner of Price Waterhouse; Professor John
Herman Taylor, a fine surgeon like his father, who has done important
research on Crohn's disease and who is always ready to give helpful
advice on medical matters; and Michael Williams, with whom I had
played when we were both in toddlers' clothes. He was one of the few of
us who suffered directly through the war, since his father was killed. His
mother was very brave. All his life Michael has been a positive, ebullient
character who makes people around him feel happy. He was one of the
first of our Hutton Mount group to get married. We used to play golf
together at the local Thorndon Club but he soon became too good for
me. As an underwriter at Lloyds and captain of Lloyd's golf he has
played on many of the greatest courses all around the world.

My father was a keen golfer, straight up and down, and disappointed
that I never really mastered the game. One needs to hold the club in an
unnatural grip. The little ball seems to me rather far away to be hit with
perfect impact each time. A brilliant stroke, which I would have a long
time to savour, would be followed by a scuff into the rough. Croquet is
another difficult game, which was set up and much enjoyed in the
garden at Mollands. Our hoops were generous. I was better when I was
younger. Tense battle was good for character. Just when in prime
position in front of a hoop you could find your ball whacked to the far
edge of the lawn. My mother had flair, but my father was most
successful, with great determination.

In 1945 I was sent away to a school in Sussex, Belmont, one of a cluster
of prep schools at the foot of the Downs. As always the headmaster set
the tone. Max Burr, with a large bumpy face, was dynamic and
imaginative, sometimes overpowering. It was the first time I had lived
away from home. I took time to get used to matron and looking after
myself. In my first year it was, of course, all very strange, and I was shy. I
stammered. When asked to call out my name I found difficulty in saying
the 'B' in Barrington. I found a way to get over it by saying 'Sir,
Barrington, Sir'. There was a boy called Wigram who would eat flies if
given a penny. Each time the word got around that he was about to
perform, quite a crowd gathered. The school had only recently returned
from war evacuation, half to Lichfield and half to the Bahamas. It was
back in a scruffy mansion, which looked as if the army had just
abandoned it, which was the case. A newly built gem was the chapel,

including the fruit of much craftwork at school. Burr taught mathematics brilliantly, making it fun. He was also an inspiration on crafts: metal and woodwork and printing. He taught me how to make two silver initialled napkin rings, which I presented to my parents and now still proudly possess – the peak of my achievement in this area.

The grounds were extensive and partly wild. We had 'drop dead' games in the woods, involving, it seemed, half the school. I played my part in all the ball games, but for some reason only watched archery, which was a speciality of the school. Nilla Burr, Max's modest self-contained wife, was Britain's national women's archery champion, which was rather surprising. In 1948, after an international tournament at Dulwich, she was declared women's world champion. Sports day in the summer, with visiting parents, was a special event. I was good at running (I had done quite well at Brentwood). In my final year at Belmont it was rather embarrassing as I was Victor Ludorum, and my mother, father and uncle Geoff all won prizes. A great annual occasion was Guy Fawkes, with a huge bonfire. One year Mrs Attlee was present and even, unobtrusively, her husband the Prime Minister, since younger members of the Attlee family had been at the school. Life at Belmont was a constant adventure. In one season we all went mad about conkers; in another we seemed to live in old trenches. There was also a craze racing snails in the dormitories at night. Typical of Burr's imagination was to mark out a grid on the terrace and have boys controlling a game of drafts from the flat roof above, with other boys as pieces. No worries about health and safety!

Most of my contemporaries had been at the school longer than I, which may have been why I hadn't been made head of the school, which slightly puzzled me. But I must have done all right in lessons. I was top in most subjects in my last term, except for Latin, and won a scholarship to Repton School. Max Burr took the trouble to drive me and a friend, Ian Thomas, all the way up to Derbyshire for the exam and interview there. None of the other staff made the impact on me that Burr did. There was the genial wise Mr Whalley, and the French teacher Mr Tulloch, with two fingers of one hand joined together. The lean Mr Pilbrow would flick you painfully in the ears if you got something wrong. Gruff Mr Bailey, teaching Latin, would come and sit beside one of the boys and try to finger our privates. We all thought it rather funny and used to wonder where he would sit next time. He suddenly disappeared in the middle of one term. Of course what he did was reprehensible, but I don't believe it did me or any other boy harm.

More serious, as I found out afterwards, were beatings. I never suffered, because I was always careful to be on the right side of the headmaster – I may have been seen by others as a little creep for that. But, after the school had closed down, and enjoyable reunions of old boys were organised, partly at my suggestion a history of the school was written. It emerged that many young boys had been traumatised by beatings from Burr, and even more so from the headmaster brought in by Mrs Burr to run the school after Max Burr had died. The writer of the book, Dale Vargas, who had been on the staff for a time, said that even he had not realised how much beating of boys had been going on. Mr Squeers had still been alive in the 1940s and 1950s.

I had happy memories of Belmont. Going for walks in the high Downs. Having one's youthful exuberance controlled, but not suppressed. Typical of Burr's approach was how he handled the last night of term when a feast in the dormitory ended in a massive pillow fight. 'Right,' said Burr, 'senior boys for a midnight swim.' Our energy was diverted to another adventure, and we eventually sank exhausted into our beds. A few days before Max Burr had spoken clearly and sensitively to boys about the birds and the bees. I had always wondered why cows had tried to climb on top of each other. There was no question of 'don't touch it or it will drop off'. Sometime later my father was greatly relieved to find, having starting an awkward conversation, that I had the necessary information.

Belmont finally closed in 1972. I didn't revisit the site until the 1980s when I was on the way to Glyndebourne nearby. The main building had been destroyed and a modern villa erected in its place. The extensive grounds were still recognisable. The beautiful little chapel some distance away had been incorporated into a separate private house.

2

REPTON. THE BIG SCHOOL

I was now going further away to a more formidable establishment. My father had known Lynam Thomas, the headmaster at Repton, when the latter had been a housemaster at Rugby during the war. I was put in his house, the Hall. The school had been founded in 1557 (as it happened the same year as Brentwood Grammar school) by Sir John Port, MP, merchant and local landowner, whose executors bought up the remains of a dissolved Augustinian priory. It went through good and bad times but was given a new lease of life by Dr Pears, headmaster 1854–74, one of the new men influenced by Dr Arnold's regime at Rugby. Some of the monastic buildings survived, particularly the iconic Arch and gracious Old Priory, giving the school a special character. The library in the Old Priory, now restored, was an important influence in my final years when I would sit and study in one of the bays and imbibe the scholarly atmosphere.

The school dominated the little village, and was surrounded by extensive terraced playing fields. Nearby towns, Derby and Burton, had little appeal, but the Derbyshire countryside, on the fringes of the Peak District, was delightful. I saw more of it when I got involved in cross-country running, one of my main sporting achievements. As I got older I was less good as a sprinter and graduated to the long haul of five or six miles. Captaining the cross-country team took me to other schools. I also met Sydney Wooderson before a mass run in London, and listened with particular interest to a talk by a Repton old boy Harold Abrahams, the Olympic medallist depicted in *Chariots of Fire*. Repton was a soccer school, playing hockey in the Easter term, so I have never been a great follower of rugby – also because of the constant interruptions by the referee, often for unfathomable reasons. The great quality of soccer and main reason for its world popularity is the simplicity of its rules and the way the action keeps moving. This doesn't stop me thinking that the British national obsession with soccer, like the addiction of the Byzantine crowds to chariot racing, could lead to the collapse of our civilisation!

At the beginning small boys had to keep their heads down. There were scary initiation ceremonies (but nothing so bad as in American fraternities, as I learned later). We each had to sing a song for prefects in the new boys' dormitory. On the whole I have found that having a surname starting with 'Ba' has been an advantage, but that night the only 'A' in the dormitory collapsed in nervous fright and I then had to do my inadequate best with 'Nymphs and Shepherds'. I enjoy singing, especially traditional hymns, and there was plenty of that belted out in the school chapel, guided by the voluble Mervyn Williams. But I do not do it well. I was at once rejected for the choir. My dear aunt Freda, who started off as a concert pianist, used to remind me that although I thought I was singing more in tune when singing loudly, that was not actually the case!

I got my own back on the prefect in charge of our dormitory, unwittingly, by sleeping under my blanket through a fire alarm practice. Down in the dining hall when names were read out there was silence after 'Barrington'. The prefect was severely admonished for not checking, and having let me burn. Martin How, one of his helpers, claims that he did wake me and I must have gone back to sleep again, but in my view that doesn't make the authorities any less guilty for allowing an innocent youth to be roasted, notionally, to a frazzle! One had to learn survival and rely on one's own ability and character. Parents, wealth and connections would not help in the least. If a group of boys, in *Lord of the Flies* mode, were determined to attack someone, it was no good saying 'not me'. Their aggression needed to be satisfied and it was best to divert it towards someone else. Dishonourable, of course. You also had to learn to share. I was given a rocket my first term by my study-holder for starting to eat by myself a cake that had been sent by my parents. 'Here we share.' And then I did. Sharing the same tubs of hot water, one boy after another, was one thing. More difficult to get used to was going to the toilet where there were no doors.

Houses were divided into studies, usually of five boys, one from each year. The two youngest were fags, junior and senior, who cleaned the study and the study holder's shoes and boots. We all favoured the system, because it meant that in the final year, when you might be a prefect or captain of games, or working hard for a scholarship, some of your basic chores would be looked after. Occasionally house prefects would shout 'fag' and those who scrambled late to the end of the line-up got given a menial job that had to be done. In theory there could have been bullying, but I saw hardly any of that. It was more likely that the senior boys, particularly prefects, would keep an eye on the younger ones, take an interest in them and alert the housemaster if they were home-sick or going off the rails in any way. As a small boy I refused to box for the house when told to do so by a prefect. I said I didn't agree with hurting others for sport. He never bothered me after this, which is rather remarkable when you think of it. Prefects took their responsibilities seriously, working as a team with the Head of House. Discipline was maintained with the heel of a hard slipper. Anticipation caused anxiety, but it was soon over. Only once, as Head of House, did I feel it necessary to beat a boy with a cane, because he had blatantly kept cigarettes in his bedside locker. I had obtained the housemaster's approval and was accompanied by two prefect witnesses. It could have been humiliating, but I don't think it hurt much. It was important not to make the victim into a hero. The boy in question went on to become one of Britain richest and most prominent citizens, so it didn't do him any harm. When we met later in life neither of us mentioned what had happened.

In the end I probably became too grand as Head of House, Head of the School (a title awarded to a senior scholar) and, above all, Head Prefect. I had numerous book prizes, some still on my shelves. I fostered a special common room for other school prefects, the heads of other houses and one or two other prominent boys, where we discussed policy and occasionally made our views known to the headmaster. There were times when Lynam Thomas listened to us rather than to the housemasters, which must have irritated the latter. I never achieved that peak of eminence until I was an ambassador, nearly 40 years later. School prefects conducted a weekly Sunday roll-call of all the boys in the school on the steps of the Old Priory. It seems a rather strange custom, which probably wouldn't work nowadays when so many pupils go home or away at weekends. But it did mean that after two years or so I knew the names of all the 400 boys in the school. It had a role in giving every boy, however quiet and inconspicuous, a moment in the limelight.

The real schoolboy heroes were, of course, those who were good at games, encouraged by house masters, some of whom at Repton played cricket and football for county teams. I developed an unspoken rivalry with a contemporary who was captain of school cricket and football; in our final year, however, we became firm friends. It helped at least that I was good at tennis, athletics and cross-county running. We all wore the same uniform, which I think is essential, to eliminate showing off family wealth, but in summer blazers carried all sorts of decorations marking sporting achievements. School prefects were entitled to a special speckled straw hat, which has provided me with the image for Milton's 'speckled Vanity', which soon sickens.

Work-wise, I did well in the School Certificate – six distinctions and three credits, just scraping through a necessary credit for Oxbridge in Latin. I think it was the final year of that exam. I then chose to specialise in modern languages, French and German. I am not a natural linguist but I had a good memory and loved the literature. In German I was able to appreciate the remarkable polimath Goethe, moving from his classical to romantic phases, and Schiller too. For me one of the great benefits of learning a foreign language is to have direct access to poetry, for example Schiller's fabulous ballad *Der Handschuh* about a lady who drops her glove into an arena of wild animals and challenges her suitor to collect it. He does this with cool courage but then throws it into her face. For French literature I had at first Ted Burrough, who would actually weep with emotion going through certain texts. Later, I was able to soak myself in all the classical writing around the court of Louis XIV at Versailles. Not only Corneille, Racine and Molière, and the critic Boileau, but La Fontaine's fables. I bought in a bookshop in Cambridge some fine old illustrated editions of their works. I also became familiar with La Rochefoucauld's *bon mots* (e.g. 'Refusal of praise is a desire to be praised for a second time'), Madame de Sévigné's letters and Saint Simon's diaries. Studying also the architecture, painting, music and politics of the period I felt I really knew what had been going on during that special period of French culture. This was very satisfying and no doubt helped me to pass the requisite A and S level exams. Recently, talking to a Repton master teaching languages, I was shocked to discover that they now hardly cover literature at all.

When I opted for modern languages I already had in mind to try for the Foreign Office, or at least to work abroad. My father travelled a good deal in his work. Business contacts would come and visit our home, opening up new worlds. One, when offered a drink, said he would like a double! Another asked to watch horse-racing on television and spent much time placing bets using my father's telephone! We became close to a delightful Sri Lankan family, the Veerasinghis. Also some Chinese Malays, the Chungs, whose sons happened to be the world's doubles champions at badminton. Their parents owned hotels in Penang, about which the mother talked incessantly.

My mother's two youngest brothers, Geoff and Dick, had an international air about them. With no jobs for them in the family woollen business in Great Portland Street (W Bill Ltd) they were encouraged by their father to seek fortune in America. They crossed the Atlantic in a cattle boat in the 1930s and ended up taking over a woollen retail business in California, 'Tweeds and Weeds', which had been a customer of the family firm. The elderly owner had suggested disposing of his business to some of the Bill sons. Dick married and settled in Santa Barbara. Geoff, his senior in age but junior in partnership, was also a salesman for the home company throughout the USA. He had learned his trade at a mill in Scotland and later helped design tweeds. He remained a bachelor. For most of his life he went backwards and forwards across the Atlantic, staying in England in the summer. In retirement he made a beautiful home and garden near Witham in Essex. During the war Geoff and Dick had stayed in America. After Pearl Harbor they took up war work – Dick in an aircraft factory in California and Geoff working at the Indian Supply Mission attached to the British Embassy in Washington. When they came to visit after the war they, and their friends, were stimulating company.

At the age of 16 one summer I did a month's swap with a French family living near the Eiffel Tower, which taught me much about how others live. Madame Franck was protective and loquacious; she showed us pictures of the family wearing the compulsory Jewish star on their clothes during German occupation. I learned that her modest husband had been a war hero: Légion d'honneur and Croix de Guerre twice, for going out at nights in Vichy and sabotaging German troop trains. I admired him greatly. With Antoine, my opposite number, I felt competitive, and with his sophisticated cultured friends, inadequate. The first night after my parents left me in the French family flat I was lost. Madame said 'goodnight' and closed the door, but there was no bed in my room. I tried to think of the word for sheets in French, which was not very easy to pronounce. Eventually she understood my concern, exclaimed, and threw off the cover of the sofa to expose white linen! Water in wine, elbows on tables and the use of 'merde' in social conversation shocked me, but it was all for the good. I got to know Paris and began to think in French. (Considering what hands might be doing under tables, I realised that it was better to have them on top.)

One of the masters at Repton who greatly influenced me was Mr Bain who taught sixth form German. It was said he had been a judge in India. He sat with bald pate, like Humpty Dumpty, behind a high desk, controlling the class with witticisms and cutting remarks. He made us copy down quotations, many of which I still remember, to squeeze into exam papers. He had a zest for learning in the widest sense: When he found I was ignorant about Jengis Khan he made me read H. G. Wells' *Outline of History*, thus stimulating my interest in world history. This came in very useful when I was posted as a diplomat to Asia. Bain was kind under his tough carapace. He invited me to his house to meet his home-loving wife, to whom he was devoted. It was several years after I had left school that she became terminally ill with a tumour of the brain. She was sent home since nothing could be done for her. She was in severe pain – 'a half-witted wreck' in the words of their daughter, replying to my letter of condolence, with no hope of recovery. I was told that he gave her poison and then took some himself, like a Roman senator of old. I could believe it of him. An heroic act, in my book. I don't know what his Maker had in mind for him. He used to tell us how terrified he had been as a small boy when he was told that if he was good he would go to heaven, sit on a cloud and play a harp for ever. For ever!

One of the things that kept me sane at Repton was that in free time I could go the art school in an old barn by the Arch to take lessons from the art master, Arty Norris. With grey curls to his neck and a trilby he was the antithesis of the dominant sports masters. A courteous watercolourist of the old school he taught us to draw portraits from life and to sketch buildings and landscapes. He used to bring old people in from the village and sit them down in front of us as models. Some of the portraits I did then have subsequently been framed. They were not at all bad. I had enjoyed drawing pictures from an early age, encouraged by my trained artist mother. Sketch books of mine have since been filled with views of different places which I have recorded by pencil rather than camera. I only rarely experimented with colours and oils. In the art school I would meet boys from other houses, for example Hugh Brogan, son of the eminent Professor Brogan and subsequently a distinguished professor himself (who is writing in his retirement a history of Repton). Numbers of my letters home talk about my time in the art school with Mr Norris. Others mention participation in the debating society and writing a paper on G. K. Chesterton. I found a letter which my mother had written to her brother Geoff in 1948 describing a visit to see me at Repton. She and my father had stayed with the headmaster. After a sherry they had lunch in the hall, sitting at the top table with the prefects, seeing me well down at the other end with the fags. They went with me to watch a boys' hockey match followed by tea in the tuck shop, which we called the Grubber. I ate huge quantities of crumpets. They looked in at the art school and saw a model sitting there. Mother described Norris as 'a most unusual type: long curly hair, bow tie. Quite an artist of note himself, son of a former dean of Westminster. Later meeting him at cocktails he confounded us by insisting on Nicholas' genius. Said in 25 years he had never seen such promise. Almost begged us to let him go later to the Slade.' Needless to say Norris never spoke to me in those terms. If I had another life again, however, I would spend a lot more time drawing and trying to paint. Going back to Repton as an old boy I have always been impressed by the great flowering of the art school into new media and eye-opening creativity. But I don't regret my more sober art lessons.

Another activity which I much enjoyed was theatre. It started with being selected to play Viola in what, in retrospect, was a splendid production of *Twelfth Night*. I played the comic farmer Acres in *The Rivals* by Sheridan, with Hugh Brogan as Mrs Malaprop. Finally I was Caesar in Shaw's *Caesar and Cleopatra*, with a false Roman nose and a rather ungainly small boy as the female lead. I certainly made an impact in the first role, because years later at an old boys' reunion I met the former senior chaplain, the Reverend Proctor, who was showing his years. When I tried to remind him who I was and that I had been in his form, he peered at me and whispered 'Viola'! Periodic reviews by the staff, calling themselves 'the Pedants', were hilarious. Amateur dramatics played an important part in my life in succeeding years. (Note that art and theatre didn't need to be on the curriculum to be experienced and enjoyed.)

There were three clergymen on the staff in those days, inculcating a straightforward brand of Christianity. Repton was very much an Anglican school, as it had been throughout its history. Archbishop Temple had been headmaster at the beginning of the century, followed by Fisher who as current Archbishop of Canterbury was Chairman of the Governors when I was a prefect and used to descend on us from time to time. He radiated vitality, warmth and humour. Archbishop Ramsey, looking like an Old Testament prophet poised on a crag in the wind, whom I was to help escort in Japan, was also an Old Reptonian. My housemaster, under the overall authority of the Head, was first John Eggar, a fine sportsman, who gave me a salutary ticking-off for not having a button sewn on when he had instructed me to do so. He was succeeded by one of Fisher's sons, Frank, who later became headmaster of St Edwards Oxford, and then Wellington. Frank Fisher understood me and other boys very well, with the right balance of correction and encouragement. He trusted us as much as he could. My first visit to Lambeth was with a group of boys under his auspices. Years later, in 1987, I went to his memorial service in Wellington, where his brilliant way of understanding boys was explained to a large congregation.

Sermons in chapel could be dull. One of the masters would put a series of coins on the ledge in front of him at the beginning for the collection and it was known that he would tip one back into his pocket every minute the sermon went over 15. I was impressed by one preacher who said that some people think there are three types of morality: to tell the truth; to tell a lie; and to cheat the government. Avoiding customs, not paying taxes and shop lifting in impersonal department stores was still being dishonest. Another fine preacher I remember was the Reverend Bryan Green from Birmingham, who used humour to keep us all interested and alert. Getting confirmed, although it was the norm, was something that I took very seriously. Privately I felt quite emotional about it. I never subsequently lost my belief in God, incarnate in Christ, although I toiled over this and other issues when I was at university. Nor have I lost my respect for the structure and wording of Cranmer's old communion service ('We are not worthy to gather up the crumbs under thy table', 'Our souls washed through his most precious blood', 'Godly and quiet life'). The service seems to me to be admirably suited to periodic self examination and getting one's priorities in order.

Lynam Thomas, an authoritative wise presence as headmaster, was supported by a very attractive wife who doled out tea and sympathy in the private side. He kept a grip on the school and on the fiefs of the powerful housemasters. He encouraged adventure activities such as climbing tours to the Snowdon area, where a group of senior boys stayed in bunks in a mountain hut, bathed in an icy stream and sang songs in the evening. In two successive years there I found the mountains exhilarating, scrambling up Tryfan and along the Crib-goch ridge of Snowdon itself. Thomas famously enjoyed tobogganing in the snow. When a national reorganisation of timetables meant that exams came earlier in the final term of the year, the last part of the sixth form's summer term was used for wider education: visits to factories, down coal mines and to theatre at Stratford, for example. An important experience was being let loose in couples at night with a map, torch and compass on a moor in the Peak District. We learned that left alone people tend to walk not straight but in a circle, and that in bad light distances are very difficult to judge. This was called the 'midnight drop'. Hours later, group by group, we staggered exhausted into the designated base for breakfast. I wonder if insurance would cover it these days.

The experience came in useful some years later when I was on holiday in Marbella in southern Spain, staying at a little house belonging to my uncle Geoff. A young American I had met in a cafe, a Panamanian and I decided we would climb a prominent peak overlooking the town and the coast. We got dropped off by some vehicle and started the ascent, up easy lower slopes, around midday. When we got to a steep tricky passage, however, the young man from Panama decided it was too much, and went back. The American and I continued, eventually climbing up a difficult rocky gully near the top. The view was exhilarating, slightly marred by the presence of a bottle with a note inside recording that a German called Hans had been there. But when we started to go down and came to the difficult bit, my American friend said that he couldn't make it. I could go on but he would go down another way. I said that we must stick together. So we started descending by a gentler slope to the north, away from the sea. That was all right for a time, but then we came to a ring of precipices impossible to penetrate. He was tired and it was beginning to get dark. I was alarmed by seeing in front of us great smooth scoops of rock, probably once worn by water, which could have trapped us if we went down, preventing us from going further up or down. We walked seemingly for miles trying to find a reasonable route. Distances, as on the midnight drop, were difficult to judge. My friend wanted to give up and let me go on, but I insisted. We kept each other going with visions of gin and tonic, and good food. It was cold. But finally, as we were clearly lost and I was getting desperate, we saw a flicker of light from a hut, which we managed to reach and where we took shelter. There was a surprised local shepherd nearby. Meanwhile our Panamanian colleague had raised the alarm back in Marbella and brought out a posse of friends to try to find us. I can't remember how they did, but we made it home and felt we had learned a number of lessons. One of them is: If in doubt, always go down the way you came up.

Besides archbishops and Harold Abrahams there were some other prominent people who came to talk to us at Repton. I wish I had paid more attention to Lord Beveridge. I shall never forget when the school was addressed by a Home Office pathologist, Dr Donald Teare, in the big school hall. I don't know who he thought his audience were but he talked about recent murders, showing slides of bloody corpses and victims of gruesome attacks. Boys started to pale; some walked out with shaky step; others fainted with a little groan. Finally the headmaster got up on the stage and said in his familiar way 'Err – I think we had better stop now'. In a letter home I simply described the talk as 'sordid and thrilling. The slides had been revolting'. I didn't mention that the headmaster had stopped the talk. George Brown was the new local MP and also came to talk. When asked a question about why the new Labour government were making mistakes he said it was like learning to play the piano. At the back of the room Mr Bolland, the acerbic maths master, said 'Get a new piano!', to general amusement.

All of us were in the corps and went on annual camps, usually in north Wales. In my last year I was the senior under-officer and had to call for three cheers for the visiting VIP, Field Marshal Viscount Montgomery. He looked at me with penetrating blue eyes and I felt the force of his personality. Which was a good introduction to the next phase of my life: two years' national service in the army.

It was an honour when Lynam Thomas suggested that I would be the best person to propose his health and that of his wife at the farewell dinner given for them by members of the staff at the Connaught Rooms in London in 1961. Frank Fisher presided over the occasion. I kept a note of some of the points I made. I said that TLT, whom we called 'The Boss', looked more like the chairman of a joint stock bank than a sentimental Mr Chips (which had been filmed at Repton). He had rare dignity without pomposity, which didn't stop him being playful, especially in the snow. He would take immense trouble to put boys first. As an example, I remembered when there had been a terrific cloudburst which had brought gallons of water flooding through both sides of the Hall, so that gym shoes and empty cans were floating in six inches of water. The headmaster had given instructions that a dam be constructed outside so that all the water was directed to the boys' side. Always the boys first! More seriously, TLT had widened all our horizons. His beautiful wife had been a breath of fresh air, treating us all as grown-ups.

I flourished at Repton. I had learned a lot, about myself and about the world. As Wordsworth suggested 'the thought of our past years in me doth breed perpetual benediction'.

During my final year it was suggested that I try for a scholarship at Worcester College, Oxford, then under a highly regarded master, J. C. Masterman. I went to Oxford rather half-heartedly, and didn't succeed. I then tried for Clare College, Cambridge, which had some links with Repton. I didn't get a scholarship, because there were few available for modern linguists. But Clare gave me entrance on the basis of my scholarship exam and I was happy to be accepted there. How much my life would have changed if I had gone to Oxford – for the worse, I expect!

That summer, after leaving school, I was given a great treat by my generous uncle Geoff. He invited me to bring a Repton friend on a tour with him of Italy, which was an eye-opener for me and a great cultural education. We started in the south of France bicycling to some of the mountain villages above the Riviera. We took in Pisa, enchanted by the three beautiful white buildings in the square, not just the leaning tower. Venice was appropriately magical. Canals and bridges, but no ugly cars. It was there, when we were leaving on a train, that a hefty porter insisted on holding his hand out to my uncle for a bigger tip. When my uncle told him that we were English, not Americans, his whole attitude changed and he embraced us affectionately! In Florence the whole city was like a museum, there was so much to see. Then finally the grandeur of Rome, culminating in the Forum, the Coliseum and the Sistine

Chapel. We all went to see an amazing production of the opera *Turandot* at the Baths of Caracalla, with thousands on stage. James Hales and I also much enjoyed our luxury hotels.

3

A SALUTARY SPELL
IN THE ARMY

University was deferred for two years' national service for all young men except medics. They were expected to qualify first and then do service as doctors. In fact national service was just about to end. Some of my near contemporaries escaped it. On reflection it was good for me; it helped me grow up. I chose the Artillery on the basis that my brain would be engaged more, and perhaps that it would be less arduous.

I duly registered in September 1952, and was given my very basic uniform. The regime at the training depot at Oswestry in Cheshire was tough, but I was lucky enough to be put in a barrack room with some good friends from Repton, including Nicholas Grantham, whose lovely old farmhouse home I had visited at St Osyth. There were others who became friends, and followed me to Cambridge, such as David Bastin and David Ramsbotham, from Sherborne and Haileybury. On the whole, public schoolboys who had been at boarding schools survived better than others. Those who had left school at 16 had been earning money, so they knew the world much better than we did, and were more streetwise; but most had never been away from their families and were homesick. Getting one's bed into immaculate shape was tiresome, as was the need to slave away at boots until they shone like glass. I took a risky step by accepting an offer from an older soldier down the corridor to take one of my pairs of boots for him to polish for cash. I think it was half a crown – worth something then. If I had had to produce them in 48 hours I would have been in trouble, but it was money well spent. They came back mirror perfect, so that they never needed more than a touch of a duster thereafter. Others who spent hours at spit and polish were not so brave, and were jealous.

As in one's first days at school it was important to keep one's head down and out of trouble. Some of my contemporaries found it difficult to be inconspicuous: For example Robin Sebag Montefiore was often asked to spell out his name, stuttering, for the amusement of some NCO who liked to mock toffs. (I don't know how a contemporary of mine at Cambridge called Twistleton Wykham Fiennes would have coped.) Bombardiers in charge of us enjoyed asserting themselves. I remember being staggered by the constant indiscriminate swearing, mainly the use of the f... word, which had not been part of my vocabulary. It still isn't in public, though I confess it can emerge when I am alone and stub my toe, or break something. I found it amusing that groups of us were often given a break for a smoke, though the only person smoking would be the instructor. My father had done a clever thing for me several years before, promising he would give me £50 if I didn't smoke before I was 21. He himself had given up smoking during the war, saying that my mother was smoking enough for two. More important than the money, which was quite a sum then, was that it gave me an excuse to resist peer pressure. When they said 'don't be a sissy and come and smoke behind the gym' I replied that I wouldn't mind but that I was waiting for my financial reward. Imagine how much money I have saved over the years because of my father's bribe, which I duly earned at 21! Not to speak of years on my life. I was never tempted to take smoking up afterwards. I recommend such tactics to all parents.

The system at Oswestry was designed to turn one into an automaton, so that orders would be obeyed without question. A guiding principle was 'If it moves, salute it. If it doesn't, paint it white'! But it was important that drill and routine should not addle one's brain. We had little contact with officers, though I cannot forget, during one exercise in the country, watching with incredulity a kilted subaltern from a Scots regiment stepping over a stile! The War Office Selection Board (WOSB), for which we went away for a few days of interviews and discussions, together with initiative tests ('With two logs and this rope lead your group over the ditch'), decided whether one would be selected and trained for a national service commission. Self-assurance was required. Most of my friends passed and were sent for officer training at Mons, near Aldershot. It was a pretty basic selection process. Some highly intelligent people failed, and spent their service in the ranks. One of my friends, something of a cynic even in early years, described in his autobiography how his manifest lack of enthusiasm did for him at WOSB, and consigned him to two years as an army clerk. However, he enjoyed visiting Korea and Japan. Once, when as a young officer I was doing a routine inspection in my regiment in Germany, I was introduced to the son of Field Marshal Lord Alanbrooke. He was an ordinary gunner who had not got a commission. My third world friends find that almost impossible to believe. Anyway, I passed WOSB; but somehow my name got lost in the system so that while my contemporaries departed for the officer training school I was sent to a holding barracks at Woolwich, south London. Conditions there were medieval. We were in large dormitories with damp running down the walls. There was a single basin outside with cold water. I remember that this was the time of one of London's densest fogs. You could hardly see the pavement in front of you. Buses were led by men with flaming torches.

It was depressing to be forgotten by the system for a few weeks, but eventually I got to Mons, where I found a new lot of friends. I never managed to take the place seriously, however, with all the elaborate drill, appropriately called square-bashing. The sergeant majors that shouted and screamed at us were stars in their own way: 'I call you Sir, and you call me Sir, but you mean it, Sir!' I never made Under-Officer. Massive Regimental Sergeant Major Brittain of the Coldstream Guards, the senior RSM of the British army, had a coat of arms on his sleeve about a foot square. His high pitched voice would reach to the furthest corners of the parade ground. 'There is an idle man there Sergeant. Not'im, not'im, not'im.'. Then a gurgled croak would come from the sergeant, 'Got'im Sir!'. Brittain kept reminding us that he had appeared in a film. At our graduation party, however, he was surprisingly kind. More interesting to me was the gunner technology itself, which we had to master. I had plenty of spare time. I spent much of it reading *War and Peace*, and Churchill's war memoirs. I remember what struck me about Churchill was that he had not tried to hide from the House of Commons what disasters were taking place, for example, the sinking of two major ships in the Far East. Also that despite all the pressures he took time to deal with small things, such as sending a minute to a colleague about a pile of unsightly rubbish outside his Whitehall offices. I also worked my way through an English translation of Proust, noting his intense observation of specific moments in time.

I then got posted to the respected 19th Field Regiment at Dusseldorf, Germany. Some of my friends had earlier seen action in Korea; others were now sent to the Suez Canal and Hong Kong. Dusseldorf, the most sophisticated of the cities in the Ruhr, was a comparatively easy option. The only action we saw was taking part in mammoth British Army of the Rhine troop manoeuvres. Our Lohausen barracks was well designed and impressive, originally built by Goering for his cosseted Luftwaffe. The Mess had a grand dining hall. A wooden practice polo pony stood in the garden. In the compound there were an athletics track, tennis courts and a squash court. At one time when we had been told that the latter was out of action, we discovered it was because an inspection was impending and that the Quartermaster was using it to hide away all his surplus stock! I played tennis, and did some running. I even clocked up a reasonable time on a half mile, to the surprise of the soldiers. I was officer in charge of hockey, and went on an umpire's course.

My letters home recorded that life in the mess was comfortable, with good food. Four times a week we dressed in Blues for formal dinner in the Mess. At one mess ball I reported that I had danced with many attractive officers' wives, nurses and girlfriends before going to bed at 5.30 a.m. Two hours later, on duty, I had counted 240 empty bottles outside the building. (There had been about 250 people present.) Laundry was done for us cheaply. Money was tight. My fortnightly pay was about £8 and my average Mess bill £3 for the same period. In one of my letters I did a reasonable drawing of my two rooms, decorated with maps and over 100 different beer mats. I learned about alcohol, which we had not touched at school, unlike modern sixth formers. I particularly enjoyed Singapore gin slings in the Mess bar. It took time before I really enjoyed the taste of beer. We were charged for what we drank, however offered, so there was no obligation to pay for rounds. I also learned a good deal about Scottish dancing. It was taken seriously, every Friday evening. Half of us had to tuck a handkerchief in front of our belts to signify the other sex. We graduated to the foursome. Down in the town I also had my first experience of nightclubs, plentiful in Dusseldorf. There was one where the well-endowed barmaid was known to lift up her sweater at one point during the evening, much anticipated and to great applause (no bra!). The regiment went for a week to Berlin for exercises where the nightclubs were even more spectacular: ladies taking a bubble bath on stage, and others with hooks on their clothes that could be lifted off with fishing lines held by quivering hands from the front rows. Berlin retained resonances of Isherwood. It was still, of course, a divided city. We saw the Soviet soldiers at their war memorial inside the Brandenberg Gate, and were taken on a coach trip through the Soviet sector to see the grand buildings and empty streets there.

With fellow national service officer friends I made holiday trips down the Rhine and to the beautiful Mosel and Lahr valleys. I visited Cologne and Trier. Looking back, I was surprised how many outside trips I was able to make. I went on a holiday weekend with fellow officer Richard Bateman and another friend to Copenhagen, where we saw the Mermaid (surprisingly small), visited castles with echoes of *Hamlet*, and crossed on a ferry to Sweden just to get our passports stamped. We caught something of the gaiety of Copenhagen in a short time. I remember that we decided to have a good meal in a restaurant only to be rather sneered at by the waiters, probably because of our scruffy civilian clothes. Determined to surprise and impress them we ordered a series of extra courses. We had them grovelling, but used up almost all our money! I also went on a trip to Salzburg, and for skiing at Winterburg, although I never succeeded in mastering the snow. Offered a lift in a senior officer's car I went to Brussels and Ghent, where a friend and I also ate well.

On one occasion a group of young officers visited an RAF station, where we were offered the opportunity of taking a flight in a Vampire jet. I accepted. There were just two of us in the aircraft. My pilot, not much older than me, did a roll and then completely looped the loop. The horizon disappeared, twisted round so that the land came up on the top of my line of vision. And then righted itself again – an amazing sensation. I was full of admiration for the skill and control of my pilot host. At one time another group from the regiment were taken to Belsen where we saw the mounds topped by simple notices, such as: 'Hier Liegen Tausend Tote', an understatement of horror. We decided that the rail terminal was so near the village that the locals must have known what was going on.

One disconcerting experience was when I was deputed to take a group of other ranks and NCOs for a few days to a Church House Christian retreat in the fir forests at Iserlohn, north of Dusseldorf. It is interesting that it was considered appropriate to educate a range of soldiers about the Anglican faith. It was also a rest. On the train on the way back I moved away from the soldiers into a neighbouring forward carriage, because I had a first class ticket. After a time I went back to see if they were OK and was confronted with a window with bare tracks behind! The train had divided, evidently common in Germany, and the men for whom I had been responsible had gone off to a completely different destination! Fortunately the senior NCO in the group had realised what had happened and got the men back to the barracks without much delay, so I didn't get major flack, although I had moments of considerable anxiety. On the subject of Christianity, I was one of the few officers who attended services fairly regularly in a basement chapel, conducted by an uninspiring chaplain. But I did take an afternoon off to go by myself to hear Billy Graham preaching in a huge German stadium. I was struck not only by his rhetoric but by his appeal to reason: 'I believe,' he argued, 'that there is a god who created us and takes interest in each one of us. If there is only a chance that this is true, it is the most important thing in the world. Be wise and declare yourself to be a follower of Christ.' I didn't budge myself, but I saw people from all parts of the stadium standing up and walking down to the middle, to register their commitment.

My job was originally Assistant Command Post Officer (ACPO) in one of the three Batteries, responsible for deploying a troop of old reliable 25 pounder field guns. These splendid weapons, designed in 1935 and unchanged since 1942, only came out of action in the British Army in 1975. We had to find them protected positions, clearly mapped, so that they could bring fire on enemy targets. Accurate calculations were necessary, which meant that, although we were such immature officers, at least we acquired some respect from the men for our technical knowledge, assuming we got it right. This was also one of the ways we gunners thought ourselves superior to the pbi – 'poor bloody infantry'. Battery captains, as observation officers, were posted with the front line infantry, noting the fall of shells and giving requisite orders so that targets should be hit. Being part of all this on manoeuvres was fascinating. Designated safety officers had to do a hurried check before each round was fired to see that direction and elevation were correct. It was quite a responsibility for a 19 year old. On one exercise with live ammunition a shell from somewhere in the regiment fell short and killed a soldier driver standing by his vehicle, half way to the front line. Tragedy, shame and consternation. Everything was hushed up as far as possible. We know now, of course, when we are much more familiar with news of fighting, that friendly fire casualties are not uncommon.

Communications played a major role in the field. They became even more important for me when I was moved to be the regiment's Intelligence Officer (IO), replacing a more senior regular officer. On exercises I became a sort of ADC to the colonel, accompanying him to high-level briefings, keeping him informed and always in radio contact with his units. His own place was with the headquarters of the Guards' infantry brigade that we were supporting. Sometimes, when communications were difficult because of the weather or topography, my unit could play a valuable role relaying messages between the guns behind and the observation officers in front. I helped reorganise our group of signal trucks to make operations more efficient.

Divisional manoeuvres were like being part of a mighty game. I travelled in my own small armoured scout car. It was a complicated operation getting the regiment on the move and finding the right place to camp at the end. On one exercise, my driver/batman, Hancock, said he was becoming too sleepy, so he stopped and said I should take over. I had barely learned to drive. The heavy little scout car, with pre-selector gear, was extremely difficult to control. A slight turn of the wheel would send it careering off to the right or left. I remember threading my way at one point in and out of trees by the side of the road. How I got to my destination I don't know. I think it was on that journey that the regimental convoy was going through a town, directed by military policemen. After a time I noticed the same truck broken down on the side of the road that we had seen before. Someone had erred in the policing, so that the regiment had gone in a circle completely around the town! Passers-by looked suitably astonished.

On big manoeuvres my job was to provide a base for Colonel Oswald with the brigade headquarters. The latter tended to take over a small village and set up an elaborate Guards' mess there, with good food and a fine selection of wines and other alcohol. I remember once seeing the brigade major, Major the Earl Cathcart, sipping port in the mess at 11 a.m.! I would usually take over some unsuspecting farmhouse for the colonel and my small group of men, where I set up an office. Memories of the war were recent. German farmers were subdued and put up with all sorts of inconvenience with good humour. I soon learned that the army sees itself as separate from 'civvy street', the civilian world. In

Germany at that time it went further. There was virtually no social contact between Germans and British.

A rare exception was a regular soldier friend Douglas Robinson, who fell in love with Ursula, who worked at the nearby airport. He asked me to be best man at his wedding. Part of my responsibility was to hire a Volkswagen and drive three of his female relatives (his father had died in Kenya in the war) 175 miles east, over German autobahns, to a village called Grebenstein, north of Kassel, in the American zone. (They were about the only motorways existing in the world at this time.) Some of the ladies were elderly, but they were full of guts. I recorded in a letter home that Ursula's parents lived in a rambling family farm with courtyard, lake and peacocks, half a mile from the old village, with its cobbled streets and beautiful church. Her father was tall and upright like a Prussian, with perfect manners – kissing hands etc. The mother was lively and full of fun. A sister was married to a man who had lost an arm in the war, in the Crimea. He still drove a car and took photographs. Everyone got on well, although neither family could speak the other's language. I was able to help Douglas and Ursula with interpreting. I noted special customs: a great family supper with fine food the night before the wedding; a garland of roses for the bride to wear; speech by her father. During the evening all the neighbours and their children came and threw old pots and pans against the door. The bridegroom had to sweep it up. I wrote that I had to calm down the rather over-excited couple the next morning. The well-managed wedding ceremony was half Lutheran and half Church of England. I had no speech to make. (Then it was a relief. Now I would feel deprived!) I did give the attractive, shy bridesmaid a little brooch, which she appreciated very much. Then I drove the ladies home.

Sadly, after army service I lost contact with my driver/batman, who was a Geordie of great character and initiative. He looked after me well, even bringing hot water bottles for my sleeping bags when we were camping. I didn't care if this aroused ribaldry. One of the merits of national service was that it provided a common experience for young men from all over the country, and from all backgrounds. It was something we all shared and could talk about. A period of common national service for men and women, not only in the forces, but for different types of community service at home and abroad, seems to me a good idea. Of course, the cost and administration required could be prohibitive.

When I wasn't required on exercises I reverted to an administration role. I was responsible for the 32 vehicles of all sorts, and their drivers, at regimental headquarters. I was supported by a wise sergeant who deferred to me politely, but who really took charge. Most of the senior soldiers in the regiment had fought in the war. Some of the young regular officers were restless because of the lack of direct fighting experience. This would not be a problem now. I played my part in routine activities such as inspections of the guard, and the compound. One of the kitchens I visited was full of cockroaches. There was a strange group of Mikhailovitch Yugoslav soldiers billeted with us. We never really knew what they were there for. I also had to collect a large amount of cash from the bank regularly and issue it on pay day. I needed to get it right, or to make up the difference.

I felt that I looked pretty smart with my dark blue number one dress for formal occasions, with a swagger stick, sometimes with a sword, and my highly polished Sam Brown belt borrowed from Billy Spratt, a friend of my parents. There was plenty of good comradeship, from which national service officers were not excluded; I took a major part in organising a pantomime one Christmas, being rather proud of a witty line in Cinderella: 'My name is Buttons and I must fly!' Regular officers had signed up for at least three years. They could be a little superior, but many became friends. Some stayed in the army and carried on to brigadier rank, like the engaging assistant adjutant, Trefor Jones, who took an interest in me. I attended one reunion some years later. Of the national service officer colleagues with whom I kept in touch, Jock Cormack became a distinguished doctor and Apothecary to the Queen in Edinburgh, Richard Bateman followed me to Cambridge then joined BP, Tim Raikes went to Oxford then joined an engineering firm. Our paths continued to cross over the years. I doubt if any of us would have expected that thousands of British troops would remain in Germany until 2019 (as now envisaged), 74 years after the end of World War II.

As I left, in the late summer of 1954, the regiment was preparing to go to Hong Kong and Korea, still commanded by the blunt, able, respected Colonel John Oswald. He had an Indian army background. He later became director of Military Intelligence as a major general. I realised that he had done me a considerable compliment by selecting me as his IO. At one of the Mess functions the local British consul was a guest. When I finally left, Oswald said he would give me one word of advice: 'on no account should you join the diplomatic service'! Looking through old papers, I found a letter from Lynam Thomas, my headmaster at Repton, telling me that Oswald had once been his pupil. We had that in common despite the difference in age. He wrote that he had advised Oswald not to go into the army!

In the summer of 1954 I went on my last family holiday with my parents and young sister. We drove to the south of France in our old Humber, which needed encouragement to get up the steeper hills. My father planned everything carefully with maps. He would never ask the way, which my mother loved doing. We visited several chateaux in the Loire, beautiful but rather like shells, empty of furniture and artefacts, which made one appreciate the treasure of English country houses in a land that had not been invaded for centuries. At the first hotel in which we were booked, mother put a mirror to the sheets, decided they were damp and ordered us out! Driving through the Dordogne we were fortunate enough to be some of the rare people who have been inside the Lascaux caves, then only recently discovered and opened. The freshness of the drawings and the colours were remarkable. Artistic sensibility must be innate in the human race considering these paintings were done 15,000 years ago. The caves were closed to the public soon afterwards because of damage from human contact.

After driving through the Gorges du Tarn we arrived at Nimes and Arles, with surprising Roman remains, and then spent some time in a little hotel on the Riviera. I began to appreciate French cheeses and wines and quality of life. It was impossible to eat badly in France in those days. On the way back we visited Avignon, where I saw, with some shock, rats in the street (recently to our shame they have been photographed in Downing Street, and no one seems to have been shocked at all). Sightseeing inside the Abbey we were impressed when a group of monks came past singing Gregorian chant in deep, melodious voices. In Burgundy country we stopped by chance at a restaurant which turned out to be one of the great gourmet restaurants of France. We were surprised to see so many cooks rushing around in the kitchen. Mother's request for an omelette was met with incredulity. My sister thinks she was unwell. I think it was frugality. Sometimes when she thought I was on the phone for too long, mother would come up miming a pair of scissors as if to cut it off.

4

MULTIPLE OPTIONS IN CAMBRIDGE

Two years' national service may have allowed me to grow up, but they interrupted scholastic habits and training. When asked for confirmation that I wished to spend three years at Clare reading modern languages, I decided to switch to a more general degree that was likely to be even more useful for a future career: economics and law. With modern languages I felt that, however well I mastered the literature, I would always be struggling with the grammar, compared with more natural linguists. My teachers at Repton had been seriously concerned, I later discovered, about this weak point of mine. One year of economics and two years of law was a hybrid favoured by the influential old master of Clare, Sir Henry Thirkill, as the nearest thing Cambridge could offer to the Oxford PPE course (Politics, Philosophy and Economics). One advantage, after two intellectually fallow years in the army, was that I started on the same basis as everyone else in these subjects, as in those days neither economics nor law featured in school curricula. Those not planning to practice law, like me, could omit the first year of a law course which contained a lot of Roman law. And economics became mathematical and technical after the first year. So they fitted well. I justified the change to myself by saying that my father had spent money sending me to a public school, and would still be giving me some help at Cambridge financially (though I did get some funding from Essex County and a small college foundation scholarship). I should therefore concentrate on studies that would be of practical use to me in getting a job. As for English literature, philosophy and history, these were subjects that I thought people should pursue privately in any case, as part of their general education, as I intended to do.

I was allocated a small attic room in the old court of Clare. It had a gas fire that was great for toasting crumpets, but that would now be condemned as dangerous. I was delighted to get my own room, despite the snag that baths were down several flights of stairs in the basement. I buckled down to learn the basics of economics under the supervision of Dr Brian Reddaway. He was a patient man, slow and careful of speech, who was not afraid of drawing out the simple principles of complex issues. He later became professor of Applied Economics, advised foreign governments, and was a source of valuable guidance on Clare's college investments. His son was a Soviet scholar, his brother and nephew both became ambassadors and his niece became married to one. He and his hospitable wife Barbara remained my friends and friends of my family as long as they lived.

Henry Thirkill, the Master, elected in 1939, had been a great operator in Cambridge University for years, ever since he had been an influential senior tutor at Clare in the 1930s. He invited groups of new arrivals for Sunday sherry after a few weeks. I didn't exchange words with him again, however, until we passed crossing the courtyard one and a half years later, when he astonished me by saying 'Good evening Barrington'. He must have studied all of the students carefully through files and photographs. The most important senior member of the college for me was my tutor, John Northam, lecturer in English and expert on Ibsen, who treated me as an adult from the start and encouraged me to have the widest intellectual interests. In due course he introduced me to the college Dilettante Society. It was in his rooms that I met Siegfried Sassoon. He and his two brothers had all been at Clare, although only the youngest, who was later killed at Gallipoli, completed his degree. I was in awe of Siegfried, tall and shy with a fine head, whose poems about World War I had moved me. In old age he had been delighted to be made an Honorary Fellow and had come back several times, under Northam's auspices, to talk to students. He left me with the sad impression that his life had virtually finished when so many of his friends and contemporaries had died in World War I. In 2010, when I myself had become an Honorary Fellow, Sassoon's papers were saved for the University Library. I helped organise an academic event at Clare in his honour.

I never misbehaved at Clare because it would have been so embarrassing to be brought up for censure before Northam, a man I already thought of as a friend. After I left he made a major contribution to the college, as senior tutor, in three areas: introducing women in 1972 (we were one of the first three men's colleges to do so), founding Clare Hall as an independent graduate college, and broadening the college's entry system so that it was less public school orientated. His predecessor as senior tutor, Dr McDonald, was a New Zealand classical scholar who occupied a corner room on the first floor of the river facade of Clare, but who normally lived in the town. If we were out late beyond the deadline when the front gate was closed, we had to navigate our way around the portal on the Backs without falling into the ditch, walk across the bridge and then climb up onto the high wall which separated Clare from Kings. From there we went in through the sash window in the senior tutor's room, which was always left open. When I look at the wall now, I can't believe that we used to do this. Once I took my Hutton Mount friend, Michael Williams, on this route as a guest. He clearly thought I was demented. The story goes that as one student was going through the tutor's rooms he realised with alarm that Dr McDonald was coming in. So he hid under a desk. McDonald sat working on his Livy texts for about an hour, and then left the room saying 'Good night' as he closed the door! One of my contemporaries spent a drunken night stuck on spikes trying to get in by a more difficult route down the service passage.

I played a little hockey and tennis for college second teams, and some squash, and buried myself in economics textbooks. Faced with some of the more complex economic theory, I began to realise, for the first time, that there were limits to my mental ability. This had never crossed my mind before. I had to accept the shocking thought that I was never to become prime minister! First year students were encouraged to go to lectures at the Economics Society. I remember once listening to a typically jargon-smothered American professor, who covered a blackboard with calculations in order to prove some theory that went completely over our heads. When it came to questions, however, a scruffy little elderly lady sitting in the front row said that she did not see the logic of one element of the calculation, pointing to the middle of the blackboard. This threw the professor completely. He had to admit that this weakness made his whole thesis uncertain. Afterwards we asked ourselves who the lady could be. It was, of course, Professor Joan

Robinson, an intellectual powerhouse who sometimes lived like a hippy in a garden summerhouse and who was so left-wing that she lauded the Chinese Cultural Revolution. I remember another example of the telling question, when I was taken by one of my parents to the law courts in the Strand, where we observed from the gallery a tedious commercial case in front of three judges of Appeal, led by Lord Goddard. The barrister droned on and it looked as if all the judges were asleep under their wigs. Then suddenly Goddard opened an eye and asked a question, which sent the lawyer into a frightful flurry, consulting in some panic his junior and his solicitor, with much passing back and forwards of paper. His case had been punctured. Goddard had not been asleep.

Cambridge had a good reputation for economics, because of Keynes, and, before him, Marshall. The latter's best interpreter was meant to be Professor Guillebaud, but his lectures were virtually inaudible. He would write something on the blackboard, with his back to us, and then rub it out before he turned to face us again! Keynes' theories were considered a little too difficult for us in the first year. But his name was constantly mentioned in Cambridge. One day I was passing by the chapel in the main court of Kings when I saw an ill-kempt old man sitting in a deckchair in the middle of the lawn, dressed in dirty brown clothes with a red and yellow scarf. Cambridge students and dons, however radical they may be, are conditioned never to walk on the green grass lawns, except Fellows of the college concerned. When I asked around who the man in the deckchair could possibly be I was told it was Professor Pigou. He had made a name for himself at the beginning of the century with a book on income, and had been the teacher of Keynes. Keynes had become internationally famous, had been covered with honours and had died. Pigou was still around, completely forgotten!

As my Director of Studies, Reddaway advised me about which lectures to attend and where it was better to read the relevant book. I was surprised at the choice. I had assumed that one had to attend all lectures. Donning a gown, however, I discovered that one could attend lectures by prominent people in any subject. I remember particularly the series of talks on poetry by a roguish Robert Graves, who began his first lecture with deliberate provocation by saying 'Why Milton was a bad poet!' He got his gasped reaction. Then there was Robert Frost who read some of his poems, including 'The day a crow shook down on me....' He said he had doubts about free verse, which was 'like playing tennis with the net down' – in his inimitable American drawl. Leavis and Raven were other lecturers attended by outsiders.

I joined the Cambridge Union, the famous debating venue, on the basis that one should start by joining everything, but found the activity there uninspiring, with few exceptions. Undergraduate speakers seemed primarily concerned to score points in such a way that they might be spotted for a political constituency. The leader of the conservative students at that time was Tam Dalyell, later a prominent maverick Labour MP. I made enquiries about dramatic societies, but on the whole found that first year frustrating. I even wrote a rather pathetic banal poem, ending in a refrain: 'Was this what I came here for'!

Coloured socks and cigarette smoke.
    Sunken in hollow armchair while folk
Talk of the army, of love and the future.
    Is this what I came here for?
Coffee and crumpets and dizzy Esquires.
    And hot gas fires.
Umbrellas, waistcoats and wasted hours.
    Not a bit what I foresaw.
A game of squash and a cup of tea.
    Then a film or a play to see.
An essay, a lecture, absorbing a book.
    Isn't there anything more?
Pursuit of knowledge, is that my end?
    Or a frank and intimate talk with a friend?
Or a feeling of fitness to try for a Blue?
    Or an effort to help the poor?
No. I am here to give me a start in life.
    So I'll earn good money and wed a good wife.
Clare should be a means not an end. That's why I'm studying law!

(The films I saw included all the Garbo canon. I was entranced by that lady.) The magic of Cambridge was eluding me. In fact, pursuit of knowledge and talks with friends became more and more important.

Everything changed during my first long vacation. Having achieved only an upper second in economics part I, I went back to Cambridge for six weeks for a long vac term for a crash conversion course in law, so I had a basis to start my two final years working up to part II in that subject. Apart from lectures I found myself with a lively cultured group in Cambridge, including some dons, interested in the arts. There was an undergraduate senior to me at Clare who appreciated the finer things of life – music, painting and literature. He was a dapper figure but he had done national service in Korea, where at times, he told me, he and his fellow soldiers were down in trenches while Chinese troops dominated the land above. John X (I shall call him) took an interest in me and introduced me to his circle of friends. He told me on one occasion 'you always listen to what is being said around you, but you rarely give your own views'. One doesn't forget such advice. I lacked self-confidence in the Cambridge environment. John later ended rather sadly as a not particularly successful lawyer, often the worse for drink. But in those early days he was a young man of some style. He introduced me to the Reverend Richard Bagley, curate at the high church Little Saint Mary's, who entertained bright young people at his house in Portugal Place, full of decent paintings and Renaissance bronzes. Besides being cultured and witty he was a wise and sympathetic counsellor. When I told him rather pompously that the only thing in life was to be kind to other people, he told me not to forget to be kind to myself also, on the basis that there are limits on what you can do to help others if you are not at peace with yourself. I have relayed this useful advice.

I started my second year following the advice of Sebastian's cousin from *Brideshead Revisited*: 'You will spend the beginning of your second year getting rid of friends you made in your first.' I had gone around with friends from school and the army, those connected with home or who were attending lectures with me. But I drifted apart from many of them. I discovered that the people I most enjoyed being with were creative and artistic. Some divided undergraduates into 'arties', 'smarties' and 'hearties', or people who only worked. I favoured the former. I was now in digs with a couple of friends on the Madingley Road (people prepared to put up students in this way have now practically disappeared, so colleges have to provide all-year-round accommodation). Most of my friends were outside Clare College, part of the university-wide group of people focused round amateur dramatics. This brought together actors and actresses, directors, writers, musicians, set and poster designers, costume people and technicians. One of the group was a young man at Kings, David Gillmore, who moved from journalism into the diplomatic service and years later became my boss as permanent under-secretary in the Foreign Office.

It was a heady time for Cambridge theatre. Julian Slade and Peter Hall had just gone down. The tunes of *Salad Days* were on everyone's lips. (When I talk to undergraduates now I sometimes tell them that they are in their salad days, but I am in my vegetable days. Adding that hopefully none of us is junk food!) Hall would soon be successful in running Stratford. Jonathan Miller was performing hilarious comedy sketches, for example on the death of Nelson and the consternation caused by 'Kiss me Hardy'! *Beyond the Fringe* was in gestation. The Footlights flourished. Marlowe performances were outstanding. I remember a dramatic Volpone. At the ADC (Amateur Dramatic Club) Peter Woodthorpe gave a devastatingly tragic performance in Arthur Miller's *Death of a Salesman*. He looked middle-aged even as an undergraduate. After Cambridge he had great success with new plays like *Waiting for Godot* and *The Caretaker*, and then virtually disappeared from view.

Partly because of an untypically theatrical Clare man, John Elwick (he wore a cloak), I joined the Mummers, the second most prominent student theatre group after the ADC, and one that had first involved women. I did a reasonable job as an heroic Hector in Giraudoux's *Tiger at the Gates*, where our Cassandra was Margaret Drabble's eldest sister, Antonia (now Baroness Byatt). One of the smaller parts was played by a friend from one of the most prominent families in Pakistan. In due course I became for over a year a committee member of the Mummers, the first of many committees I have sat on. I like the definition of a committee as a group of people who individually can do nothing and collectively decide that nothing can be done. But this one was useful. This one I enjoyed. John and Ann Tusa were both committee members with me before they got married and created such a good partnership. John was a convincing Proctor in Arthur Miller's *Crucible*, on which production I assisted. I acted with Clive Swift in *The Merry Wives of Windsor*, supporting as Falstaff David Buck, the outstanding actor of our period, who died quite young. That was a production for the ADC, the main undergraduate theatre group. I even got a good review in *The Times*: 'Nicholas Barrington, his delivery as crisp as a hammer-tap, made the welsh pedant, Sir Hugh Evans, more than usually comprehensible.' (I had drawn on my mother's Welsh forbears!) Clive, who has never been out of work since turning professional, married Margaret Drabble, who was soon to produce a series of compelling novels. The director of *Merry Wives* was Clive Perry, later a successful professional director at Leicester. He was meticulous in demanding what he wanted, even in youth, and he got results. Julian Slade's younger brother was also in the cast. I played Bassanio in *The Merchant of Venice*, alongside another of Cambridge's best-known actors Robin Chapman as Shylock, with his girlfriend Jill Booty as Portia. We pretended to be a troop of actors strolling through the audience in Kings Fellows garden to perform on a small square stage. I became a member of the Footlights but didn't perform. I was on the fringes of the best undergraduate theatre, and it was stimulating.

The most spectacular production in which I took part, although in minor roles, was *Troilus and Cressida*, by the Marlowe Society. I was rightly pipped for the leading part by the handsome young Julian Pettifer, a year younger than me at Johns, who spoke poetry beautifully. Dan Massey was Achilles, Bamber Gascoigne Paris, Johnny Bird Nestor. Chapman was a ghastly Thersites and David Buck a brutish Ajax. (I have always loved that passage of Pope's about the importance of sound seeming an echo to the sense, including the couplet 'When Ajax strives some rock's vast weight to throw, the line too labours and the words move slow.') The play was directed by George Rylands and John Barton. It was in full costume. We would go to the room of Dedie Rylands to be told how to speak Shakespeare's verse with absolute precision. I remember not being able to put down my drink because every surface of the table at my side was covered in nick-nacks of one sort or another. John Barton, then a young don, later a greatly respected director at Stratford, rehearsed us thoroughly for all the individual fights making up the total battle scene. We had heavy shields and solid swords that could injure if the routine was not followed correctly. During the battles Judy Birdwood, the aristocratically connected costume mistress, with vast bosom full of appropriate pins, would give us bloody gashes in make up, indicating injuries, before our next appearance. When the last act of the play was all put together for the first time in one of the final rehearsals it was exciting as it all came alive.

The most distinguished of my contemporaries of Cambridge was Michael Frayn, then journalist and critic, subsequently a brilliant playwright and novelist, a man of quiet charm and modesty. Bamber Gascoigne was a golden boy, whose review, *Share my Lettuce*, was put on in London while he was still an undergraduate. He then wrote a good book on the Moghuls and soon embarked on many years creating and starring in *University Challenge*, master of the new television medium. Graeme MacDonald, the supreme stage manager for all undergraduate productions, became head of one of the national television channels. Jan Pienkowski, poster designer, became a successful illustrator. Theatrical friends took me to sit at the feet of E. M. Forster, holding court benignly and saying little in his rooms at Kings. I admired his theories of the supreme importance of friendship.

We were all pretty well behaved in those days. However, one of my foreign friends came to me in some desperation saying he was in trouble because a girl he had been with needed money for an abortion. I gave him £50, which was quite a lot to me then. He had asked for a loan, but I preferred to consider it a gift and forget about it, so that it didn't affect our relationship.

Looking back, it is amazing how much activity we crowded into three short terms in three years. In my final year I put in a bid for a spacious set of rooms on A staircase in the old court of Clare, and got lucky. The panelling was all a gloomy dark brown, which the bursar wouldn't change. But my father generously offered to pay to have it painted off-white, and the bursar didn't object. This is remarkable when you think of it. I have never heard of such a thing happening before or after. It could be because the bursar was a neighbour of my aunt Freda. Anyway my rooms were a great place to live in and entertain that final busy year.

John Northam got me to run the college's Picture Guild. During my time we organised three exhibitions in a large room in the old court. One was of wood cuts and other illustrations by Darwin's granddaughter, Gwen Raverat, whom we used to see being wheeled out for sketching from her house opposite the Mill (now part of Darwin College). She was, of course, a direct link with the glamorous days of Rupert Brooke. She was laconically pleased with our efforts and invited me to choose two small, signed woodcuts at the end. Thanks to the contacts of uncle Geoff, who collected modern art and patronised a number of modern artists, I organised an exhibition of paintings by the group of artists who lived at the village of Great Bardfield in Essex, all of whom my uncle knew: John Aldridge, Edward Bawden, Michael Rothenstein, Clifford Smith, Audrey Cruddas and others. I had visited most of them with him. This was also a success, as was the show Northam arranged through the Whitechapel art gallery, after which several pieces were purchased for the college's own collection. Bamber Gasgoigne got me involved with the Cambridge Contemporary Arts Trust, sponsored by the flamboyant director of the Fitzwilliam Museum, Michael Jaffe. This allowed undergraduates to have experience of living with and borrowing original paintings. (I don't tolerate reproductions in my houses.) Sadly, despite best efforts over the years, Clare remained something of a desert in terms of visual arts.

Later the college became outstanding at music. A few years before my time the organ scholar had been an older friend from Repton, Martin How, who, as it happened, had preceded me as captain of school cross-country running. As opposed to my dilettante approach to life, Martin, the son of the senior Anglican clergyman in Scotland, concentrated on two things which he did supremely well: cross-country running and music. He took trouble to give me advice on running the school's cross-country team in letters after he had left. As organ scholar at Clare, Martin had done his best with little support. He ended up highly respected as a teacher in the Royal School of Church Music. One of my contemporaries at Clare, a chorister but reading English not music, was Roger Norrington, later to become a distinguished conductor and advocate of traditional music. He took me to visit his father, then master of Trinity College Oxford and the inventor of the Norrington tables. It has been a pleasure watching Sir Roger's career from a distance, especially when he took charge of the *Last Night of the Proms* in the Albert Hall.

The elegant college chapel was a lively place because of our clerical team. The dean, John Robinson, was later to become famous as author of *Honest to God* (1963), which dared to suggest that the supreme being might not be a white-bearded old man sitting on a cloud. He never talked down to us in his sermons, which merited careful attention. He promoted a good tradition that at breakfast in college after Sunday communion the remains of the sanctified loaf were passed around. Robinson and his wife were socially very shy. Not so our chaplain, Bill Skelton, who got on particularly well, as a sportsman himself, with the games crowd. I never found out until afterwards, however, that he had a DSO and DFC and bar as navigator on numerous bombing trips over Germany. People didn't talk about their bravery in those days. Nor did we know that he was related to the Dukes of Somerset. Thirdly, as a bonus, we had as a Fellow in Clare the Lady Margaret Professor of Divinity and former dean, Charlie Moule, whose brother had been one of the chaplains at Repton for a time. Charlie was a man of immense scholarship, combined with transparent goodness, with whom I was lucky enough to keep in sporadic touch until he died in 2006. He never forgot a thing, taking great pains with personal relationships, reinforced by letters in a beautiful hand. To me he was something of a saintly hero. It emerged that he had been quite firm, however, in dealing with shoddy scholarship.

A macabre event happened during my last year. There was scaffolding on the tall towers of Kings chapel not far away from my rooms. One night, the dean or chaplain of Kings (I forget which) climbed up the scaffolding to the top, high above the ground, and threw himself off. His mind had clearly been disturbed. We wondered if he thought he could fly like an angel or that they would bear him up. There has been a troubled history of clerics at Kings. In 2009 the dean committed suicide after being accused of sexual crimes against young people way back in the past. It is almost as if the great building, with its sublime fan-vaulting and medieval glass is so ravishingly beautiful that no common human is worthy of it. One of my friends who became a school master nearly ended his life because of some accusation from the past which had to be gone into by the authorities, although I would judge there was no substance to it. Who knows what the truth was or what prompted somebody to make such a cruel accusation years after the event. I gave my friend support. I am afraid my unfashionable view is: complain at the time, or cope with it!

Religion in Cambridge in those days was more talked about than politics, which we rather despised. There were the artistic high church people around Richard Bagley, and the Catholics patronised by the resident chaplain Father Gilbey, related to the gin family, who lived in considerable style. I noticed he had original Zurbarans in his rooms. Mervyn Stockwood was a strong force as vicar of Great St Marys. Above all there were the evangelical members of CICCU, the Cambridge Intercollegiate Christian Union. This was a fairly recent phenomenon, strengthened by some role model sportsman such as the cricketer David Sheppard, a legend who had just gone down. He later became bishop of Liverpool. One of my charming cultured friends from army days, David Bastin, tried, rather embarrassingly, to convert me, but I stuck to the middle of the road Anglicanism I had become used to at Repton. I did thrash out with friends over coffee religious beliefs as well as politics and other issues, the sort of thing that university is for. In my view one of the main purposes of university is to find out about oneself. Technical colleges may prepare some people better for earning a living in the world.

Successful entrepreneurs such as Branson can do without a university education at all. Not all with good degrees find appropriate jobs. But the process of exposure to all the possibilities at a university like Cambridge, and then plumbing one's own character, beliefs and interests is very much worthwhile if one can have the chance. Someone once said that the job of education is to replace any empty mind not with a full mind, but with an open mind. It is also to find out about yourself.

I was pretty ignorant of world affairs in those days, though none of us could fail to be affected by the Hungarian Revolution in 1956, which drew several courageous and therefore admired undergraduates to Budapest. Also by Eden's invasion of Suez around the same time. Hungarian refugees started to appear in Cambridge. I went to one social occasion when a group of them, as special guests, toasted independent Hungary and then smashed their empty glasses against the fireplace. This may have been a local custom but their host was not very happy! Clare gave a place to one Hungarian student from a refugee camp in Austria. I made a point of getting to know Zoltan, since others seemed hesitant about doing so. He had been a pentathlon champion at Budapest University and, as one of the most prominent students, had been roped in on a student committee to support Nagy and independence from the Soviet Union. The tide turned, and Russian troops moved in. My friend was going home one day when he was warned that the local KGB was after him. He therefore joined a number of people trying to get across into Austria. He told me he was on a train heading for the border when a security official came to the carriage and started to question everyone. When asked the reason for his journey he said that he was going to a village that he knew was near the frontier. At this point one of the other passengers, whom he had never met, spoke up and said that indeed he was from that village, where everyone knew him. Thus he was saved.

Off the train he and a ski-jumping athlete friend found a local guide who, for a fee in advance, was prepared to take a group of about 40 people at night through the woods and snow across the frontier. It started well, but after some hours, he and his friend, who were out in front, realised that their guide was leading them in the wrong direction, towards a police post. They didn't tell the rest of the group, to avoid panic, but got hold of the guide, put a knife to his throat, and forced him to conduct them all through completely unknown territory and across the border, where they were rescued by Austrian guards. My friend learned good English and got a BA degree in four years. He distinguished himself as promoter of the pentathlon at the university and won a fencing Blue. Eventually he joined Unilever, married a delightful Spanish girl, and ended up as a respected citizen of the Canary Islands. I remember one thing that he told me was that despite all the communist brainwashing, Hungarian students had not been as cut off as we had imagined, but had been perfectly well aware of what was going on in the wider world. We kept in touch. I visited him and his wife in Tenerife.

The Suez adventure, about which we protested, caused general concern, although we were not aware of the duplicity of the Eden government, denying collusion with the Israelis and the French. British policy seemed, at best, dubious, however irritating Nasser had been. The long gap between the British/French ultimatum to Egypt on 30 October 1953 and the eventual landing at Suez on 5 November, while our fleet was going through the Mediterranean, was particularly disturbing. It had allowed international and domestic criticism to build up. With lack of American support there followed the humiliation of defeat, withdrawal and Eden's resignation. An apt comment was in one of the review numbers at the Establishment nightclub in Soho (which continued the burgeoning trend of political satire and of which I was proud to be a founder member), suggesting that all sorts of bad decisions by politicians could be mocked by saying 'he was a sick man at the time'.

I sometimes felt that I did not really achieve as much as I should at Clare. I was not awarded a Green Cup, nor made secretary of the junior common room. I was quite proud on the other hand of being one of the few people invited to join three very different college societies. First, the Dilettante, which I later helped to revive after retirement. John Northam was the prime mover. I presented my first ever paper at one of their meetings, on art forgery. I had always been fascinated by the story of Van Meegeren's creation of fake Vermeers. Research at the British Library raised some eyebrows. Under the title, 'The forger as artist', I also considered whether a forgery was as 'beautiful' as an original. The paper still reads quite well. I have collected material on art forgery ever since. The second society was the Clarence, an appropriately named gourmet wine tasting and dining society. Our royal family is descended from Edward III's son, Lionel Duke of Clarence, whose wife was the granddaughter of Lady Clare, founder of our college. A subsequent

Duke of Clarence, brother of Edward IV and Richard III, was, of course, reputed to have been drowned in a butt of Malmsey wine. So the name was appropriate. Clarence presidents, or grandmasters, were chosen for a term and would organise their own distinctive meal for the group, with a special guest. I brought the painter Clifford Smith. My friend Max Cropper brought Jaffe, the director of the Fitzwilliam Museum. The Falcons Society, thirdly, was composed of sportsman but admitted some all-rounders. I was, at least, one of those.

It was a mark of distinction to be selected for the prestigious Mellon Fellowship to go for a year after Cambridge to Yale. But by that time I had passed the Foreign Office entrance exam, and having already lost two years in national service felt it was time for me to start a career and help my father by earning some money. So I declined. I also had the fear that once prolonging the pleasures of university life I might find it difficult to get back to the real world. Clare has benefitted hugely over the years by the fact that Paul Mellon, son of the US steel king Andrew Mellon, went to Clare and has been a major benefactor. A series of exchanges of graduates between Clare and Yale has long continued. Mellon fellows at Clare in my time were impressive, and good company.

I coped with all the pressures those last two years by doing the minimum amount of work during the year, but studying extremely hard during the run up to the exams. In the final months I used to lock my outer door ('sport my oak') and work until late at night. That included careful analysis of previous exam papers and preparing quotations and illustrations that I would inject into my answers come what may. I took the line that if we were going to be tested by exams I was going to do my damnedest to do well in them. My law supervisor was the young radical and very sharp Fellow of Clare, Bill Wedderburn, subsequently Lord Wedderburn. One really had to be on the ball for his supervisions. A major influence at this period, to which Wedderburn drew our attention, was Lord Denning, judge in the Court of Appeal, who was making the law more flexible by developing precedents about what a reasonable man would do. We heard his west country recorded voice and enjoyed the elegant simplicity of his written judgements. In fact, all the top judges' judgements were models of concise and elegant prose. I enjoyed Professor Jennings' lectures on international law, of some marginal benefit to me as a future diplomat. Wade on the constitution was boring. Supervision on criminal law by Turner in Trinity Hall was an experience. He gave the impression that he never moved from his study up a long flight of stairs. As he gleefully plotted crimes and asked our reactions, we wondered if Turner was a great lawyer or a great criminal! His daughter married Robert Runcie, then dean of Trinity Hall, subsequently archbishop. Fortunately I had a good memory for case law, spending many hours in the old law library. When I didn't understand any issue I always made a point of thrashing it out with someone who did. This is, of course, a key principle in education: if you don't understand, don't be afraid to ask.

Usually I consulted a fellow student with whom I had played hockey, John Roch. He was planning to be a lawyer and was more hard-working than I was. Anyway, in my final year, to surprise of many, I got a First (I dare to say it was more difficult then). The news came to me in a telegram from Wedderburn while I was playing a part in a Marlowe production of *As You Like It* on a tour in Holland after term had finished. I think the telegram made clear that my supervisor was a little astonished, because of the exclamation marks. Years later, when I was back in Clare as an Honorary Fellow after retirement, and helping the development office getting in touch with former Clare men who might be interested in donations, I asked for news of John Roch, but the college had lost track of him. I remembered that he had a good friend, John Boot, an appropriately named solicitor from Nottingham, and got the latter on the phone. I asked him what had happened to John Roch. He said 'Oh, you mean the Rt Hon Sir John Roch, Lord Justice of Appeal'! It has been a pleasure to regain contact with a man who helped me get my First, and to be entertained by him at Grays Inn.

Thinking back on it I was very lucky to have contact with so many fellow students from such a wide variety of backgrounds. It was immaterial whether they were Etonians or council school boys. Talent, ability and character were what was important. We didn't take drugs, nor did we drink very much. Coffee rather than beer; coffee houses rather than pubs. I used to give sherry parties in my rooms, mixing fellow students from different areas of my life, with sympathetic dons and some outsiders. Social contact with Fellows was quite extensive and a few became friends.

There have been two major changes since my time. The first has been the arrival of many more girls. In my day there were so few women's colleges that entry was very competitive. Newnham and Girton usually got the highest exam marks. My time coincided with the first year of the third women's college, New Hall. I and my friends knew all of the 20 or so pioneer New Hall girls. Most of them were able and attractive, with distinctive personalities. They operated from the old Darwin family house that is now part of Darwin postgraduate college, in a good site near the Mill Pond. (In due course New Hall moved to a larger complex on the Huntingdon Road. After retirement I met up with a number of my old New Hall friends at a ruby ball in 1994, and at the college's 50th anniversary celebrations in 2004, for which I was one of the patrons. In 2010, to acknowledge a major donation, New Hall became Murray Edwards College.) Girton has now become mixed, as have all the men's colleges. In a reversal of the old pattern, women now tend to be underachievers in the class lists. Paucity of women meant that there was competition to invite them to May balls. I had some good times. For my first May ball, however, I invited a daughter of one of my aunt's closest friends. Bim remained dear to me for the rest of my life. After that first May ball my aunt laid on a full breakfast for about 20 people on her terrace in Barrow Close. I don't know how all my friends got there after late night punting, but we had a great time.

The second major change has been the large number of postgraduates doing PhD, MPhil and similar degrees. If there are 12,000 undergraduates in Cambridge nowadays there are probably 5,000 graduate students. In the 1950s they were very rare birds. Postgraduate work can be rather isolated and lonely. Many come from overseas. So colleges now make an effort to ensure that they are part of the community.

One of the great merits of Oxbridge, of course, is the multidisciplinary nature of the colleges, both among the undergraduates and at the high table. Mathematicians sit next to theologians, linguists next to biologists. This means you are likely to make friends with people in all fields of study, pursuing eventually widely different careers. Friendships can be very intense in the short incubation time that undergraduates can enjoy. It is important, in my view, to maintain contact with friends, particularly with those in different walks of life. Perhaps I made more of an effort on this than others because when I went abroad as a diplomat I made a point of keeping in touch with friends by scribbling over Christmas cards, and when I came home, I would keep contact by at least inviting them for a meal or some other function. If you leave the gap too long the relationship may disintegrate.

Many of my Cambridge friends stayed friends. Apart from the theatrical crowd there was the medical student, Peter Barbor of Clare, with whom I played hockey and tennis. Because of his successful back-specialist father, and well-organised mother, I even tasted for a time the London debutante season, though it wasn't really my scene. The official presentation of debutantes to the Queen, sanctifying the class structure by linking it to the monarchy, was finally stopped in 1958, so I got a glimpse of its last throes. It wasn't the Barbors' fault but I remember finding many of the debs empty-headed and their escorts, the 'debs delights', the converse of delightful. Peter became a distinguished paediatric oncologist. I have always felt privileged having him as a friend, with his lovely wife whom he met on a skiing holiday.

Roger Berthoud (Trinity Hall), son of a punctilious and strong-minded ambassador father, became a successful journalist and writer. He specialised in the art world, writing authorised biographies of Sutherland and Moore. Dry and clever, Roger was good company and another firm friend. Donald Reeves, who studied English at Queens and played the organ, joined the British Council and later the Church. He became well-known as the liberal rector of St James's Church, Piccadilly, which he made a vibrant centre of all sorts of activity, as a church should be. After retirement he played a significant role in bringing together different religious factions in former Yugoslavia. Alan Griggs, a year before me at Trinity Hall, with whom I had played tennis as a child, ended as a canon in Leeds, a man of transparent goodness who with his wife greatly helped the local community. Julian Pettifer became a prominent radio and television journalist, distinguish-ing himself particularly in Vietnam. He later took an interest in wildlife programmes and became president of the Royal Society for the Protection of Birds. With these and many others it didn't matter that I was often separated from them in remote parts of the world. We always caught up and stayed close.

Christmas and Easter holidays I usually spent with my family, including my lively, attractive, growing sister. At one time she had an alarming series of boyfriends – one I remember was very unsafe behind the wheel of a car – but she eventually married John Symes, who was sound, kind and in tune with the countryside, that was his business as a farmer. In his modest way he was artistic. He painted, played the piano by ear and became an accomplished potter. I have felt much indebted, over many years, for the way John made my sister happy.

One Christmas I stayed with Cambridge thespian friends in a big house belonging to one of my uncles at Frinton. We did Footlights material and other sketches in a sort of cabaret in various private houses in the area. I can't remember how our hosts, who paid for our performances, were chosen, but in a couple of cases they also expected us to take part in some embarrassingly sexual games, which shocked my then puritanical soul. Not being at home for Christmas had been a gesture of liberation. Frinton was normally an exceptionally staid place where, with the Barbor family and others, we played tennis in the summer. One year, I took out, once or twice, a tall young actress in the local repertory company. It was Vanessa Redgrave. Fifty-five years later, when I congratulated her on a British film award which she had accepted graciously, she told me she had not forgotten Frinton, her first professional job, when she had good experience of playing ten different characters for £7 per week, of which £4 was for lodging and breakfast.

The summer break, the long vacation, was a period that needed to be spent wisely. Part of my first was spent attending law lectures on the conversion course. I also went to the Riviera with Roger and another companion where, in Antibes, we became friendly with the daughters of Harry Wheatcroft, the pioneer English rose grower. I then went on down to Spain to stay in uncle Geoff's villa in Marbella. I visited the Alhambra at Granada, my first taste of the orient, which was to be such a feature in my life. I fell in love with it. I greatly enjoyed exotic flamenco and I must confess the drama of bullfights, where men were playing with their lives before one's very eyes. Many got injured. It wasn't an entirely one-sided affair. Bullfighting is an extraordinary survival from Roman amphitheatre days. I relished the costumes, the colour, the music and the drama. One could argue that motor-racing drivers put their lives on the line behind their helmets, but you can actually see the matador's face as he is risking life and limb. It was a few years later in Marbella that I fell in with a rather louche crowd. A striking looking Cambridge acquaintance, another Peter, I met on the beach and found to my surprise that he was operating as a gigolo with older American lady tourists. His Spanish girlfriend Menchu took a shine to me. One of their acquaintances was a young man who had lost a considerable fortune as a gambling addict. He continually tried to wager on anything he saw around him. At the local Jacaranda nightclub there was a spirited Filipino band, and one met at the bar April Ashley, a young Briton who had changed sex, with her partner, an English peer! Also Rosemary Strachey, sister of John, painter of cats.

Part of this long vacation was also spent on a visit for several weeks to Reckitt and Colman in Norwich, arranged by the university careers service to introduce undergraduates to industry. I did this with Robin Steward, a Repton contemporary although from another house, who was also at Clare and who had Norwich family connections. He and his wife Val ended up in Cape Town and years later organised a magnificent holiday for me there, introducing me to the many culinary pleasures and natural beauties of the Cape and its vine-growing hinterland. In that long vacation, Robin and I were shown all over the Reckitt and Colman group of factories, mostly by the experienced floor managers, sort of NCOs. I was surprised to find that the company produced not only Reckitt dyes and Colman's mustard, but Robinson's barley water, Three Bear oats, Cherry Blossom boot polish and many other products. The secrets of the famous mustard were guarded fiercely. A small slit was opened in a steel door before we were allowed into the mixing area. It was a classic monopoly with profits made, to some extent, from material left on the plate. We were told of a lady customer who had complained vociferously that she was changing to another type of mustard. They refrained from telling her that this was also produced by Colmans! I found it particularly educative to go out one day with a travelling salesman, visiting numerous village stores and trying to keep his customers sweet. We picked up some criticisms and suggestions coming from the floor managers which we put into our final report for the directors, just as management consultants recycle views within organisations, at great expense. Both of us liked the general atmosphere of the company. I applied what I had learned about work study to the organisation of my personal kitchens and offices later in life.

For my second and last long vacation I was more ambitious. My uncles had invited me to visit California. I took an economy passage to New York on the *Queen Mary*. We slept in crowded conditions, four or six to a cabin, but for food we were allowed to eat our way right through the extensive menus. With a companion, I found ways of going through secret doors so that we could enjoy ourselves in the second- and even first-class areas of the huge vessel, although it was mildly embarrassing when we were spotted by an officer. The arrival in New York with the Statue of Liberty and silhouettes of Manhattan skyscrapers was suitably spectacular. (The later twin towers made the vista aesthetically less pleasing.) I stayed cheaply at the YMCA with good swimming pool, near Central Park. Dollars were difficult. I did the sights. Much of the time I was invited to meals by the friends of my uncles. On one rather unpleasant occasion I was taunted as an Englishman by an Irish lawyer from Boston, which put me off the Irish for a long time. But most people were very hospitable and friendly.

I went across the country by Greyhound bus, an excellent way to get an impression of its vastness. I stopped for a few days with a family who were friends of my uncles just outside Chicago, in a mansion with a garden going down to Lake Michigan. It is easy to forget what a beautiful setting that city has against the lake. The young daughters of the house gave me a drink as a special treat which I did not recognise. They said that they thought all English people loved tea. I told them I had never had it iced! One could get off the bus anywhere and pick up another later; it would stop at out-of-the-way places where you caught a glimpse of the real America. In Omaha and Wyoming one could appreciate why many Americans were little concerned about what went on in the wider world; they were over 1,000 miles from the sea. At the Wyoming bus stop I saw real live red Indians (now native Americans) with brown lined hatchet faces. Also cowboys walking in such fashion down the road that one could see light between their curved legs, conditioned to horseback. At Salt Lake City I visited the Mormon centre.

I was met at Los Angeles by uncle Dick and driven to his comfortable home in Montecito, a suburb of Santa Barbara, where his business 'Tweeds and Weeds' was based. Uncle Geoff was in England but loaned me his car. They had found for me a job as extra hand at the San Ysidro Ranch, a luxury hotel part owned by Ronald Colman and part by a state senator, Al Weingand. The ranch was an exclusive place favoured by very wealthy prominent people, partly no doubt, because of Colman's Hollywood connection (I only met his wife), but mainly because Weingand, from a family of hoteliers, cosseted all his guests. He stayed in charge for 40 years. He jealously protected his clients' privacy. Among those who stayed there in the past, I later learned, had been the Kennedys, the Nixons, the Vanderbilts, Somerset Maugham, Fred Perry, Frank Sinatra, Vivian Lee and Laurence Olivier. Colman and Weingand lived on the estate and created a discreet family atmosphere. They had met and travelled together, decided to start a special hotel and had paid $50,000 for the ranch in 1935. There were central buildings with Filipino cooks and waiters, but most of the accommodation was in a series of different cottages, furnished with antiques, with open fireplaces and their own terraces and private garden areas. They were all set in an extensive garden of flowering shrubs falling down a gentle hillside. About 70 guests could be accommodated.

I was to act as chauffeur meeting people at the airport. One day a week I looked after the pool, and another the private beach. The young students earning money by helping out at reception became friends. One told me horrific stories about hazing in fraternities at Stanford. Occasionally I accompanied groups to barbeque picnics in the hills. The conductor Eugene Ormandy was one of the guests. Another was a Texan oil rancher who asked for congratulations one day because he had just had another gusher! I was struck by the egalitarianism. There was little difference in accents, unlike in Britain, and rich children played happily with poorer sons of employees. On the other hand people were somewhat puritanical. They made me change my too skimpy swimming trunks after someone had objected. I did my best to be useful to Weingand. Sometimes when I met couples at the airport they were distracted by my English accent. I would hear them whispering together to see if I would be offended if they were to offer me a tip, at which I spoke up and made it clear I would not be offended at all! I cannot forget driving up to the ranch one day and seeing a dark object moving in the middle of the road. I parked my car and for some minutes peered forward, keeping a good distance, watching a very large tarantula quietly progressing along the central reservation. Hairy, with a lump on the back, it was not an attractive sight. I was very much aware that if pressed spiders can move as fast as racehorses for their size.

Uncle Dick was one of those people who emanated vitality. I suspect that he had always had an eye for the girls. It was rumoured that one reason he was sent off to California was that he had become involved with a very attractive young married woman from an unsuitable background. She later told her son by her second husband, who became a colleague of mine in the Foreign Office, and later worked for the Royal family, that she had indeed had an affair with Dick. In Santa Barbara he drank lethal dry martinis with only a whiff of vermouth, played tennis and golf hard, and ran a successful business with four outside branches. Mixing with clients socially was part of his job. I stayed with him but visited his wife, who he was in the process of divorcing, at the beach house where she was living with her two sons, my cousins. Divorce was something I had not encountered in the sheltered life of Hutton Mount. I was surprised to find myself at parties where both divorced parties were present. Nor had I come up against people with the drink problem from which my aunt Spinney suffered. She had once been a good athlete. There were plenty of alcoholics and former alcoholics around. I was never sure of the reason for the split between uncle and aunt, but Dick was already starting to court the divorced wife of Al Weingand. It didn't affect the two men's friendship. Beverly was not young but attractive, feminine and highly strung, nice to me because she was hoping to marry my uncle (which she eventually did). I had to keep neutrality with all that was going on around me. It was always a pleasure being with my two lively young cousins. One day I was invited to the beach house when the grunions were running. At some times of the year hordes of this fish, some six to nine inches long, would be thrown up on certain beaches on high tide. The females would come first and lay eggs, and the males, on the next wave, to fertilise them. At night torches would reveal hundreds of flickering silver bodies in the sand trying to get back into the sea. We went first to the right and then to the left picking up loads of fish which we put into buckets and then took home for a feast – easy fishing.

I played tennis with Dick and his friends and went with him to a variety of parties, some with aspiring Hollywood stars. At one I danced with a glamorous young woman with bright lipstick and eye shadow who told me she was hoping to be spotted by a film director. But when she told me she was only 14 I quickly recoiled. At some events I was told I should meet friends from my own country, but those who claimed to be titled, or from Eton, often turned out to be nothing of the sort after a few questions. Several of Dick's friends proudly traced their ancestry to Spanish colonisers, who had transferred California to the USA in 1848. Santa Barbara had a Spanish air about it. I saw a fine fiesta procession with respectable citizens arrayed in Spanish traditional dress. Some things shocked me. Dick expressed surprise that anyone of Jewish origin should be admitted to his precious golf club. I was proud that this sort of prejudice didn't exist in Britain, as far as I had ever heard.

Returning home was another adventure. Through his shipping connections my father had arranged for a Norwegian ship-owner friend to secure for me a working passage home from Los Angeles to Antwerp.

The Olson Line freighter, with a dozen passengers, needed painting and I was to do some of the work and be a general factotum. I was given the cabin boy's room near the bridge. I had plenty of contact with the officers, watching them in action and noting that if it looked like there was even the remotest risk of collision with another vessel steaming in our direction they would always alert the captain, even waking him at night. I used to eat with the boatswain and the ship's carpenter, on a diet full of fish. As the boatswain told stories he would sharpen a matchstick with his knife and use it as a tooth-pick, whereas the carpenter would pick the tail of a large piece of fish up with his knife and whip it into his mouth. I noted that the repair man, who made up our table, sometimes took six helpings of stew.

There was too much strong coffee; I had to beg the cooks for tea. I have never really been a fan of coffee since. I sat chatting to the radio operator. Painting on the deck I was sometimes accosted by a passenger trying out some phrase in Norwegian. 'I am terribly sorry,' I used to say in exaggerated English, 'I don't speak a word of that language.' Most of all I remember the silent companionship as many of the crew leaned over the rails each evening to watch the sun set. The sea could be choppy, wild, or smooth as glass reflecting the sinking orange sun. Shoals of whales would spew up air from their blowholes. Flying fish would leap out of the water. Dolphins would ride at our bow. The boat sailed down the west of Mexico and through the Panama Canal. That meant going up many different locks and then down again surrounded by vivid green, tropical vegetation. We stopped briefly at Curacao, with Dutch houses in the town and a busy lagoon with oil depot behind.

Arriving at Antwerp I stayed in the boat for several days before arranging my passage across the channel. I accompanied sailors to a series of drinking places by the port, sometimes returning up the gang plank with difficulty, and finding the room spinning around in different directions when I got to my bunk. Emptying my pockets I found an extraordinary amount of beer mats to add to my collection! This whole transatlantic trip was not only a good experience for an immature young man but a good talking point for my future Foreign Office interviews, which I was increasingly feeling was the way I wanted to go. It couldn't do any harm to have shown such enterprise.

For the record I should mention that after completing national service I had an obligation to serve three years in the Territorial Army. This was never satisfactory since gunnery involved technology on which you had to keep au fait, and that wasn't easy when your mind was on university study. There were annual camps. At first I was posted to a regiment that seemed rather strange. On arrival I was told it was a parachute regiment. I said 'You must be joking,' and immediately sought a transfer. While working at Cambridge I wasn't going to throw myself out of an aircraft and hope my parachute would open! I was then posted to a Yeomanry regiment that contained some of the rather grand Essex county families. My heart was never in it and I took an option to leave after a year or two.

I think it right for young people to be radical. I used to quote the adage, in its French version, that anyone who is not socialist at the age of 20 has no heart, while anyone who *is* socialist at 30 has no sense. It seemed to me that one of the strengths of Cambridge, where undergraduates are enveloped in the manifest beauty of its gardens and old buildings and conscious of a continuing tradition over the years of scholarship and enquiry, is that it is impossible for young people to be completely anarchistic. The past cannot be portrayed as all bad. Round the two pound coins, neglected in many of our pockets, are Newton's words: 'We are standing on the shoulders of giants'. Cambridge's influence stayed with me, reinforced when my parents moved from Essex to Trumpington, and sanctified when just before retirement my college did me the honour of electing me as an Honorary Fellow. So I became even more part of the college family and involved with university and city.

PART II

5

THREE FOREIGN OFFICE POSTINGS

I took the Foreign Office entrance exam during my last year at Cambridge, and passed – not to be taken for granted. Required to learn a 'hard' language, I chose Persian. I then spent nine months in full-time study at the School of Oriental and African Studies (SOAS) in London, followed by a further nine months attached to the British Embassy in Tehran. I drove out in the Spring of 1958 in a Land Rover I had decided to call 'Josephine', in Napoleonic vein, accompanied by my friend Peter Barbor and one of my Persian teachers. Desmond Harney, who had studied with me in London, was married and already in post. His son Richard became my godson, my second godchild after Priscilla, the daughter of one of my cousins. In due course I was honoured to be asked also to be godfather to Peter Barbor's eldest son Edward.

One of the most interesting and lively characters in the Tehran Embassy was a young Iraqi who had studied at the American University of Beirut and was working under the counsellor on the commercial side. Willie Amin made sure that those around him enjoyed life. He came from one of the most prominent Kurdish families in Suleimaniya, eastern Iraq, where his ancestors had been chiefs and rulers. One of his family was usually to be found in every Iraqi cabinet of whatever hue. But Willie didn't really like to talk about this political background. He later married Patricia, a blonde English girl, daughter of a businessman in Tehran. They had three sons. The parents were of mixed faith, but Willie acceded to Patricia's proposal that since the sons were growing up in England they should be baptised. When I agreed that this made sense

I was asked to be godfather to all three! I kept in touch with the family over the years, through thick and thin. After my retirement Patricia was struck down by motor neurone disease but kept, with friends and family around her, at home. Visiting her was distressing as she swiftly deteriorated. In due course the middle Amin son Paul married the daughter of the well-known British race-horse owner, Robert Sangster, who had been in my house at Repton but a few years younger than me. I hadn't seen him since. He had been heir to the Vernon football pools fortune, but had been treated like everyone else at school. Because his life-style featured often in the tabloids I expected to find him arrogant. Not at all. He had collected three high-profile wives, and had had a publicised liaison with Jerry Hall, but was surprisingly modest and unpretentious. The wedding, however, was pretty spectacular. Too soon after, Sangster died.

At SOAS I had become attracted to Persian poetry: profound thoughts expressed in simple, beautiful language. I was in Tehran when the father of my Repton school friend Nicholas Grantham, who had been the chairman of the Chartered Bank of India for 20 years, made a visit to open a new branch. I got invited to some of the functions in honour of that tall distinguished-looking gentleman, with black waistcoat and gold chain, who had spent much of his life as a trader in Bombay. I was able to do some services for his wife, for which she was grateful. People I met at one of the bank's events discovered that I was interested in poetry. As a result I was invited to one or two gatherings where poets recited their verses, to great acclaim. Among them was Forough Farrokhzad, a young woman of pale face and dark straight hair, now an iconic figure, who composed free and fairly explicit love poetry. I have a book of her poems she inscribed for me in Persian 'to Mr Barrington. I shall never forget the pleasure of meeting and getting to know him. Spring 1958.' This is quite a treasure now. She died young, killed in a car accident, perhaps fortunate not to see what happened to her country.

I was told in Tehran to concentrate on my language studies and not to get involved in embassy work. I travelled in Josephine throughout the country practising Persian and visiting historical sites. To get away from English speakers in the capital I was sent for two months to the provincial city of Meshed in the north-east, a place of pilgrimage because of its ancient shrine.

My closest friend in a group of young local Iranians there was the son of a wealthy landowner in Nishapur, Siavash. He was incredibly hospitable and generous. He gave me a beautiful striped turquoise and black ancient pot which had been discovered recently on his land, and was not damaged. It dated back to the time when the great city of Nishapur, not far away from Meshed, had been so destroyed by the Mongols, with every living thing killed including cats and dogs, that a horseman could ride over the ruins without stumbling. This had been the penalty for resisting the Mongol armies. Siavash introduced me to his elderly father, a very small man confusingly called Big Saidi because he was the eldest member of the family. His cousins were in local and national politics. Siavash concentrated on his farming. We made a point of visiting the tombs of two great poets in Nishapur: the small blue dome and run down garden belonging to Fariduddin Attar, and the rather basic building with an attractive garden linked to Omar Khayyam. Khayyam was known as a brilliant scientist and mathematician rather than a poet in his lifetime. I had always been attracted by the *Rubaiyat*, a copy of which had been among my parents' books. I became more interested when it emerged that friends of my sister lived in the former house of Edward Fitzgerald, who had freely translated Khayyam's verse and given Persian poetry, for the first time, popular appeal in the West.

Two hours' drive away from Nishapur I also visited one of the only fully functioning turquoise mines in the world, which I was told had been worked for over 2,000 years. After a walk of half a mile in a tunnel, we arrived at working places where there were veins of soft blue and white turquoise in hard rock. Powerful hammer blows were needed to extract the stone, which was of varying quality. In parts of the East, turquoise traditionally wards off the evil eye. I also visited nearby a huge cave of salt. There were numbers of men up ladders chipping away at the salt walls. The flickering light of their candles spread like stars against the background of glistening salt, making me feel I was in Aladdin's cave.

I was felled for a time in Meshed by a bout of old-fashioned yellow jaundice. It stopped any pleasure I got from alcohol or rich food for some time. In fact, I think that I have never been able since that time (and I caught hepatitis B lightly when I was in Cairo) to consume any great quantities of alcohol. I have tended to get ill before I get drunk, which is probably no bad thing. It was while I was in Meshed that I went once to see a foreign film in a local cinema, for the experience. At first I couldn't understand why all the audience were speaking out loud so one couldn't hear the soundtrack. It was because those who could read were speaking the subtitles for their neighbours who couldn't!

I enjoyed Iran and the Persians, my first experience of the East. Then I drove on to my first proper job in the British Embassy in Kabul where I was to be the junior political officer, called the 'Oriental Secretary'. Persian, with a different accent called 'Dari' was widely spoken. Travelling around the country was part of my job and I made an adventurous trip to Nuristan that years later ended in a book. The Russians and Americans were beginning to compete for influence in Afghanistan, but London was hardly aware of our existence. Nevertheless I did my job reporting events via the diplomatic bag. Helped by being able to communicate in the language, I began to value many Afghan friends.

I played a lot of tennis. The Kabul Amateur Dramatic Society (KADS) was very active in a society devoid of amusement, a focus of social life among the international community and some Afghans. I was president for a time. I directed a play-reading of Sartre's claustrophobic *Huis Clos*, as well as a full production of *The Crucible*, which was a success. I enjoyed playing a sober Jack Worthing in *The Importance of Being Earnest*. We put on an ambitious *My Fair Lady* which was a sell-out! Since Afghanistan had not signed up to the copyright convention we were able to put this on before it was normally available. We could occasionally watch for recreation the wild nomadic sport of Bozkeshi when the teams came into Kabul.

We had good parties. One sticks in my mind. It was a Roman fancy dress event and I got myself suitably prepared, but found to my distress that Josephine wouldn't start. There was no telephone in my little house in the embassy compound so I had to change back and go down to the office (I couldn't have appeared in ridiculous costume in front of the guards) and telephone my American girlfriend who had been waiting for me. She came and collected me. By the time we arrived the party was in full swing. Our American hosts had laid tabletops on the floor so that we drank and ate at a feast with elbows on the floor in Roman style. Menus were in Latin. To get the party going they served a mixture of vodka and cointreau that slipped down very easily. I was anxious to catch up and join the fun. As a result I drank far too much and for the first and last time in my life woke up in the host's guest bedroom! I was told that all husbands and wives from that party had gone home separately!

People are unimaginative these days and don't do fancy dress parties, or I don't get invited to them. In Cairo it was fun going to one party where the invitation said 'come so you will not be recognised'. I parked some way down the road and crept in as a tramp with make-up including false nose, altering my height and shape. I danced with many ladies whom I knew but who had no idea who I was. On occasion the hostess would look around wondering how many of the people had really been invited. In Brussels Rosenmontag was the occasion before Lent when married women took their rings off for parties. The idea was to do something for which you could then atone. One enterprising colleague had two different costumes so that when he appeared in the second disguise some people talked about him indiscreetly thinking he was not present, although he was sitting next to them, a mistake they realised with a shock! One of the best fancy dress parties I gave myself was in Brussels in honour of friends who were members of the Béjart ballet. It was a pyjama party. I turned my main room into an exaggerated bedroom with beds, dressing tables, mirrors, scent bottles, clothes horses, and so on. Some of the ladies came in baby doll outfits. I had plenty of spare pyjamas so that those who came in ordinary clothes had no excuse. They were chased off into the spare bedroom to change! It is best that a fancy dress party should have a common theme which is not too difficult to fit in with.

One difficult time in the Kabul Embassy that I don't think I handled very well was when one of our two secretaries, Valerie, an attractive girl, said she wanted to leave and marry an Afghan pilot. She was young and quite naive and I tried desperately, perhaps too hard, to persuade her to give up the idea. I told her about *purdah*, how wives had little freedom, and how in collective family compounds everything would be controlled by the mother-in-law. She wouldn't be persuaded and became more determined to go her own way. It didn't help that I had no high opinion of her future husband. When I went back to Kabul six years later on a visit from Pakistan I arranged to meet her briefly. She said she was all right, but she did say that she understood why I had tried so hard to make her change her mind. Only recently at a feast at Clare College I was introduced to a man who said he had had a relative living in Kabul at my time. I was astonished to discover it was Valerie's brother. He told me that her husband had died and she was now back in the UK with her children.

We were always happy to entertain the few visitors that came through. My father took the trouble to visit me in Kabul, coming up by air and returning by truck to Peshawar, on the precipitous road which he later described as hair-raising and ghastly. He was somewhat comforted by travelling with the clergyman who used to visit us once a month to take services. The only Christian priest allowed in Kabul those days was part of the Italian Embassy. It can't have been easy for my father to make the long journey, a diversion from a business trip to Singapore. I much enjoyed being able to entertain him with my Indian cook's good food and introduce him to friends. We had long talks about everything under the sun. I helped him purchase a carpet. Bargaining was fun in the Kabul shops. It was wise not to reveal those items in which one was really interested. A good technique, if time was no object, was to walk out of the door and hope to be called back. Besides carpets I bought two interesting old Afghan Jezails, finely decorated. The firing mechanism in both cases had been stolen from East India Company recruits whose names with dates were inscribed. The Afghans had been skilful at constructing a longer barrel around the British mechanism, which made their weapons more accurate. Sometimes small boys, left in charge of stores, would cope with a complicated sale knowing exactly how far to make concessions.

I never really appreciated enough what my father did for me when I was young. He had taken me to see the Olympics in 1946, watching the flying Dutch lady, Fanny Blankers-Koen, tear down the track and win the 100 metres. He took me to watch rugby at Twickenham, tennis at Wimbledon and even to watch Arsenal beat Liverpool in a soccer Cup Final. That was in the stands before seating became the rule. I was taken to Bertram Mills circus, with performing animals, trapeze artists and great clowns like the Caroli Brothers, a spectacle denied to modern children. He took the family to the ballet and opera. We saw the incomparable Joan Sutherland in *Lucia di Lammermoor* and Margot Fonteyn dancing. When, as a treat, he took us to see *Oklahoma!* from a box, we were met by a costumed flunkey and thought we had strayed behind stage.

Father tried to get me to understand about accounts and investments – which he advised should always be spread as far as possible. He was frustrated that I didn't know how much I earned and spent, only that what was coming in was more than what was going out. I learned from him not to get into debt, following advice to Laertes. In my radical phase after university I use to say that it was very unfair that some children had the advantage of a private education. This caused father mild apoplexy, saying that he had sweated blood to send me to a private school. He only hit me once when I was younger. It was my job to fill up the bucket with wood to keep the drawing-room fire going at Mollands. One day, when I was being lazy and difficult, he reproached me and told me to fill the bucket immediately. I went out and brought it back full of bricks! Not surprisingly he went ballistic! But that was not his style. Many people loved my father because he had the gift of showing interest in everyone he met. He could draw out the shyest wall-flower. I loved and respected him but didn't show it enough. Like old-fashioned British men we did not embrace. I liked to think he was proud of me. Not long before he died when he and my mother visited me in Tokyo we all got on extremely well together.

My godfather and special uncle Geoff, whom I discovered had also made a contribution to my university expenses, arranged to meet up with me in India while I was posted in Kabul. I took local leave, drove down to Peshawar where the Parsee Mr Gai, agent for our baggage and stores, was his usual hospitable self. He was one of the few to recognise the value of Gandhara Graeco-Buddhist sculpture, collecting pieces brought to him in exchange for a little money. He had a fine library of books. All were sadly dispersed by his unmarried daughters after he died. I had seen a good deal of Peshawar on my occasional trips with the diplomatic bags, usually staying in Deans hotel. This was a traditional establishment like a motel before these were invented in the West, for you could drive your vehicle just outside your rooms. These would consist of living area, leading to bedroom, leading to bathroom, all on one floor. Meals were in a central building. Elderly turbaned servants abounded. Similar hotels in Pindi and Lahore have now all disappeared.

To link up with Geoff I then drove down the Grand Trunk road to Lahore and across the border to Amritsar, where the Sikh mystic Sant Fateh Singh was staging some sort of religious protest in the Golden Temple. Holy men were crawling around the sacred pond and there was an air of religious sanctity combined with political tension. Driving beyond, towards Delhi, an old man on a bicycle suddenly veered out into the middle of the road in front of my car. I braked but hit him softly and he fell down. I got out, distressed and apprehensive. An Indian driving just behind me also stopped and said that he had seen exactly what had happened. The old man had gone right out into the road without warning. I could quote him as a witness if necessary, but he advised it would be best simply to offer the old man some monetary assistance. I did this and he got off and walked away, content and seemingly unhurt. That incident endeared me to Indians for life.

Uncle Geoff was on a tour of the world with an easy-going young companion. The idea was that once I arrived at Delhi he would pay for a holiday for the three of us, seeing the sights in the triangle of Delhi, Agra and Jaipur. I admired particularly Homayun's tomb, the Qotb Minar and the Rajasthan palaces of Jaipur. One of the latter was a hotel in which we stayed. In Jaipur the stars were favourable and everyone was getting married. Young boys, sitting high up on lavishly decorated elephants, were being taken with music and drums to the houses of their brides. Most spectacular of the things to see was of course the Taj Mahal, which is one of those exquisitely beautiful creations of man that never disappoint. I have seen it now at all hours of the day, in all lights, both at a distance and in close-up with its many inlaid semi-precious stones. Its beauty leads me to question the Darwinian thesis that everything in the world has been a product of a series of mechanical natural selection accidents. Everyone should see the Taj Mahal if they have the slightest chance to do so.

Geoff wrote an account of his world trip, which he had printed privately, called 'Flying East'. Each round-the-world ticket, stopping off where he wanted, cost £500. Aircraft were usually half empty. His journey started with Rome and Greece, Egypt, Lebanon and Iran to India. Then on to Thailand, Indonesia, Japan and Hawaii, back to his familiar California. I used to dismiss the book as a simple travelogue, but it is an interesting record of what all those places were like in 1960 when there was little tourism and development. Geoff had good powers of description. He told me afterwards that the three things in the world that most impressed him were the temples at Luxor, Persepolis and Angkor Wat. I have yet to visit the latter.

I saw more of the world in other journeys to and from Kabul. I flew the cheapest way for home leave by Aeroflot through Moscow – mechanically reliable but with minimal comfort. We stopped at

Tashkent where I found I was able to speak in Persian to several people waiting at the airport. It had been the language of educated people over a wide area of Central Asia, and particularly strong among craftsmen and shop owners in the cities. I visited the Kremlin and Red Square. I noted the bare shelves in the department stores and the grim bureaucrats, often women, who seemed to be running everything.

On my final return home I visited Beirut and the magnificent Roman ruins at Baalbek. Also Jerusalem; the city was then controlled by Jordan, not Israel. I tried to get cheap lodgings in one of the religious houses. As I traipsed around, accompanied by a helpful Arab boy, I found that they were all full. It was Orthodox Easter. Eventually I agreed that I would look at the Arab's own house where a bed was on offer. They showed me a large well-decorated room with double bed, so I accepted for a reasonable price. I came to realise that the whole family were living in another large room next door. In the morning, when I woke up, a little face was peering at me over the board at the foot of the bed. Eventually more faces appeared each higher than the others. There must have been eight or nine! My friend had many younger siblings. I was duly impressed by the Dome of the Rock and the Al Aqsa mosque on their platform, and the narrow arched-over lanes in the old city. The church of the Holy Sepulchre, however, was a confused jumble and a disappointment. Some Arabs told me, more in sorrow than anger, how they missed their lands now occupied by Israel.

I never lost my interest in and love for Afghanistan. Posted home I was given a job dealing with Scandinavia. Scandinavian countries presented few problems, except perhaps Finland trying to evade Soviet embrace. Organising the King of Norway's state visit was a significant achievement. I was also selected as one of the four Resident Clerks, bachelors, who had apartments in the Foreign Office buildings so that they could take turns covering emergencies out of office hours and at weekends. It taught me much about how the office was run, about which I had been completely ignorant.

It was while I was a Resident Clerk that I was contacted by a Mr Charles Barrington asking about my parentage. He was interested in Barrington genealogy and had spotted my name in some list in *The Times*. He said he had a son called Nicholas. His other son was the national squash champion Jonah Barrington. I explained that as far as I knew my family were very ordinary. My grandfather was Frederick Barrington (I never knew whether it was deliberate that his two children, my father and my aunt, were named Eric and Freda). I had made enquiries at Somerset House going back, as you could, until 1837, the start of Victoria's reign, and discovered that my great-grandfather was Frederick Gottfried, and his father Arthur John, apparently from Essex. Charles Barrington came to see me. He told me that the Barringtons had been the hereditary foresters of Hatfield forest and that their pedigree could be traced back to people called Barenton at the time of the Norman conquest. One of the Hatfield Barringtons had a younger son who had gone to Ireland and was the ancestor of numerous Irish Barringtons, Protestants, including himself. Amongst them was the former Chief Justice of Ireland, Jonah Barrington, who was a prominent social and literary figure in his day and from whose entertaining personal sketches I have quoted. Charles Barrington lent me some sheets of the family tree and gave others to me, all hand written, suggesting I should find out how my own branch of the family might be connected to the Hatfield people. I still have the scrolls. Looking at them recently I saw that some had been copied in my parents' handwriting. No doubt these were the ones which had had to be returned. But I went abroad and lost touch. Only recently did I learn from Jonah himself that his father had died shortly after we had been in contact. I told him how grateful I had been to him.

With the help of a professional genealogist I have recently made the connection that Charles Barrington was asking about. For a start I have solved the mystery of why my father never seemed to be in touch with any relatives on his father's side. I found a letter from one of his uncles from Australia explaining that my great-grandfather Frederick Gottfried had been a prosperous merchant with a large Georgian house with 16 rooms in Southgate, north of London. There were ten acres of land with extensive outbuildings, orchards and lawns. In 1895, however, he had had a 'severe financial setback' from which he never recovered. He became heavily in debt and was declared bankrupt. Responsibility fell on my grandfather, who was the eldest of 16 or more children (I remember him only slightly as a genial gentleman living in Worthing who worked for Bovril). He gathered a family conclave and arranged simple accommodation for their mother. His father could not adapt to his new situation, nor settle into any new job. He became despondent and mentally ill and died in an institution. It must have been accepted that since there was no money the children would all disperse, some to Australia and Canada. It was difficult to keep in touch over long distances in those days. It must have been a dreadful disgrace and family tragedy.

Arthur John Barrington had been a wholesale milliner and his father John Barrington an impecunious seventh son who worked as a farm foreman. For a time the latter was a butler in London, married, probably to another servant of the house, in St Georges Hanover Square. Beyond John there were several generations of farmers in Essex and Suffolk, often also younger sons, so that land holdings were dissipated. The line goes back to a Thomas Barrington, son of another Thomas who was a younger son of the Hatfield family. An elder son of the second Thomas was progenitor of a group of prominent Barringtons who were members of parliament for Colchester. One of them was private secretary to Cromwell's son Richard. It is a coincidence that in the Hatfield line there were several Sir Nicholas Barringtons.

My grandmother, called by us 'Grandy', was a strong character who long outlived her husband. She claimed to be one of the first women to ride a bicycle in bloomers at the beginning of the twentieth century. As a widow she spent some time with my parents, some time with my uncle Tom and aunt Freda in Cambridge and Norfolk and some time in the Garden House Hotel in Cambridge. When I was an undergraduate she would invite me periodically for lunch. The most distinguished individual in our family was her youngest brother, Sir Donald Allen, who had been a hero in World War I, but never talked about it. He had won a Military Cross and bar in the Gunners. He had then studied law and devoted his life to charity as Secretary to the London Parochial Charities, the charitable funds of the London City churches. On his retirement after 40 years' service in 1965, tribute was made to his superb administrative competence, his invariable courtesy, his awareness of the needs of his less fortunate fellow men and his burning zeal to help them. He was always good company, proud of distributing money in an imaginative way to a series of good causes with minimal overheads. He had no use for charities such as Barnardo's who, in his view, spent far too much on administration. Uncle Donald was not much older than my father and in many ways a mentor to him. He told good stories and played tricks with coins to amuse children. My father followed him into the Reform Club. His work brought him into contact with the Duke of Edinburgh, and Lord Longford (both of whom he respected) and many others in the charitable world. I remember my mother thinking he sometimes talked too much about these contacts, but I wish I had asked him more about his work. He kept a benign eye on my career until he died.

We didn't have much contact with the Allen family, except for uncle Donald. Aunty Maud, famous for making rice puddings which I didn't care for, was married to uncle Cecil Powditch, who was steward of St Bartholomew's Hospital. I remember visiting them during the war and seeing people taking refuge from bombs in underground tunnels.

My father's only sibling Freda was a woman of great character and talent who had been a prize pupil at the Royal College of Music but gave it up when she married Tom Bird, from an old Cambridge family. Tom's sister was married to the eldest of the Chivers brothers. An aunt was one of the founders of Benenden school. Freda was blessed with perfect pitch. When I played any of the piano keys she would tell me what note it was. She liked painting and was a good cook. Her only child, my cousin Susan, is a professional artist who studied at the Courtauld. She has a great gift for drawing objects excavated by archaeologists and was in demand at various digs around the world. For a time she was in charge of graphics in the Greco-Roman section of the British Museum. She has been like another sister to Sara and me.

My next posting was to Brussels to be part of the tiny permanent mission to the new European Communities. I arrived in time for the collapse of our first negotiations, vetoed by De Gaulle. My work was with common market personnel and institutions including covering the European Parliament in Strasbourg. We had to keep London informed and interested. It was important work.

I had two fine apartments provided for me in Brussels. The first was a place of considerable character in Avenue Winston Churchill in Uccle. It was fully furnished with a library. It was there that I heard the shocking news of Kennedy's assassination. Some evenings I would keep my colleague John Robinson company on long walks that he needed to combat his low blood pressure. After one of my better dinner parties in that apartment, I was told that one of my guests had German measles, and other guests should be told in case any of them should have been pregnant. When I checked I found to my surprise that all the women had been pregnant! But fortunately they came to no harm. When the trusting owner returned I moved to a larger but less attractively furnished apartment in the Rue de la Loi in Tervueren. It was there that I gave the pyjama party. I had maids on hand in both places. I never cooked for myself. I hadn't yet been taught the basics by my sister. I took advantage of Brussels' marvellous restaurants, providing a combination of meals with French quality and Dutch quantity, with everywhere fine Burgundy wines. I developed a taste for moules in the little restaurants near the Grande Place. There was a fish restaurant in the Quai aux Poissons where the head waiter would recognise me – a great incentive to go there often. Comme Chez Soi had a legendary owner/chef who would sometimes tell you to stop talking and get on with the food.

Some little things I remember. There was a bright attractive secretary or registry clerk in our mission who spoke with a charming Welsh accent. She had well-tended longish blonde hair and used to join us for meals occasionally, where she was popular. She held her knife and fork, however, in a strange way that many would think was impolite or crude. I wrestled with the decision whether or not to suggest to her to change to a more normal way of eating. But I chickened out. It might have been kind of me to say something, but our relationship would have suffered. When you are someone's direct boss it is easier to point out things that might affect their work.

I used to do this in later life, drawing on some of the advice in a paper circulated to us on 'Guidance on diplomatic usage' (marked confidential!) for those going to first postings. Personal habits are different. A lot of things in the booklet were considered excessively pretentious and out of date, but much made sense. For example, if you go to a large official reception and your ambassador is there, go and greet him briefly in case there is anything he may like you to do. You might even help him escape from being pigeonholed by a tiresome fellow guest. Generally show your head of mission respect not only by calling him 'sir', whereas for everyone else in the mission you use Christian names, but escorting him to the door where appropriate, particularly in your own home. Others watch how staff members treat their heads of mission. Sometimes they can even draw wrong conclusions if staff members don't shake hands with each other. You should never criticise your government or your ambassador in the presence of outsiders. The ambassador's reputation is important for the success of the government's objectives. Sadly some politicians have not always shown appropriate respect when overseas and thus damaged the ambassador's effectiveness on their government's behalf. If someone has entertained you, when you next see them make a point of saying how much you enjoyed the occasion, even if you have written a thank-you note, which you should normally do. Of course you must fit in with local customs. In Brussels it used to be normal to send flowers to your hostess before going to dinner.

I met a number of Belgians through contacts of my father – charming cultivated people. I used to go with mixed groups of young people to stay in chateaux in the Ardennes, and to villas on the coast at Le Zut. Somehow I got onto a circuit of some rather exclusive Belgian families. I was invited to a huge gourmet dinner laid on by the Janssens banking family for Prince Albert and his beautiful Italian wife, later King and Queen (there were 150 for dinner under canvas. 200 more arrived later for the ball). Also to a memorable dinner by the banking Camus family, where for the only time in my life the servants would enter the room and announce the name and dates of the wines before serving them: 'on annonçait le vin'. At that dinner was the brilliant economist Barbara Ward. Also Mr Winant who had been US ambassador in London. He had lost an eye, caught in a hook when fishing. Since then I always give casting fishermen plenty of room. The big banking families were top of the pile in Belgium. I also met some of the aristocracy such as the Princesse de Ligne and the Duc d'Ursel, as if they had emerged from the pages of Proust. This was mainly at functions organised by Countess Florence de Lannoy in her house near the Bois de la Cambre. She was one of those hostesses who do not serve lavish food but always have a variety of interesting people as guests. Much more important. Everyone knows that they will have a worthwhile evening and attends if they possibly can. I was grateful for her hospitality. I drew passable portrait sketches of some of the young ladies I met in those days (see Plate 18).

Living in Brussels was extraordinarily easy and comfortable. Traffic moved smoothly thanks to the big inner ring road around the city, where the old walls had been. It took no time to get to the Forêt de Soignes, where one could enjoy nature at peace, and beyond to the site of Waterloo – a good place to take family and visitors, where it was easy to envisage the whole course of that great battle. It was slightly distressing that most of the exhibitions in the area were about Napoleon rather than Wellington, but I believe this was later corrected. Smart Belgian society would go to the music concerts in honour of their Queen mother Elizabeth.

I enjoyed even more the exquisite Theatre de Monnaie in the centre of town, particularly when the Béjart ballet were performing, or the Royal Ballet visiting. I became a great fan of Béjart whose works were always stimulating and original and often a little erotic. In that respect he was a sort of successor to Diaghilev. I remember seeing the great Massine at one of the productions. At a party for the visiting Royal Ballet with Nadia Nerina I talked to one of the Béjart dancers, Jaleh Kerendi, with whom I had a link because she was half Iranian. She was married to one of the male stars, Paolo Bortoluzzi, who was a dancer of brilliant technique and a delightful individual. We became friends. I saw them several times in London, then, sadly, lost touch. I believe they started a ballet school in Turin.

Later, when in London, working in the Private Office, I used sometimes to drop in to theatre or ballet performances on the way home from work to Islington. Once I did this for a Rambert ballet production and found myself sitting in a spare seat in the front next to a trim little old lady with swept back grey hair who was following the ballet with great attention. She was interested in my comments. I said I didn't suppose that she was by any chance Madame Rambert herself. She was. I told her sincerely how well she looked and that I was glad to see an institution so well preserved. We struck up quite a good relationship, fuelled by my fascination with her firsthand accounts of people like Diaghilev and Nijinsky. I met her again at a ballet six months later when she greeted me warmly and took me out for a drink with the American choreographer, Alvin Ailey, talking away at a great pace. A few months later I achieved a coup by taking Madame Rambert to the first night of one of the programmes of the visiting Béjart company in London. I think it was *The Firebird*. She was on cracking form with plenty of stories. 'Here's Mr Baluncheon, come for luncheon!' I reconnoitred the way and took her during the interval behind stage where she met Béjart himself, introducing me. Also there, on the vast platform, was Anton Dolin whom she said she couldn't stand but greeted warmly. He was together with John Gilpin, a former pupil of hers who she said he had ruined. She did a pirouette, bag and all. Dolin asked her to do another, then picked her up and spun her round twice. We held our breath but they were relaxed after this little exhibition. Not bad for her 80 plus years! She ran to the imaginary audience and blew kisses. She then went up to congratulate Paolo and Jaleh in their dressing rooms. The trouble with my 'here one day and gone the next' peripatetic career was that such remarkable friendships drifted apart. At least I have great memories. One visit to Sadler's Wells I particularly remember. It turned out to be the first night of a ballet based on a Noel Coward short story. At the curtain call the chairman of governors spoke to the audience from the centre of the dress circle saying they might like to know that Her Royal Highness Princess Margaret was present. This was greeted with applause. Also, he added, Dame Ninette de Valois. Much more applause. And, as a bonus, the master himself, Noel Coward. Huge applause, as the great man stood and waved.

There was an active amateur theatrical group in Brussels called the English Comedy Club. I was chosen to play a suitably dignified and pompous, and at the end pathetic, Malvolio. Of course it is a great part. Critics were kind but I don't think I got the most out of the cross-gartered scene. I also played Archer in Farquhar's feisty *Beaux' Stratagem*. It was a classic restoration comedy in full costume. The actor playing the man to whom I was really a friend but pretending to be a servant had theatrical connections which I found fascinating. An uncle of his had been killed by lions in Wigan. He was a lion tamer. One year, on tour in Wigan, some of his lions almost got out of control, and created an incident. The following year, in Wigan again, they got him! I don't know how I found time to do all this amateur theatre, because if you take on the commitment, you must of course stick to it. You can't let all the other people down.

I played regular tennis in a Belgian club with good indoor courts. One of my partners, Prakash Shah, later became permanent secretary of the Indian Foreign Office. He was a highly intelligent Jain. We kept up a correspondence for several years. I enjoyed the fine galleries in Brussels. I would drive in my pale grey Ford, Zuleikha, to Antwerp where there were more good pictures. That city had quite a different atmosphere. A friendly family there had a son who was an enterprising Belgian diplomat. It was better to start off talking to people in English rather than French in the Flemish areas. I also enjoyed Ghent and Bruges, with its lovely little-known Michelangelo Madonna and child. What I never did, and should have done, was to visit the World War I battlefields. On French soil there are memorials to two of my uncles. Visiting the galleries and museums in the Netherlands, a little further afield, was also easy. I stayed there with hospitable friends. I particularly admired the glorious Vermeers in the museum in Delft.

One Belgian family I visited as a result of a contact proved to be a nightmare. When I knocked at the door there was aggressive barking. Once inside, a medium-sized brown dog rushed at me. When I sat in an easy chair drinking tea, the dog was haunched at the other side of the room baring its teeth at me. Then it moved around to my right-hand side and started to snap at my arm. 'Don't worry,' said my host and hostess from the beginning, 'he is perfectly good natured, and won't hurt you.' The wretched dog was in no way discouraged but snapped again at my jacket. 'Don't worry,' said my host. 'Don't worry?' I replied, standing up, 'He's got hold of my sleeve!' At this stage the couple looked disturbed, more critical of me than of the dog, and said, 'Oh well if you don't like him we will have to put him outside.' Which they did, with reluctance and great fuss. But that was nothing to the fuss the dog made! It ran backwards and forwards snarling and yelping outside the French windows, making clear that it was extremely angry and unhappy. After a period my hostess said, 'Oh dear, we should probably let him in again.' At which point I said goodbye and made my exit as quickly as I could! A diplomat's life does not work owning pets, but if anything I am a cat man. I find dog owners are usually blind to their animals' faults.

6

FIRST TOUR IN PAKISTAN AND A PLUM JOB IN THE PRIVATE OFFICE

I was allowed to go by ship (unthinkable nowadays) to my next posting to Pakistan, where I was to be first secretary political (internal). I arrived in Karachi in the autumn of 1965 as fighting was erupting between India and Pakistan over Kashmir. It was in Britain's interest to stop it. I was soon given the task of establishing and coordinating a small unit at Rawalpindi, far to the north, where President Ayub Khan and his foreign minister Zulfiqar Ali Bhutto were based, nearer to the action.

As I was working there, flat out, a message came from home that my father had suffered a heart attack. Fortunately, at the last minute, his condition improved. This first heart attack probably gave him ten more years of life as he decided to retire early and take it easy. I strongly urged him to do this in my letters home. In the spring of 1964 my sister had married John Symes and they had moved into a farm that family funds had enabled him to purchase in Martlesham near Woodbridge in Suffolk. Their view looked down over the fields and sea wall to the Deben estuary, an incomparable setting. Shortly afterwards, my parents had sold Mollands and moved to a neo-Georgian house with terrace and walled garden in Trumpington near Cambridge. It meant that they were close to Addenbrooke's Hospital when father was ill and he was well cared for. My uncle and aunt, Tom and Freda Bird, had been living in Cambridge, though they now moved to Cley-next-the-Sea in Norfolk. It was always a pleasure to visit my parents in Cambridge and take friends there. A spacious garage was converted into a study, bedroom and bathroom I could use which we called the 'summer palace'.

When things calmed down I started to get to know many Pakistani friends in Rawalpindi, especially the very hospitable family of General Shahid Hamid. His eldest daughter was engaged to a dashing young officer and polo player.

Though I am not a horseman it was a delight to watch Jaffer and the other polo players disporting themselves in the afternoon sun on the Pindi racecourse. There was a polo crowd that seemed to come straight out of the Raj, for example Colonel Hisam Effendi, with brushed up moustaches, descended from the old exiled Afghan royal family. Two of his sons became professional polo players. Personally, I never had a good experience with horses. My parents thought I should learn to ride and for some time when I was very young I was taken out by a girl who sat me on top of her large, broad and placid horse. She would leave me outside on this beast while she went to have coffee and gossip with various friends in the neighbourhood. I was far too high up to get down so I was stuck and quietly fuming. In contrast there was a family party at my uncle Arthur Bill's house in Kelvedon, Essex. They had a field attached and a pony, on top of which they placed me for all to admire. Then my uncle gave the animal a sharp slap on its rump, after which it took off round the outside of the field like a bat out of hell! I was terrified, clinging on for dear life and everyone else was laughing. Never again, was my unspoken sentiment after I got down. It didn't help that in those early days I seemed to lose quite a few girlfriends to their love of horses.

Many people overseas expect a British diplomat, especially an ambassador, to be a good rider, but I am afraid I disappointed them. Nor have I been keen on shooting wild birds, though I was effective at small bore when I was at Repton. I think of the birds that end up wounded in ditches. I enjoyed the response of Sir Denis Greenhill, a distinguished permanent secretary at the Foreign Office who had an early career in the railways. He would say that he knew more about shunting and hooting than about hunting and shooting! I must also add that I have never been too impressed with the intelligence of horses, for example when you see a big creature shying away at a tiny jump. But I do admire equine beauty, so well depicted by Stubbs, and it was easy to admire the splendour of the polo ponies as well as the skill of their riders. The game must be a refined form of those wild games played by Central Asian horsemen as shown in Afghanistan's violent Bozkeshi. World history changed when the horse was domesticated and ridden into attack, when cohorts of horsemen from the north descended 'like a wolf on the fold' on the peaceful agricultural communities living in the fertile river valleys where agriculture had developed. It is a remarkable thought that for thousands of years of man's history the fastest that he could ever travel on land was on the back of a horse.

During the Kashmir crisis I shared a large house on the edge of Rawalpindi with two fellow diplomats. Eventually I had the house to myself. It wasn't luxurious but it was spacious. I had it painted a warm off-white and filled it with personal things so that it became a home. My former bearer from Karachi had come up with his wife to run the place, together with the cook, who could produce good meals. The garden in front seemed to be full of zinnias, sometimes six foot high, lovingly tended by the gardener. When once he came back from leave, it was said that he had been responsible for a revenge or honour killing in his village. I decided not to probe. There was also a one-eyed chowkidar, that is a night watchman, who was the sort of person you would not want to meet at night. It was a general protection system. In April, when the weather was splendid, I described my garden as looking very good. Masses of phlox and stock, antirrhinum and roses, cornflowers, sweet peas and pansies in pots. I had just removed all the plantains from the grass lawn. At night, in the hot summer, I would sit out in the garden, reading with the help of a standard lamp with a very long flex, while crickets chattered and the shrubs pushed out a heady scent. A particular joy was to see hoopoes in the garden, such an attractive bird. It was designated king of the birds in the great poem by the Persian sufi Attar, because of its crown-like crest. I was also very conscious of buffalos just behind the house. Their milk was rich and delicious. Buffalo steaks were excellent.

Servants were generally loyal but had to be watched. One day looking for some reason through the drawers of a little-used spare bedroom, I saw a couple of my shirts. I discovered that the system was first to remove some items to a distant part of the house for a period to see it they were missed. If not, after a considerable time they would disappear.

One serious problem in my Peshawar Road house taught me a lesson. When I went into my bedroom at night I started to hear a continuous gentle scraping sound. It was very slight. I thought something must be wrong with my hearing. But strangely, when in exasperation I loudly shouted 'Shut up,' it would stop for a minute. Then I began to notice some powdered wood dust by the doorways and, on the walls, little channels of light-brown mud linking one part of the woodwork to the next. I had termites, white ants! The landlord took immediate action. Exterminators came in to pump insecticide into various parts of the house. Much of the woodwork had been hollowed out and had to be replaced. The noise I had heard had been thousands of white ants munching away. I was there when they found the queen, a disgusting, large, slug-like creature hidden in the woodwork in the bookshelf area.

Part of my job was to travel as a way of getting to know the country and its people. Reading through my letters home I was not then, it seemed, as interested in antiquities as I later became. I did visit Taxila, near Islamabad, where there were extensive Buddhist remains. I purchased one or two carved Gandhara heads. It was before the fake industry got underway. I visited the dramatic new dam being built at Mangla, halfway down to Lahore, on the border of Azad Kashmir where the American contractors had created a purely American isolated camp. It was the flooding of villages near Mangla as part of the vital UN Indus Valley Treaty scheme, designed to ensure adequate irrigation water for Pakistan after partition, that led to the first south Asians in quantity coming to the UK to work in Yorkshire woollen mills. Their homes had been inundated. Their relations followed. As a complete contrast I went with friends up the narrow Kaghan Valley along tricky roads, where we eventually climbed across snow to the dazzling blue-green Saiful Moluk lake, surrounded by wild flowers.

I accepted an invitation once to stay with a Punjabi landlord, a member of the National Assembly, on his estate near Multan. He spoke good English and in his home territory was clearly boss of all he surveyed. He showed me the traditional Punjabi 'tag' game of Kabaddi. He took me across his lands to call on a neighbour, the aristocratic maverick radical Nawabzada Nasrullah Khan, famous for always being in opposition, who was sitting in a field wearing a fez – just as hosts in country houses in England take you to see their neighbours, perhaps showing off both ways. My Punjabi friend's house was divided by a curtain so I never met any of the ladies behind it. In the evening when I asked politely where I might relieve myself, I was given some water, cloth and a trowel and asked to find myself somewhere in the scrubby area in front of the house! That was a bit of a shock. Fortunately by that time it was dark.

I also visited East Pakistan as part of my job and got to know many of the very different people there in the days before the breakaway of Bangladesh. It was scorching in summer. The trick was to visit in winter.

Back in Rawalpindi, besides football and tennis, there was an active Scottish dancing group led by an American who had been president of the Scottish Dancing Association of Oxford! A lively Christmas cabaret was largely organised by me in 1966. I found myself organising cabarets in other posts as well. My own contribution would often be an old Footlights 'vampire' poem which starts 'Though this is how you see me here, immaculately dressed, I may not be what I appear – I'm not a welcome guest!' I might also do the 'Cleopatra' song from *Salad Days* or *The Stately Homes of England*.

There was an active amateur dramatic group, appropriately called RATS (Rawalpindi Amateur Theatrical Society) which did rehearsed play readings in costume. I had a go at Thomas More, getting as close as I could to Scofield, and inciting a few tears in the audience over the final walk to execution. Particularly successful was a production which I directed of *Lady Windermere's Fan*. I played the Lord. My lady was Raana Sherwani, an extremely bright and attractive neighbour and friend, the daughter of a Ministry of Finance official, who later became a force in the creation of Pakistan television. She married a senior diplomat. She reverted to her career during Benazir's second term as prime minister. She organised a brilliant musical fashion show at the Barbican for the second of Benazir's official visits to London.

Lady Windermere was performed to an appreciative audience at the back of the house of Iqbal and Shahida Saigol. The Saigol family were a feature of Rawalpindi society that must be mentioned. Four brothers of the older generation had neighbouring houses along the Peshawar Road near their highly efficient cotton spinning factories. We rarely met them but the children, several of my age, had been educated in Britain, including Oxbridge, and were excellent company. They were starting to take over the reins of the growing successful business. There were several cousin marriages among them, as with Iqbal and Shahida. Typical of their *élan* was the party that they gave that same summer around their swimming pool. It was a beach party, for which about 20 lorryloads of sand were imported; barbecues, deck chairs, coloured umbrellas and towels turned this into an extraordinary oasis over 800 miles from the sea! Most of the younger guests ended up in the pool.

My own house and entertaining became well organised, judging from my letters home. On one occasion I invited 80 people on my lawn to watch a film about Churchill. I recorded a dinner I gave for my High Commissioner Sir Cyril Pickard and his wife in January 1967. He had succeeded Sir Morrice James. I described my new boss as intellectually brilliant but socially rather shy and awkward. On this occasion he 'was more wide awake than usual'. Other guests were the aristocratic Chief Election Commissioner and his young American wife (the Mueenuddins), Sardar Aslam Khan and wife, Secretary General of the Muslim League (a charming straightforward member of the National Assembly embarrassed by some of the excesses of the regime), Mr and Mrs Aslam Azhar, a modern-minded television executive, and Tariq Afridi, a young polo player working for Pakistan Tobacco. I gave them thick turkey soup followed by salmon with mixed fish and mushroom in a vol-au-vent shaped like a fish, with Pouilly Fuissé, then half a roast stuffed chicken, tiny new potatoes, peas in tomato cups and a dish of spinach and carrots. Good claret. A hot golden syrup souffle was followed by coffee, liqueurs, fudge, fruit and nuts. Someone once said that one of the nicest things about life is that we can regularly stop whatever it is we are doing and devote our attention to eating. I used to think I was living a fairly primitive life in those days but it doesn't seem to have been too bad!

In exploring the wooded hills north of Pindi I had come across a special place where the road on a high stone bridge crossed a gully where a stream poured out of the hill from the right in a series of rock pools. The route was not very well frequented, and driving along it one could easily miss the spot. I used to take a few friends there occasionally for a picnic and swim. I gave a special farewell party there for about 30 people for my American diplomat friends, the Quaintons. For my own farewell party I invited a lot more people, including Pakistani friends who had no idea that the place existed. It was about 20 miles and one hour's drive from Pindi. Guests had to be given maps and careful instructions. My servants went ahead to cook the supper and cool white wine in the shallows of the stream. Carpets were laid out in flatter areas and flaming torches erected to give the place a dramatic ambience as night fell.

Recordings of Bach or the Beatles competed with the sound of water. There was a small pool above the bridge and a larger deep pool further down fed by a waterfall, where people could swim. My servants supplied a loo with blackout curtains. Cocktails were provided followed by a full supper with rosé wine, as guests sat in groups by the stream in the moonlight. There are parts of the world where opera and nightclubs are not available but one can create spectacularly enjoyable events. It was sad that when I returned to Pakistan as ambassador the whole area of this magical spot was out of bounds because it was near to the nuclear research facility of Kahuta. Perhaps one day it will be rediscovered.

I had been conscientious in my work in Rawalpindi and must have secured good reports. I was posted home in 1967 to one of the European departments, logical after my earlier tour in Brussels. The plan was then for me to spend some months working as private secretary to Morrice James, now permanent secretary of the Commonwealth Office, then to move to be number two private secretary to the foreign minister, Michael Stewart. He was about to take charge of the merged Foreign and Commonwealth Offices. These were busy years.

Back at home I needed a London house. Searching for it was a serious business. I could visit my parents in Cambridge for weekends, but I couldn't commute from there. After a search I settled for a little eighteenth-century terraced house in north Islington. A mortgage, and contribution from my father, made purchase possible. This was before the Victoria Line was built. (Communications with central London were greatly improved when it was opened in 1969.) Parking was available by the Foreign Office and it was perfectly easy to commute by car. The house was in an area of Islington that was being rediscovered. In medieval times you would travel north out of London up through green fields to the playgrounds of Sadler's Wells, where there were pleasant springs and people practised archery and other sports. A famous inn at the Angel crossroads was the point from where coaches and horses would set off up the east side of the country to Cambridge, Norwich, Lincoln and York. Beyond was the village of Islington with, on its north side, an old priory that became the town house of the family of a rich merchant who had been mayor of London and had acquired the title of Marquis of Northampton. Part of the old tower building, where at different times people like Anne of Cleves and Oliver Goldsmith had stayed, still survived along with plenty of big trees. This part of Islington was called Canonbury, after the earlier religious establishment.

Houses in Islington had originally been well built with large windows, but the area had gone through a bad period at the beginning of the twentieth century. When I arrived there were still local slums, gradually being swept away. It was artistic people with little capital who had discovered the area first. Over my garden wall I used to converse with my neighbour, the actress Beatrix Lehmann. Despite her deeply lined face she had a beauty that shone through. She had been one of those intellectuals in the 1930s who had been persuaded that communism was the fairest way of organising society. She had joined the party. But she left when she began to realise what Stalin had really been doing to impose party control. On my other side neighbours had bought their house from Flora Robson. Bernard Miles moved in down the road. The architect Basil Spence lived nearby. His scheme to demolish some of the houses in the area for a big new project was fortunately blocked. While working in London during the next four years I was mostly very busy and had no time to get involved in local activities, but I do remember a splendid street party for the Queen's Silver Jubilee with tables full of food and drink right down my little street, Alwyne Villas. It helped us all to get to know our neighbours.

I explored the antique shops of East Anglia to find furniture for my house helped by a loan from uncle Geoff. Influenced by him, and my parents, I went for comfortable easy chairs, traditional antique mahogany tables, decent lamps (my uncle always said that lamps should be 'important'), and a variety of original pictures, both traditional and modern, so each sets off the other. Not for me bare walls and sparse pine furniture. I entertained a lot of people in that little house: Béjart dancers and my Cambridge acting and writing friends. Also, a good example of name dropping, two British foreign secretaries, Alec Douglas-Home and Michael Stewart and their wives, Jean Monnet, Arnold Toynbee, George Weidenfeld, Professor Freddie Ayer and Ursula Vaughan-Williams! The last was brought by my great-uncle Donald. What they all thought, cramped into a small space in a house with no central heating (only storage radiators) and only one loo, I can't imagine!

While I am doing routine desk-work on Europe it may be an opportunity to say something more about my mother's family, the Bills, with all my uncles. They originated from around Tenby in south Wales, undertakers and general merchants who began to specialise in the clothing trade. My great-grandfather came to London and set up a business in Bond Street in 1846, retailing and wholesaling fine tweeds, cashmeres and other cloths. My grandfather, William Bill, lived in a large house in Gidea Park near Romford. He and his wife and their ten children are well represented in a family photograph (Plate 2). My grandfather, whom I never met, loved books, some of which I inherited, and read the bible aloud to his family, but didn't go to church. He kept strict discipline at home, using a switch if hands were placed on the dining table, and not allowing children to leave until they had consumed everything on their plate. His gentle wife came from English reputedly county stock. With her small frame she must have been exhausted producing a steady stream of children, who all appeared to have survived in good health.

The six eldest were boys who all fought in World War I. Uncle Bernard, who had the air of an absent-minded academic, knew the Latin names of all the plants in the garden. He was commissioned but had a quiet war. Uncle Ned, the second son (sitting next to his father in the picture), had no children. He was a small street-wise man of sharp intelligence who had been called up as a bombardier in the horse artillery, supporting General Allenby's campaign in the Levant. He became the powerhouse of the family firm, W Bill Ltd, after his father's death, keeping the company going through the difficult World War II period and expanding the wholesale export trade. The firm had an excellent reputation, featuring in some of the better guidebooks on London for American tourists. Fielding's *Travel Guide for Europe* for 1973 wrote that 'W Bill Ltd was the finest woollen specialist we have ever found in the British Isles.' Uncle Bern's two sons David and Brian, my cousins, carried on the firm in the next generation, but in the fast-moving economic climate of the 1960s and 1970s it had to expand or fade away. My elderly uncles could not bring themselves to borrow enough money to pay increased rents for what were then five premises in London, including in Bond Street. The ethos of the company was that the interests and pensions of the loyal staff were of paramount importance. Eventually the firm was sold.

The third Bill son, uncle Jack, had been a dispatch rider during World War I. He had crashed into a shell crater and lost his leg in a battlefield operation. He never complained but his artificial leg clanked and always hurt. He went into finance, becoming an adviser to Lord

Inverforth. The story was that he invested judiciously, including, for instance, buying Malaysian rubber shares during World War II when they were at rock bottom. This was on the good principle that if we lost the war what matter anyway, but if we won the shares would be worth a lot. Uncle Jack entertained generously in an attractive house in Essex with a succession of housekeepers, the last of whom, the daughter of an admiral, he eventually married. Their love of corgis had helped bring them together. Some of uncle Jack's inheritance eventually came down to me as descendant of one of his two sisters.

Charlie and Arthur, the fourth and fifth brothers, were superfluous to requirements in the family firm and went to Canada to farm on new lands being opened up there just before World War I. When war broke out they immediately joined up in a Canadian unit and found themselves in the European trenches. Charlie, we discovered later, had been a regimental runner taking messages back overland across the lines – one of the most hazardous jobs. It was not surprising that he was killed. Uncle Arthur survived. It was only later in life – he lived until the age of 99 – that he was prepared to talk about his experiences: the mud and the rats in the trenches, the constant shelling and the barbed wire. He told me that one day when his group had gone over the top for an attack he was badly injured in the arm, was retrieved and sent for medical attention. He was waiting to be taken up out of the trench to an ambulance, when another man more seriously injured was brought in. Arthur said this man should take priority. That man was then duly taken up to the surface only to be killed at the top by a sudden shell which also destroyed the ambulance. After treatment Arthur worked in a training capacity and didn't return to the frontline. He was a man of gentle character who never seemed to harbour an unkind thought. He took infinite pains with customers at the Bill shop. He was incredibly fit, playing good tennis into old age. I remember that when I was young he would do a standing jump over a thick hedge at Mollands, as a show piece.

Frank, the sixth son, of whom my mother was particularly fond, had probably lied about his age to join up early. He died in the dreadful flue epidemic that swept across France immediately after the Armistice and is buried there. This was tragic for his parents and family but one can only imagine how dreadful it was for the boy himself, not having played a role as a soldier to which he had been aspiring and dying quickly without family around him in a foreign land. It makes me think of one of Wilfred Owen's most poignant war poems: 'Move him, move him into the sun,' which ends bitterly: 'O what made fatuous sunbeams toil to break Earth's sleep at all?' It is not surprising that my mother found it difficult to be sympathetic to Germans. It can't have been much fun at home as the letters came in from the six sons with continued anxiety about their fate. The four youngest children must have been very aware of this. These were my aunt Lena who died fairly young (whose daughter Jane is the closest to me of my Bill cousins), uncle Geoff, my mother and the youngest uncle Dick. I have already written about Geoff and Dick's travels to America.

Working in the Private Office meant keeping long hours. It helped for entertaining that I had been a member of the Royal Commonwealth Society since I left Cambridge in 1957. It was situated near the Foreign Office, served an excellent cold buffet luncheon and had private rooms for parties at reasonable prices. All my family were members, including the ladies. It was sad when health and safety rules made it impossible to maintain the old building which had certain style and character, so that it was replaced by an unexciting hotel and an efficient but colourless conference centre and restaurant. Sadder still when in 2013 it lost the premises altogether. I had stayed out of loyalty but was much happier when, during my next home posting in 1977 I joined the Athenaeum. This was at the suggestion of my parents' old friend and neighbour, the surgeon Herman Taylor. One of the attractions of the Athenaeum was its academia aura, with rooms full of books from floor to ceiling. Ever since I had returned from Kabul I had started nosing around the bookshops near the British Museum and acquiring an item or two. I had joined the Central Asian Society which later became the Royal Society for Asian Affairs, where I found many congenial spirits and attended interesting lectures. Through the scholar Dr David MacDowell I had become a founder member of the Society of Afghan Studies, which, when activities in Afghanistan became difficult, turned itself into the Society for South Asian Studies, linked to the British Academy. I was attracted by the idea of being thought of as someone who had academic credentials – slightly bogus though it was.

I might mention here that at some time in 1969 I was driving through Knightsbridge and Hyde Park when I saw mass of cars and many people walking to some event. Full of curiosity I managed to park my car and join the throng. Thus I witnessed the famous Rolling Stones concert in the Park at which Mick Jagger pranced around in a white outfit and released a host of white pigeons in honour of his colleague who had recently committed suicide. The atmosphere of this, the only 'gig' I have ever attended, was extremely good humoured. The music was, of course, full of life. I still prefer The Beatles, but I never saw them play live. The only singer I paid to see was probably the seductive-voiced Eartha Kitt, to whom for a time I was devoted.

In the Private Office I was responsible for relations with Europe and defence. I often accompanied my ministers on European trips. I watched the last stages of the negotiations for British membership of the European Union, which were finally successful after the death of De Gaulle, and was present for the signing ceremony in Brussels. I went on trips with the foreign minister to India, Pakistan, Japan and Hong Kong as well as to the UN in New York. I was involved with the crisis in Pakistan that led to the creation of Bangladesh, also the agonising to-ing and fro-ing over the independence of African countries.

As number two private secretary to two foreign ministers (Stewart and Sir Alec Douglas-Home), both of whom I came to respect, I had arguably more influence on British foreign policy than at any other time in my career. The relationship involved trust and inevitably became close.

I found myself flatteringly lionised because of my position. I was invited to evening parties by Ronnie Grierson, a director of the well-known General Electric Company (GEC), who had offered me a job at one point. He was a superb host in his house near Hyde Park Corner. There was nothing special about the food and drink but everything special about the quality of the guests. There would usually be three to four cabinet ministers present and a similar number from the shadow cabinet. Prominent media personalities like Robin Day would rub shoulders with duchesses. The disgraced but now rehabilitated and admired John Profumo would be there with his beautiful film star wife. During the course of the evening, Ronnie would take the trouble to come up two to three times to each guest to introduce them to others. People were so sure they would meet interesting individuals that they would come on from other dinner parties, so that between 10.30 and 11 p.m. there would be a new influx of guests. It was through Ronnie that I also became invited to several of Lord Weidenfeld's parties along the Chelsea Embankment. 'Come to a small gathering,' he said, which turned out to be a glittering array. One would meet people like Tom Stoppard, Evelyn Rothschild and Harold Wilson himself, once he had retired. I remember Marcia Falkender saying there how much she admired Mrs Thatcher. Sitting at a dinner table with Weidenfeld once, I blotted my copy book by making an expansive gesture and sweeping a wine glass to the floor where it shattered. My courteous host said that it did not matter though I could see that the glass had been valuable. I think I was invited there less often afterwards which was understandable! I am sure that I needed taking down a peg or two in those days.

I have a confession to make about my time in the Private Office. In principle I hadn't kept a diary. In fact, after about 1½ years with Michael Stewart I decided that, fiendishly busy though I was, I was doing the most interesting job that I never expected to do, so I really should maintain a diary, for history's sake. For the next two years I did keep a frank and intimate record which I shall leave with my papers, wherever they should end up.

I had forgotten about such things as the couple of talks I was asked to give to new Foreign Office entrants, which seemed to have gone down well (those who were present may know better). I did all I could to frustrate the recommendation to ministers of the chief clerk (then Oliver Wright, later a successful ambassador in Washington) that the Foreign Office building should be demolished and rebuilt, if necessary on another site. He claimed to have support for this throughout the Office, which I doubted. It was essential in my view that the Foreign Office stayed where it was, right next to No. 10 and not far from the House of Commons. If absolutely necessary it might be rebuilt behind existing dignified facades.

I had forgotten about some minor incidents such as the letter in French to the home secretary from 'the President of Sealand', on which his Private Office asked for advice. After checking, I told them that this was some buccaneer sitting on a fort in the Thames estuary trying to establish international credentials. No reply, should of course, be given. 'It looks as though this gentleman is your pigeon,' I wrote to my opposite number, and commented, 'one up on the Home Office!'

My diary records the rudeness and truculence of the new Labour prime minister of Malta, Mintoff, who was trying to blackmail us into paying a hugely increased subsidy for stationing our forces on the island.

We called his bluff. Without doubt he was the most abusive of any foreign statesmen with whom my ministers had to deal. Qaddafi came close. I recorded the lack of tears when Obote, the most unpleasant of new African leaders, was toppled by a coup – though it turned out to be a question of 'out of the frying pan' with his successor Amin.

I noted that Alec Douglas-Home, basically right-wing, tended naturally to be critical of corrupt black governments. I had to work with my boss Johnny Graham to keep him on track, about the unacceptability of racial discrimination.

Some of my comments in the diary on individuals were pungent. Talking of De Gaulle's foreign minister, Couve de Murville, I exclaimed 'What a sour man!' When Michael Stewart had spoken in favour of direct elections to the European parliament 'He looked as though he was going to be sick all over the carpet!' I described Giscard d'Estaing as a classic over-brained egg-head, the prototype of a specially built intellectual man who used a good deal of his brain power not to show his disdain for the indifferent mental material of others! On Sadruddin Aga Khan: 'If he is to be the UN Secretary General he must learn to talk less and listen more'. Kissinger, for all his brilliance, was 'out of order' when he tried to undermine Secretary of State Rogers by letting us know that the latter was not fully in President Nixon's confidence.

There was childish ribald humour. We giggled in the Private Office about a telegram from Tripoli, reporting the activities of a local individual called Mr Fartas. It prompted an under-secretary to tell us that in his last post there had been a Swedish ambassador called Herr Bugger, along with a Soviet military adviser, Colonel Fukovsky and a Danish ambassador, His Excellency Mr Axel Sporranfiddler! The best story I heard was perfectly polite. It was told by the Canadian foreign minister to Mr Eban, and passed on to my minister. Two Jewish ladies were talking together and found that each had the same problem: they had brought their sons up as good Jews and then sent them to Israel and each had come back Christian. They went to see their rabbi, who acknowledged that he had suffered the same experience. His well-brought-up son had been sent to Israel and come back a Christian. The three of them went to the synagogue and prayed: 'Dear Lord, what shall we do? We brought up our sons as good Jews, neglecting nothing, sent them to Israel and they came back Christians.' In response, after a pause, there was a booming sound, followed by a voice from the heavens: 'Same thing happened to me!'

The diary records a series of conversations that have nothing to do with foreign policy, such as my exchanges as Madame Rambert. Occasional disturbing tummy troubles, probably due to stress, were noted in the diary, as was my first discovery of a white hair. Recording that one Christmas I had given out more presents than I had received I commented that this was another sure sign that I was growing old!

Douglas-Home himself was quite artistic. He enjoyed arranging flowers and in ministerial meetings his doodles, often of flowers, were attractive. At one point I got into the habit of collecting up doodles of ministers from their pads at the end of sessions. The Dutch Foreign Minister Luns used to draw battleships, while the Belgian, Spaak, did pictures of pretty women. Sometimes when I was at less than exciting meetings, or later seminars, and not taking notes, I would start sketching other people around the table. I got quite good at it. When they noticed I might be drawing them, people would adjust their hair or tie to show themselves off to best effect. I love drawing in restaurants where there are paper tablecloths. Sometimes I have torn the work off and presented it to surprised subjects at other tables.

The Private Office with four private secretaries and a number of lady assistants and typists was a collective operation often working at full stretch. Occasionally there were pastoral responsibilities. The girls in the outer office were specially chosen for their intelligence and typing skills. One of our young women suffered a terrible tragedy. She was staying with her fiancé at the top of a London hotel that caught fire. Their rooms filled with smoke and they thought they had no alternative but to jump out of the window. Judy, a lovely girl, was impaled on the spokes of the railings around the hotel and died. We kept closely in touch with her family. I went to the coroner's court with some of them to give what support we could and wrote a piece for *The Times* diary. Her boyfriend also died. As it happened the coroner was Dr Thurston, who had been our family's GP in Essex years before, but I had no chance to speak to him.

When I first went overseas my mother had warned me not to marry an exotic foreign princess. She hoped I would marry a nice English rose. As I was preparing to go abroad over ten years later and was still unmarried, she changed her tone. 'Marry anyone, anyone at all!' My trouble was that the women I was attracted to were not the women with whom I felt intellectually in tune. Many of the latter had careers which could not fit with the life of a Foreign Office wife. By this time also a few of my friends had made disastrous marriages, which had split up with distress and acrimony. One indicated to his wife that he had been intimate with many of her friends, pointing out how some of their children resembled him! Much of this was excuses. I was nervous of the commitment that would be involved. I was later told of the difference between Eastern and Western marriages. Several of my Muslim friends had accepted marriages arranged by their families and had fallen in love subsequently. An Eastern marriage is like a kettle being put on to boil, they would tell me. A Western marriage is like a kettle of boiling water being taken off the stove! Fortunately my sister had three fine boys, each of them clever and talented in different ways, so my parents had grandchildren to fuss over. If people asked me why I was still unmarried, I would say, looking cheerful, that being unmarried was, of course, very miserable. I would repeat the saying that 'Life for an unmarried man is incomplete; when he is married it is finished!' (My lady-friends don't find that very funny.) I did sometimes feel guilty for not playing my part in propagating the race. When one of my nephews fell and gashed his head I commented what a terrible responsibility it was to bring children into the world, 'but someone has got to do it!'

7

JAPAN, HANOI AND LONDON AGAIN

After the Private Office I could virtually choose my next posting. Tokyo won over Athens because of Japan's new role as an economic power and the responsibilities of being Head of Chancery in a major embassy. Besides my political work and coordination role I also soaked myself in Japanese art and culture.

I soon became very fond of my new home in the embassy compound, and of Yamada San, the lady cook and housekeeper who served there. The garden was dramatically beautiful with a wide terrace, lawn, and beyond a great bank of shrubs and trees – some flowering, some clipped into geometric shapes and some allowed to grow naturally. Good lighting helped. The place became a venue for many memorable parties, including those for members of visiting British companies, such as the Royal Shakespeare Company and the Royal Ballet. Prominent Japanese from all walks of life would enjoy meeting such people and the response was mutual. A Japanese actor-friend, Yoshi Oida, had helped train members of the Royal Shakespeare Company before their visit so I had a special connection. Pauline Munro, Bob Lloyd and Gemma Jones (Titania) remained good friends ever after. (Pauline's son Sam became a treasured honorary godson.) For such big occasions I would find teams of jugglers, puppeteers or drummers to provide entertainment. Quite often we would all end up swimming in the embassy pool over the road in the compound.

I had read up about Japan and cultivated a few Japanese that I knew, particularly Yoshi, then working with Peter Brook, and Carmen Blacker, a Cambridge academic. They helped with introductions. Among new friends I soon made were members of the political Aso family and the delightful Chako Hatakeyama, and her husband Seiji. The latter had a house in Tokyo which drank in the garden view.

They also had a traditional house in a citrus orchard on the Izu Peninsula, south of Tokyo, which was an excellent base for walks among the local scenery: rivers, fountains, rocks and natural flowering trees and plants typical of the countryside throughout Japan. At the far end of the house was a large bathing area fed by a natural spring. Bathing is an important part of Japanese culture, which I embraced. The bathroom often had the best view. The form is to wash first from taps near the floor and then, once clean, to soak collectively in large hot basins. I am sure this custom leads to the calm temperament of the Japanese and their longevity. I spent many happy weekends at this Atagawa house not far from the conical Mount Fuji, glorious when not covered in cloud. There were also weekends at the Hatakeyamas' cottage by the sea at Zushi and, with a quite different more European atmosphere, in their ranch-type house in the north island of Hokkaido. Would you believe it, I also visited their house in the cool woods at Karuizawa, even nearer to Fuji. Visiting a traditional Japanese house on the other side of Japan Seiji, something of a modern Samurai, taught a group of us how to behave in traditional Japanese mode, including the correct lotus posture. We walked around the garden and lake, admiring and absorbing the view in one or two resting places. Then we stooped to enter a classical teahouse where Seiji performed the ceremony for us, with appropriate good conversation.

It was a Japanese academic friend Shuichi Kato, whom I came to respect, who explained most clearly for me the significance of the tea ceremony. Traditionally it took place in a small tea house built of natural material which was entered through a low doorway, often after touring and admiring a garden outside. The keynote was refined simplicity. Bending to enter was a sign of humility. The space was deliberately too small for a samurai to wield swords. They were left outside. The host would arrange a special scroll in a niche (tokonoma) with a carefully chosen vase and flower arrangement appropriate for the main guest and season. Dishes for the (ill-tasting) tea carefully chosen by the host were to be commented on and admired. Perhaps they were ancient artefacts, perhaps the work of the host himself. Numbers were small enough to encourage conversation. Each event was, according to

Kato, a unique work of art, which with those people, in that place, and with that exchange of ideas, would never be repeated.

Chako would join me and a group of close friends in expeditions to various *onsens* or bathing resorts, especially those which had open-air, hot spring baths called notenburo, or rotenburo. Typically we would go for the weekend in a group of about 12 to 16, Japanese and foreign, both married couples and singles. My favourite destination became Takaragawa *onsen* in Gumma prefecture north of Tokyo, to which I had once been taken by an American diplomat. I introduced the delights of this traditional Japanese *ryokan* and nearby mixed bathing to many friends including, as a first experience, quite a few Japanese. After a train and bus journey we would arrive at the old-fashioned inn hidden in a secluded river valley. I would book two large Tatami rooms into which we would divide sexes for sleeping. Down a path by the river were large natural pools of hot spring water. The experience was best in winter when, up to our necks in very warm water we would see every tree, every over-hanging branch, and every twig, covered in pristine snow. Our bodies would retain the heat long enough to get us back to the mother building. We bathed three times a day: once in the morning, once when we returned from a long walk in the surrounding countryside taking with us simple sandwiches, and once in the evening after supper. This would be a Japanese feast sitting in a circle in one of the rooms. The only problem was breakfast. Sometimes a kindly meant fried egg would be sitting on a plate for several hours accompanied by a piece of salt fish. (With age I have become more and more conservative over breakfast: fresh orange juice, tea, toast, marmalade and honey.)

We thought of the Japanese countryside as beautiful and benign but there could be dangers. It was popular to go for walks at all seasons around Lake Chuzenji, north of Tokyo, where our ambassador had a holiday house. One winter a group of my friends found themselves in a severe blizzard. A young French woman diplomat walking ahead of her party, mistakenly confident that she knew the way, got lost and was missing. A search the next day discovered her body frozen in the snow. I had not been one of the party but I knew the lady. We were all of course deeply shocked and distressed.

Japanese towns are ugly, but there was so much attractive countryside to explore. With a group of 20 people from the embassy I climbed Mount Fuji. The Japanese say that anyone who doesn't climb it is foolish. Also foolish are those who climb it more than once! The form is to go up in summer when there is not too much snow, but at night, so that the snow cap that remains is hard and can be walked on. We purchased wooden staffs with little bells at the top, which were branded at each stage where there were manned stops for rest and refreshment. Mine proudly has the sunrise station mark recording 12,395 feet. Some carried torches. There was a full moon. The idea was to reach the top to see the dawn breaking. It was quite exhausting, especially when the path got steeper and more slippery. The lights of towns and villages twinkled down below.

We eventually reached the top at about 3.30 a.m., after six hours of walking. The view was sensational. Fuji was so much higher than anything near it (like Ararat, which had impressed me on my original overland journed to Iran). Massed clouds lay below with a much greater sensation of height than in an aeroplane. On the sweep of the horizon one could see distant mountain tops emerging. We walked part of the way round the circular volcanic crater. At sunrise a streak of yellow and orange slashed across the eastern horizon. Then a blood red crescent appeared, cutting through the banks of white clouds, and the orb of the sun finally emerged triumphant. It began to warm our frozen fingers. A truly inspirational experience. Around 4.45 a.m. there were about 60 people on the peak watching. This account comes from my letter home soon after. The descent was much more difficult, not surprising if you think of the steep slopes of the mountain in pictures. We started at 5.30 a.m. and stuck together, branching off the route to go down a scree. Going down is, of course, painful on legs and feet, bringing unused muscles into play. We ended up in woods and had some difficulty getting back to our bus. We managed to get transported in jeeps down dangerous muddy roads that were partly washed away. We reached the bus at noon and after a snack were back in Tokyo in the late afternoon. I tottered into bed and slept.

Through Yoshi I met the beautiful and fascinating actress Tetsuko Kuroyanagi, who was such good company, already becoming Japan's best-known and immensely popular television star. Through her and with the help of Robin Duke, head of the British Council, and his Anglo-Argentinean wife Yvonne (an accomplished artist) I was lucky enough to meet a range of people in the Japanese theatrical world. Like the English, the Japanese are natural actors. I saw several first-class productions of Shakespeare. He was beginning to be more accessible to the Japanese public thanks to modern free translations by Professor Odajima, who became a friend. I struggled a bit trying to appreciate the very formalised Noh theatre, comparable to classical Greek theatre, though it helped that I got to know one of the families that preserved the Noh tradition, and Yoshi himself had been brought up in the Kyogen/Noh discipline. I claimed to be one of the first foreigners to have appreciated the ultramodern dance guru, Hijikata, who created a concentrated minimalist type of dance/drama, now called Butoh. Actors would have powdered faces. I watched the spectacular all-girl Takarazuka troop productions.

But most of all I was entranced by Kabuki, the form of drama that can be compared in many ways to Shakespeare, because of the period when it developed in the sixteenth and seventeenth centuries, and because women's roles were played by men. It was always for the people, whereas Noh was for the elite. The Kabuki stage was wide with elaborate sets. A walkway came through the audience. Costumes were colourful. But above all the intensity of the acting focused attention. Like opera in a foreign language the meaning of what was happening on stage was usually explicit, helped by a synopsis in the programme. The great actors belonged to famous families, with their own fan base from whom there would be shouts of approbation when a particular line was spoken and pose struck, as if ready for a photograph. Some of the most renowned actors played women's roles, the onnagata, even to an advanced age. It was said that Japanese women would model themselves on their deportment and gestures. I was invited to sit in on a few occasions when an important actor was going through the long preparation process for performance, treated by acolytes like a god. First the full, mostly thick white, make-up. Then the elaborate wig. Then the costume, layer after layer. Understanding who was who in the Kabuki world was complicated since famous names were handed down from father to son, and sometimes to adopted sons. Using practised family-tree skills I produced a chart showing recent generations of the six or seven great families. Tamasaburo, friend of Tetsuko and popular onnagata, had been adopted into one of them. He was praised for his beauty, but I admired above all his acting which could convey such strong feelings of emotion.

Tetsuko gave some parties at which I was one of the few non-Japanese. On one occasion I remember the conversation turned to tattoos, which in Japan are often whole-body multi-coloured works of art that make Western tattoos look like haphazard doodles. Actors liked tattoos but could only have them in areas of the body that would be covered by clothing. Several of the guests said that one of the actors present should show me his special tattoo. A group of men went with me to the next room away from the ladies. The tattoo was on his penis! Ouch!

I read plenty of Japanese novels now being well translated (my Japanese was just about enough to enable me to travel around the country). There were many other aspects of Japanese culture that I found attractive. Gardens of course. I visited many, some of great antiquity. Wooden temples and other old buildings had often at some stage burned down and been rebuilt, but their gardens were virtually original. After many visits to Kyoto I produced a cyclostyled guide to the temples and gardens there which remained in use at the embassy. I suggested forgetting some of the more popular places and discovering little-known treasures, such as the Miroku Bosatsu sculpture in otherwise dull Koryuji, the painted screens in the magnificent gardens of Samboin, the great hillside vistas at Shugakoin Palace and the abbot's garden at Kiyomizudera, not normally open to the public. I was particularly fond of Zen temples, such as Daitokuji where the monk Kobori San resided, who became a friend. I produced maps that helped identify which sub-temples were most rewarding and accessible. Sometimes perseverance was needed. I would knock and say that I had come especially to visit this temple. I would be refused. But I would not go away. Knocking again, I would politely say that I had come from far away and would be deeply disappointed if I was not allowed in. Eventually the monk would let me in. I would look round, take my shoes off and sit contemplating in front of the best piece of garden view, perhaps a glossy mossy slope with large stones judiciously placed. When he saw I was genuinely interested the monk would bring me tea, show me round his temple and perhaps let me see some of their treasures. Behaving with politeness and respect was the key, plus gentle persistence.

The Japanese were in their element at festivals around the country. They loved dressing up, celebrating and having a day off for families. I used to make special expeditions to see festivals where I could, for example in Nikko, in gloomy woods north of Tokyo, and in Kyoto. One could see the local butcher proudly parading down the street dressed as a samurai preceding a tumbril full of dignitaries in splendid garments. The most spectacular festival I managed to get to see was the Hadaka

Matsuri, or naked festival, at Okayama, which I visited with a small group. We watched some of the participants beforehand dressed with a minimal loin cloth, immersing themselves in a local river, though it was February and cold. In a spacious hall attached to a temple we were given places on a high balcony overlooking a mass of near-naked bodies from which steam rose, periodically doused with water. Perfumed batons were thrown into the melee by priests. Groups of men teamed together to get hold of them and conceal them, then to extricate themselves with fierce struggles and win a prize by producing the batons at a designated place. As the sticks were thrown several men who had climbed to positions on beams in the roof launched themselves down into the crowd. There was nothing too violent. A surreal event.

So much of Japanese culture, for example the elaborate textiles, the carved objects, the woodblock prints, of which I bought quite a number, showed great artistic sensibility. This, along with Japan's growing economic strength, attracted many visitors from the West. I was delighted to be asked to give lunch to Iris Murdoch and her husband whose books I had avidly consumed as they were published. I honed up on her recent novel, where one character had been a diplomat and collector of porcelain, and suggested when she arrived that I might be in the mould of this gentleman. The name did not register with her at all! She told me that she forgot about her books and the personalities in them immediately after they had been written! Other visitors included my Cambridge contemporary Michael Frayn, to whom I introduced my theatrical friends. On return to the UK he wrote a couple of typically brilliant pieces for *The Observer*. I was rather upset that he had ended on an apocalyptic note that all Japanese achievements might end in an earthquake disaster. We had a slightly strained exchange of letters. One could argue, however, that the recent Fukushima disaster, many years later, justified his prescience. I saw a bit of the great potter, Bernard Leach, who had, of course, many Japanese friends. Lord Jellicoe, a social acquaintance, came out promoting Concorde, which was one of our priorities. I was able to entertain old friends like the Fries family (from Brussels) and Ronnie Grierson, as well as other family friends. Having a contact on the ground made visiting Japan much easier.

I still tell Japanese that what I particularly loved about Japan was Zazen, Kabuki, rotenburo and Sumo. I was privileged to see a great celebration of Japanese martial arts at the Budokan, laid on by the right-wing rich benefactor Mr Kodama. This included judo, aikido, kendo, sword fighting and naginata (how women in villages could defend themselves against swordsmen with long pikes). Many of the great masters of the day were present. But on that occasion there was only a taste of the popular sport of Sumo: wrestling between men of great bulk and nimble feet. I got tickets when I could for the three or four Sumo contests that took place in Tokyo each year. The atmosphere in the stadium was tense. Referees in brilliantly patterned kimonos presided over a ceremony in the small ring, which led to a brief dramatic contest. Putting any part of the body on the sand other than your feet, or being expelled from the ring, meant defeat. This was always accepted with dignity. Combatants had to fight every day for 15 days in the top group, after which if they had more wins than losses they would advance up the ladder to honorific positions and titles. A mixture of strength, skill and psychology was involved, which was absorbing to follow. I claimed to have spotted champions such as Chiyonofuji early. In our culture big, fat people are despised. In poor countries a good belly often commands respect, since it indicates wealth. In Japan it was interesting to see how the Sumo giants outside the stadium were respected by and gentle with children. They had nothing to prove. It was a time when one or two foreign wrestlers were breaking through to the top ranks. More recently this process has accelerated, no doubt because fewer Japanese are prepared to put themselves through the extremely tough training and discipline involved. As a Sumo aficionado I found some later reports of corruption in the sport distressing.

I had to confess, to the dismay of several Japanese and Japanophile friends, that I never really liked Japanese food. Much of it was raw, with lots of fish. Traditionally there would be a whole series of dishes, each artistically presented, but the taste was bland. I could not stand tofu nor the inevitable soya sauce. My worst experience of food was when my friend Yoshi kindly took me to a sort of week-end retreat with monks in a temple at Nara. Almost all the food was plain rice with soya sauce. Thank heavens I had secreted some cheese and fruit into my week-end bag! Sometimes at dinner parties raw creatures would be winking at you still alive, it seemed, as they postured on your plate (it is said that it was a brave man who first ate an oyster). The final bowl of rice was tasteless. We have come to like rice cooked and seasoned in different ways. The Japanese enjoy the delicate taste of rice itself, which passes me by. I suppose it is rather like the way that we can enjoy different flavours of our own staple food, bread.

While on the subject of food I should add that I was sometimes invited home to dinner by Japanese friends. Their wives would be rushing around in the background serving us with dish after dish, and it would need a specific request by me to allow her to join us for a moment. Much washing up afterwards, no doubt. Plenty of sips of sake helped, especially after some exquisite-looking morsel that tasted dreadful. Strong liquor does not go well with delicate tasting food, which is a mistake made in my experience by many Chinese, offering whisky. I would always opt for tea. At this time plenty of my Japanese friends had wives who were highly intelligent and doing worthwhile jobs. But except for the super elite, they almost invariably adopted a submissive posture at home. The men would go out after work drinking with their colleagues, sometimes going to a bar where they had developed a relationship, probably not sexual, with the lady proprietor. What was difficult to understand was that it was quite normal for these men to expect their wives to wait at home for them and not even to telephone to say whether they were coming home for supper.

The priorities of the embassy were mainly economic and commercial but we also wanted to keep alongside the Japanese politically as far as we could, encouraging them to play a greater role in international affairs.

Fondness for Japan helped when I found myself playing a major role in organising the Queen's state visit to Japan in May 1975, the first by a British monarch. It all went well. I drafted the Queen's speech for the Emperor's banquet. Among the things I noted that we and the Japanese had in common was the love of theatre and gardens. Also driving on the left.

Because we have to change sides of the road when we cross the Channel we in Britain tend to think that all foreigners drive on the right, which of course, is not so. As well as Japan most of the old Commonwealth and Empire countries, except Canada, drive on the left, including India and Pakistan. Where you drive now may be a product of the cultural rivalry between Britain and France. In the days of horsemen and swords it would have been logical for one always to pass on the left so that right-handed people, the majority, could attack or defend to their right. It seems that the French unusually deserted logic when choosing to drive on the right – perhaps because the right has traditionally seemed superior to the left, or perhaps just to be different. They seem to have persuaded countries such as the USA and China. They did not persuade the world to adopt a ten-day week. But they did succeed in making decimalisation the standard for most of the world's measurements.

My pastoral duties as Head of Chancery in Tokyo were not onerous, but there were a large number of staff to keep an eye on, working closely with the administration officer. I took pains at the beginning to invite all members of the staff for lunches. I started a tradition of Boxing Day football matches to help morale; the Embassy team of 11 would be on one side of the pitch and as many other people as wanted competing with them on the other. I warned the Office in London, tongue in cheek, that the allowances for our shorthand typists were so low that some of them might be tempted to find part-time work in the expensive bars in downtown Ginza. I did not expect that some months later one of our brightest girls was spotted working there as an escort (not of course, of the sexual variety)! Japan was expensive.

Some of our young diplomats worked very hard. One day as I was leaving the office I noticed one young man looking rather tired and strained and asked if he was all right. He said yes. But later that night he took an overdose of pills. It was a cry for help. Sick in bed he telephoned one of his colleagues, who fortunately was at home. He was rushed to hospital, pumped out and saved. He had left a poignant note for me, which I got the next morning, saying that because of my interest, I had 'almost saved him'. I called on him in hospital expressing sympathy and concern, and tried to figure out what had been going through his mind, since he seemed to have a bright future in the service. He indicated that life for him under pressure had seemed to be full of great monsters with which he just could not cope. He went home. The Foreign Office treated him well, but I believe he could only manage routine jobs thereafter.

I think I reached my peak in some ways as I was leaving Tokyo. I wrote in a letter home, 'I can hardly remember a time in my life when the days dragged.' I was 41 – about the prime age for an astronaut. I had a hugely diverse range of contacts and friends, including large numbers of Japanese. I have a tape taken during a farewell party I gave, which for me is very evocative. It includes voices of politicians, diplomats, academics, theatrical people, artists, businessmen, even people concerned with judo and Japanese rugby, mostly saying kind things. There is a background of drummers and a guitarist is singing *I'm Leaving on a Jet Plane*. Departures were emotional and once in the aircraft leaving for home I cried a little.

* * *

There are a couple of things to mention before I leave Japan. From the beginning I tried to persuade my parents to visit me there. Eventually they came in the autumn of 1973 for a visit they greatly enjoyed. I took them to the major sights including down to Kyoto on the shinkansen express train. Over the years I had had differences with my father, being earlier more radical in my views. Sometimes my mother would have to intervene as she had when father and uncle Geoff began to dispute over the merits of the USA. But on this visit there was nothing but warm good humour between us all, not the slightest discord. It was great being in their company and introducing them to Japan and many of my friends. These good memories helped when some months later in 1974 I was woken at night in my house in the embassy compound and told that my father had died of a heart attack. He had been on the golf course with a friend, had struck a ball (which I like to believe was a good shot) and dropped dead. The Foreign Office said they would consider whether they would pay for me to fly home on compassionate grounds. 'To hell with that,' I replied, 'I am going.' I needed to be with my mother and sister. (They coughed up two months later.) At the funeral service in Trumpington church several people appeared who said they owed my father a great deal but whom we had not known about. Father was 72 and should have lived longer. Reading recently through his letters I remember what a generous, thoughtful father he was, full of wisdom and enthusiasm for life. In my diary I had described him as a man 'of generous energy'. He was good man, respected by all with whom he came into contact.

My concern, and my sister's, was now for my mother, since the marriage had been so close. She had relied on him for most practical questions, especially anything financial. It goes without saying that the closer the marriage the greater is the distress when one partner dies. In the event mother lived on for over 20 years. I had always written home regularly but I promised myself, after father's death, that I would be particularly careful to keep the letters going, which my mother appreciated. We used often to end our letters to each other with the letters ILYAYK, meaning 'I love you as you know', which we both found an apt phrase. One of my last letters from my father in early 1974 described a grand dinner he had attended at the Reform Club, where he had spoken both to Sir Alec Douglas-Home and to Michael Stewart. Each had said that they had had a Christmas card from me. Father thought it pretty good that Sir Alec knew that I had just been in Hanoi. I hope that these exchanges gave him pleasure.

Over the Christmas of 1973–74 I was sent to fill a gap in Hanoi for two months, being promoted to counsellor as a sweetener. It was an interesting experience driving through war-torn South Vietnam and peaceful (then) Cambodia to the grim communist state of North Vietnam. I was head of a team of only three people living in frugal conditions. There had been a temporary ceasefire after the Kissenger–Le Duc Tho talks. We had no access to Vietnamese and the Diplomatic Corps were mostly Eastern European.

Diplomats gave parties for each other in Hanoi on the slightest excuse. I am still distressed to remember one occasion when I courteously offered to light the cigarette of the young wife of a Romanian diplomat sitting near me. The badly made local match split and a piece of glowing wood made a hole in the green silk dress which must have been special for her. She was clearly upset but tried to pretend it was all right. I apologised profusely but what could I do? I could not offer money. I did send her later a fine new woman's scarf I had brought in my bags for contingencies.

Mostly we were thrown on our own resources. Books, of course. A couple of packs of cards proved useful, for playing bridge and patience. There is only one worthwhile type of patience in my view, which if you carefully make the right moves has about 20 per cent chance of success. I spent hours fiddling with what I later came to know as a set of pentominoes, the 12 only possible arrangements of five blocks on the same plane. I had bought a set in Pindi made in China, years before, as a toy. There were numerous possibilities which I now had time to work out. Some years later when I was posted to Cairo, and among other things was responsible for our aid effort, a splendid character came out from home to promote educational toys for Egyptian children. Jack Pettican was a salt-of-the-earth Welshman, wonderful with his hands, who was frustrated by the poor organisation of the project he had been paid to conduct. But he got on very well with me, particularly when he found I was interested in what he told me was pentominoes. He made a special set for me which I still enjoy.

After Christmas a tennis competition was organised for foreigners at the shabby local International Club run to keep the Diplomatic Corps happy. There were three separate small leagues whose winners had to play each other in the final. In my group I beat a young Romanian, the Indonesian military attaché and the French ambassador (a charming, experienced colleague). In the final I managed to defeat a stalwart Pole, but had a terrible tussle with a supple young Indonesian. I started so badly that I got audience sympathy and he was well ahead. But I finally beat him, showing what British underdogs could do! At the prize-giving the Russians won the volley ball and the ping pong and Laotians won the badminton. Then we all drank Hanoi beer in a friendly atmosphere.

There was not much that I could report from Hanoi but everything we sent was snapped up because there were so few sources about what was going on there. My brief Southeast Asian expedition was an interesting glimpse of a different world.

On one period of leave from Tokyo I visited Sri Lanka, meeting friends of my father. I had an introduction there to the charismatic Chitrasena, leader of a traditional dance group, and spent time with his delightful family. I visited Anaradapura, Solannaruwa and the great rock palace of Sigiriya. I got stuck for an extra day in Nairobi on the way home where I was fascinated by an afternoon's visit to a local safari park, an interest I was able to develop after retirement. I was now set for a period at home.

Back in the Foreign Office I was made head of Information Department, promoting and explaining British interests overseas. Part of my time was spent in liaison with the BBC external services for which the Foreign Office paid the bills without controlling editorial policy. I had to fight to preserve the best of our operations against a superficial and aggressively cost-cutting review.

During this time in London I was busy in the Office, partly because, as head of a non-geographical department, I could not expect to have the brightest and most ambitious of young diplomats on my staff. Much of the drafting was therefore up to me. I also enjoyed an active social life, in particular taking the opportunity of going regularly to the theatre. I seized every chance to watch those great actors who were still active on the London stage: Laurence Olivier, John Gielgud, Ralph Richardson, Paul Scofield, Alec Guiness, Peggy Ashcroft, Wendy Hiller, as well as comedians such as Robert Morley. Even Deborah Kerr, Douglas Fairbanks Junior and Wilfrid Hyde-White from the film world. Youngsters like Ian McKellen and Judi Dench were beginning to make an appearance. It certainly seemed a rich time for British theatre. There was no shortage of attractive girlfriends to escort! I kept several of the programmes and have thrown lots away. In the more adventurous area I was suitably seduced by *Hair,* and inspired by *Jesus Christ Superstar.* On one special evening I took a group of friends including Terence Stamp to see Kabuki at Sadler's Wells. I have continued to be an advocate of Kabuki on the rare occasions it comes into town.

Anna Cropper, only sister of my school and college friend Max, was often on the stage at this time. I would see her and take her out afterwards. I had known Anna since she was a teenager. She was no classic beauty but full of sparkle and charm and a good actress. In 1961, when I was a Resident Clerk, she had married an extremely handsome young man she had met while working in a repertory company. This was William Roache, who became known throughout the country as Ken Barlow from Coronation Street. He started about that time and was still a popular star in the soap 50 years later. They were a glamorous young couple delightful to know, living in Islington. Sadly Anna's theatre work in London fitted ill with Bill's television schedule in Manchester and they divorced. In his autobiography *Ken and Me* Roache blames his dalliance in the north with other women for the break up of his first marriage. I used to think of myself as honorary godfather to their son Linus, who became a fine actor himself.

One summer Anna persuaded the headmaster of Linus' school Littlemead, near Chichester, that I should be invited to give the annual speech at speech day. I accepted, appreciating the honour, and worked hard on something worthwhile to say which could appeal both to pupils and to parents, and to staff – so no risky jokes. It seemed to have gone off well. Linus told his father, who sent me a kind letter, that the children had actually 'listened' to my speech, not a common occurrence. It became the pattern for other school speeches when I was ambassador in Pakistan. Making such an address (best to break the ice with a joke early on) is rather fun, especially if you can capture the children's attention. What I found less enjoyable was shaking the hands of hundreds of prize winners! I gave a tribute to Anna Cropper at her funeral in Chichester in the 1990s. Linus and his sister were there, but sadly neither her brother (who said he was unwell) nor her former husband could be present.

1 Author aged six months with mother, looking rather beautiful (mother).

2 The Bill family. Back row from left: Frank, Jack, Bernard, Charlie and Arthur. Middle row: Lena and Ned either side of the author's grandparents Selina and William Bill. In front: Mildred (author's mother), Dick and Geoff.

3 Parents and young son.

4 Paternal grandparents Frederick and May Barrington.

5 Great-uncle Sir Donald Allen, war hero and charity administrator.

6 Painting by the author of Mollands, the house and garden in Essex where he grew up.

7 Expedition of Belmont prep school boys to the nearby downs in Sussex. Author in the middle.

8 Belmont Headmaster Max Burr with his wife Nilla visiting Cambridge.

9 Headmaster of Repton Lynam Thomas accompanying the Queen during 400 anniversary celebrations outside the Old Priory. With Archbishop Geoffrey Fisher (Courtesy Repton School and Leicester Mercury).

10 Drawing by the author of an old man brought in as a sitter in the Repton art school.

11 The beginning of a teenager's enjoyment of amateur dramatics, playing Caesar at Repton School.

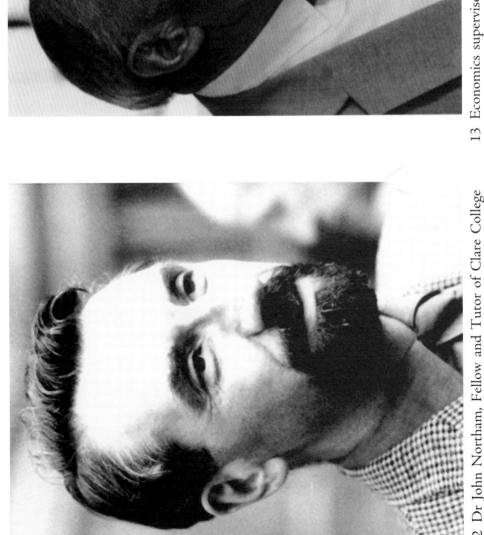

12 Dr John Northam, Fellow and Tutor of Clare College Cambridge, friend and guide (Clare College).

13 Economics supervisor at Clare: Dr Brian Reddaway, later Professor of Applied Economics (Clare College).

14 Treading the boards at Cambridge. Playing Hector in the Mummers production of *Tiger at the Gates*.

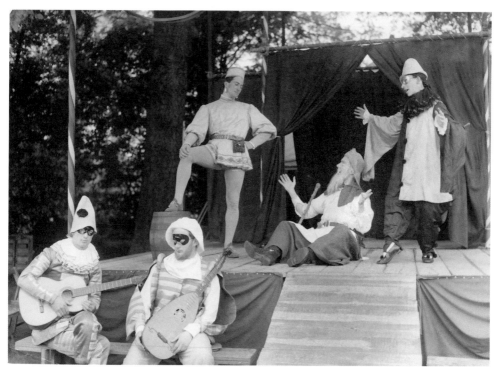

15 As Bassanio in the University Actors' production of the *Taming of the Shrew* in Kings Fellows garden.

16 As cowardly Welsh teacher Hugh Evans (at left) in Cambridge ADC production of *The Merry Wives of Windsor*.

17 With family at the Senate House after receiving Cambridge MA degree.

TROILUS AND CRESSIDA

Dramatis Personae:

PRIAM, *King of Troy*
HECTOR
TROILUS
PARIS   *His Sons*
DEIPHOBUS
HELENUS
MARGARELON, *a bastard Son of Priam*
AENEAS   *Trojan Commanders*
ANTENOR
CALCHAS, *A Trojan Priest, taking part with the Greeks*
PANDARUS, *Uncle to Cressida*
AGAMEMNON, *the Grecian General*
MENELAUS, *his Brother*
ACHILLES
AJAX
ULYSSES   *Grecian Commanders*
NESTOR
DIOMEDES
PATROCLUS
THERSITES, *a deformed and scurrilous Grecian*
ALEXANDER, *Servant to Cressida*
HELEN, *Wife of Menelaus*
CASSANDRA, *Daughter to Priam, a Prophetess*
CRESSIDA, *Daughter to Calchas*

Trojan Soldiers, Myrmidons, Trumpeters and Attendants.

The play will be presented in two parts with an interval of fifteen minutes.

The Society wishes to express its gratitude to
The Governors of the Shakespeare Memorial Theatre, Stratford-upon-Avon, for
the loan of costumes and properties, and to Miss Judy Birdwood and Miss Sheila
Scott for supervision of the wardrobe.
Armour by Bapty & Co., Ltd.   Wigs by Nathanwigs, Ltd.
Jewellery by A. Robinson & Son.   Furniture by Old Times Furnishing Co., Ltd.
The setting, designed by a member of the Marlowe Society, built in the Cambridge
Arts Theatre Studios and painted by Roger Beck.

For The Cambridge Arts Theatre Trust:

Resident Stage Manager	...	ARTHUR HEWLETT
Box Office Manageress	...	ENA VARLEY
Chief Electrician	...	KENNETH REEDER

18 Marlowe Society programme for *Troilus and Cressida*, revealing some signatures
of future Cambridge luminaries.

19 With US Embassy colleague Kendrick travelling in remote Nuristan, Afghanistan.

20 View of Nuristan while staying at a village high in the mountains.

21 Portraits of four lady friends from Kabul, Brussels and Rawalpindi.

22 Playing Malvolio in *Twelfth Night* in Brussels.

23 As Noel Coward's Gary Essendine in Cairo, with Ambassador's wife Hilary Weir.

24 As the doddery Rev Chasuble in *The Importance of Being Earnest* in Islamabad.

25 Author in Lotus posture creating a surprise in Takaragawa onsen, Japan.

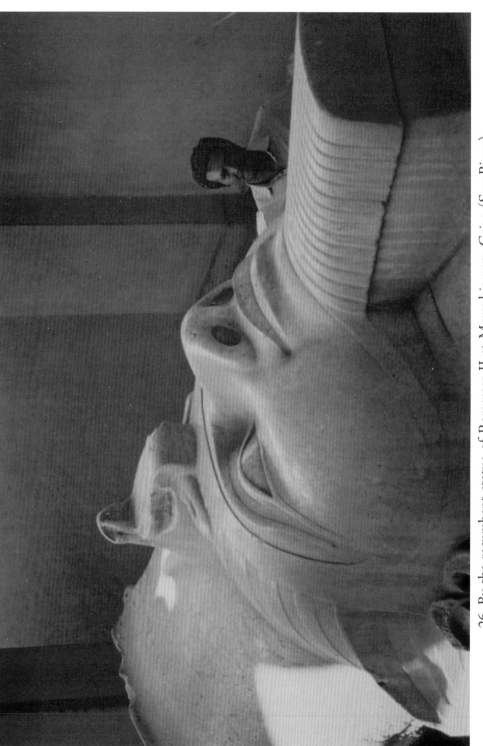

26 By the recumbent statue of Ramesses II at Memphis near Cairo (Sue Binns).

27 The Royal dubbing. An original pen and ink drawing by Gino d'Achille, using his imagination. A gift from cousin Susan Bird.

28 Chief bearer in Islamabad Lall Khan with one of his flower arrangements.

29 Islamabad cook Rahim with one of his confections, in this case depicting a bridge between East and West (castle and mosque).

30 Visiting Swat with Prince Aurangzeb (on right) with his wife Naseem (in dark glasses) and old Hutton friends Michael and Susan Williams.

31 Kay Hartenstein in one of the beautiful pavilions at Lahore Fort.

33 Poster for *The Tempest* in Islamabad.

32 Author as majestic Prospero with magic staff.

34 Roger Mear, mountaineer, adventurer and friend with his new wife Ghazala.

35 Collage of pen portrait sketches drawn by the author surreptitiously over the years while attending seminars and meetings.

36 Aunt Freda Bird with her artist daughter Susan.

37 Generous benefactor uncle Geoff with much-loved dog at his house in Essex.

38 Willie Amin at wedding of middle son Paul.

39 The author's sister and brother-in-law at Hill Farm with Pakistan wildlife expert Tom Roberts.

40 The author's three nephews. From left: Rupert, Cris and Andrew with wives Alison, Lai and Camilla at Hill Farm with views over the Deben estuary, Suffolk.

41 With Roger Cooper, former prisoner in Iran, visiting Cambridge (Copyright Hana Valyi).

43 Painter friend Harry Webster with some of his works at his retrospective exhibition.

42 In Cambridge with astronaut Michael Foale, modern hero (Rhonda Foale).

44 The committee of the Clare College Dilettante Society, with its patron in 2005 (from left, Ben Pearson, Richard Charlton, Richard Hadden and Tim Wogan). Over the mantelpiece is a painting by Clare academician, Algernon Newton, presented to the college by the author (Dr Richard West).

45 The Ancient India and Iran Trust building in Brooklands Avenue, Cambridge, drawn by the author in 2013.

47 Shield and arms granted to the author by the College of Heralds. Note the motto 'With Kindness to Wisdom and Peace'.

46 The Cypress Tomb in Lahore, one of the many minor monuments under threat in Pakistan.

8

THE RICHES OF EGYPT AND TENSIONS IN TEHRAN

My next job was to be counsellor and deputy to the ambassador in the British Embassy in Cairo, which I welcomed. Egypt was a country of critical importance, with a fascinating history.

Advice was that the safest way of making sure that you got your car to Egypt was to take it out with you by land and sea. Accordingly, in April 1978, I took my new British Ford across the channel. There was a minor panic when once on the ferry I closed a self-locking boot thinking I had left the only keys inside. I hadn't. Relief! The car then went on a train with me to Milan, after which I drove down through Italy to Naples, where I was to embark. As I was coming into Naples in the yellow evening light, approaching the end of a motorway, I could see the city and busy port down below me. Just before the exit booths I ran out of petrol! A minor but essential indicator in the new car wasn't working properly. Even though almost all my luggage was packed tightly into the boot I was reluctant to abandon the vehicle, in view of the Italian propensity for robbing cars. Years before I had been given a lift in a young American's car coming from Patros in Greece to Brindisi and then up to Naples. In a small town where we stopped for the night his car was cleaned out of all its contents, to his great distress. But what could I now do? My ship was leaving the next morning. I explained my predicament to a man in the exit control booth. 'You're in luck,' he said, 'the road goes down-hill from here and at a curve on the right there should be a garage,' I managed to get the car moving, jumped in, coasted down, and there was a little one-man petrol pump! A heavenly garage! A stroke of incredible good fortune! Sometimes the gods are with you. Once on the extensive pebble beach at Cley in Norfolk I found that my car keys had slipped out of my pocket. Retracing my steps I saw them wedged between grey stones.

My most extraordinary piece of luck took place years later in 2010 when I was driving in my little Honda from Canonbury to Cambridge and Ely to attend the funeral of a diplomatic colleague. In north London, stuck in a line of cars at a traffic light, I noticed a tiny man with a wizened, pointed face gesticulating at me as if something was wrong with my car. I could see nothing from behind the wheel but I wound down the window. In a foreign accent he said, 'Oil. Come and look.' I quickly got out of the car and saw to my horror that oil was all over the lower part of the radiator grill. The little man said, 'Come over to the other side. I'll show you.' I extracted myself from the line of cars and parked at a lay-by opposite. I opened the bonnet and saw that oil was all over the bottom of the engine. 'You were lucky,' he said, pointing at a photograph and card round his neck on a ribbon, 'I'm a mechanic. Your oil pipe is broken.' His English was not good but I got the gist. 'If you drive back 50 yards and turn right I can get a new Honda oil pipe and fit it for you!'

Unbelievably this is what the little man did. I parked 200 yards down a side road. He disappeared into a building and came out with a new pipe. Lying on his back in the road he fitted it in about ten minutes, showing me the broken pipe. He said it would cost me £60, 'More expensive in a garage.' Still somewhat dazed, I gave him £80 which by good fortune I had in my wallet. I asked where he came from. He said Iran, but didn't understand my Persian. It emerged he was from the north-east of the country where they speak Azeri Turkish. He said his name was Ali Ismaili. To me he was an angel, a funny looking little angel, but an angel for sure. I could only guess the chances of discovering engine damage, during a journey of an hour and a half, right by a man who had access to and could fit a new oil pipe! There could have been a burn-out and serious accident anywhere further along the motorway. I confess that driving ahead smoothly I looked up at the clear blue sky and imagined a smiling bearded god figure looking down at me and saying, 'Now, what do you think about that?!' I reckon that my luck is now exhausted.

I inherited a spacious, if rather run-down, house in Zamalek island in the middle of Cairo, with a garden full of flowering shrubs and trees.

Head of my domestic staff was bulky Nabawi, the cook, who operated from a large kitchen in the basement, where, if I ventured at night, there were likely to be plenty of cockroaches too big and brittle to squash. The saffragi, who we would have called bearer in Pakistan, was a rather feckless and temperamental young man called Amer, who used to fall asleep at the drop of a hat. Sometimes I would come home to find that waiting in the hall in case the telephone rang he would be lying on his back with arms and feet in the air like a sleeping kitten. The two of them coped with plenty of entertaining, getting in assistance as required. A large pregnant maid cleaned upstairs. They were not ideal servants. Wherever I was posted I was always reluctant to change staff, partly because loyalty was two-way and partly because servants dismissed were often the direct or indirect cause of subsequent household robberies.

I got used to an unusual rhythm of life: in the office at 8 a.m. early in the morning and working straight through to a late lunch after 2 p.m. Then a siesta in the midday heat, watching tiny geckos on the bedroom ceiling. Away from high summer it was possible to sunbathe in privacy on the flat roof. In the late afternoon there would be tennis or swimming, usually in the extensive grounds of the Gezirah Club close by, of which I became a member. There might be pingminton in the garden. Sometimes I would go back for an hour or two into the office.

My main responsibility was to supervise the economic, commercial and aid work of the embassy, which was a good experience. But I was also often in charge of the whole embassy when my ambassador was on leave, or between ambassadors. There was a change halfway through my time, during which it fell to me to report on President Sadat's agreement with Prime Minister Begin at Camp David. The Egyptians thereby achieved the reversion of the Sinai Peninsula.

Cairo itself was a great metropolis with many surviving medieval buildings. The call to prayer from minarets in Cairo, sometimes exaggerated by loudspeakers, was one of the features of living in the city. As well as a series of mosques there are many tombs, remains of old walls and, what is unusual, a couple of large houses showing how rich men lived a couple of hundred years ago. In the third world, places of worship and tombs are buildings most likely to survive from the past; it is quite rare to find furnished houses. (One of Britain's unique assets is of course the number of fine country houses, still fully furnished with carpets, pictures, silver and crockery, with their gardens, that have survived almost intact. No other country has comparable riches.) In the Bayt Suhaymi and Gayer Anderson House one could note the warren of rooms and inner courtyards, and the main reception rooms with a little fountain where guests would be entertained sitting on cushions. There would be lattice windows above, from which the ladies of the household could observe.

Egyptian mosques tend to have a rather dull brown exterior, lacking the dramatic features of the coloured tiled domes of Persia, but they have fine brick and plaster workmanship and interesting interiors. One learned to distinguish Fatimid, Ayubbid and Mamluk architecture, and later Ottoman buildings. The Citadel which dominates Cairo was developed by Salahuddin (Saladin), the leader of Kurdish origin admired by some crusaders as a just enemy. But one could climb down the 300-foot-deep Joseph's Well there, with vaunted magical properties, which is believed to date from Roman times. Saladin was also responsible for many of the city walls, which still survive. It is sometimes claimed that Nasser was the first Egyptian to rule over the country for 1,000 years. The Fatimids, a Shia dynasty originally from Tunisia, built what can claim to be the oldest university in the world at Al Azhar. The Mamluks had been brought in as mercenary Turkish slaves. It was an early Mamluk ruler who finally put a stop to Mongol expansion in the Levant. The Mamluks gave way to the Ottomans and it was an Ottoman governor who founded the Farouk dynasty. He was proud to be an Albanian. In a vibrant city like Cairo with growing population there were constant pressures to encroach on and demolish old buildings, thus the need for efforts to create conservation areas. UNESCO helped. I suspect that despite best efforts several of the monuments that I saw, the towers, the street fountains, the old brick archways, may not have survived.

I cultivated a wide range of Egyptian ministers, officials and business leaders so that I was in a position to give help and advice to our many visitors, as well as to departments in London.

There was a strong Coptic Christian community, with its problems. They were much in evidence in Cairo's social life. Though rarely found in senior governmental positions they were prominent in the professions. Two of the best embassy doctors were Copts. One of them successfully diagnosed and treated my fortunately mild attack of hepatitis B. There were prominent Coptic academics and artists. With my particular interest in art I got to know a group of painters, including a special

Coptic lady, Inji Efflaton. She gave me one of her paintings, as did the respected senior artist in Cairo at that time, Salah Taher, who was good company. The redoubtable Coptic theatre director, Laila Abou-Saif, who staged *Mother Courage* at the Citadel, became a good companion. She was a feminist who introduced me in New York, later, to the famous Gloria Steinem. What particularly concerned her and other human rights activists in Egypt was the cruel practice of female circumcision, often performed in the villages in a crude and insanitary way. It was a tradition specifically designed to prevent women getting any pleasure out of the sexual act. I have reservations about aspects of feminism, for example I don't agree with giving women jobs they don't deserve on quotas, purely for sex equality. But I was convinced that female circumcision was a wicked practice that should be eradicated.

Living in Egypt was full of interest. Egyptians were devout, but also fun-loving. There were imaginative cabaret shows at the principal hotels, especially the Mena House near the pyramids. In those days belly-dancing was very much a feature of social entertainment. For special occasions, such as a marriage party, it was *de rigeur*, like champagne is in the West. One would watch young bridegrooms seated next to their richly but modestly bedecked bride on a couple of thrones, trying to adopt the right attitude when watching a voluptuous belly-dancer, in other words showing appreciation but not too much! The only concession that belly-dancers made to Islam in my time was to wear a flimsy gauze over their normally bare mid-riffs. I began to realise, after watching many performances, that it was not so much the physical beauty that commanded admiration but the personality and character of the women that determined how they held their audience. My favourite was Fifi Abdou, even though I didn't understand the risqué remarks in colloquial Arabic with which she would favour some of her patrons. During a visit by the Duke of Edinburgh I discovered that he would be entertained at a dinner at which there would be a belly-dancer. I made it clear that there should be no sitting on laps or photographs. In fact Fifi Abdou handled the occasion with her usual aplomb.

Cairo was a popular venue for visiting film companies. One of my friends was an enterprising young American who worked for an organisation hosting these companies. Sometimes Elly arranged for me to give parties for them. Thus Charlton Heston was my guest at one time, accompanied not by his mistress, masseur or valet but by his tennis partner. Also the delightful Susannah York. The most glamorous of these visitors was Lesley-Anne Down who had become well known in the UK when appearing in the long-running TV serial *Upstairs Downstairs*. Working on a film in Egypt she decided, for some reason (which puzzled many of us), to get married to the rather scruffy assistant director. Their informal wedding reception took place in my house. My mother, sister and brother-in-law were visiting at the time. My sister has never forgotten that the star borrowed from her a white belt which she never returned. Later we caught a glimpse of Lesley-Anne filming in skimpy attire at the Ramesseum in Luxor.

I felt particularly honoured to entertain Wilfred Thesiger, one of the last of the great explorers, whose books on the empty quarter of Saudi Arabia and the marsh Arabs I had greatly enjoyed. He had also visited Nuristan, which gave us something in common. At this time he was mainly living with the Masai in Kenya, whom he thought the noblest of mankind, after the Arab bedouin. Thesiger was brought to dine by Mark Allen, a young Arabic-speaking member of the Embassy who had become a sort of Lawrence of Arabia character. He had written a book on falcons and kept two of them, hooded, in his guest bedroom. He would train them in my garden. Mark distinguished himself at the end of his career by his efforts to persuade Qadaffi's Libyan government to discard nuclear ambitions, for which he was knighted.

I used to arrange very good parties at my house. The only entertaining disaster was when I gave a buffet supper for visiting Foreign Office inspectors to meet a large number of embassy staff. I didn't want it to be too lavish in order not to give the inspectors the impression that our allowances were generous. But half way through the buffet the cook told me that everyone was eating so much that the food was running out. Staff had to be sent out into the neighbourhood to purchase chickens, at any price, that were then roasted on the spot! I didn't handle that inspection well at all. I insisted on taking pre-arranged leave though I knew it meant that I would be away half the time the inspectors would be in town. The absent are always wrong. The eventual report suggested that I contributed very little of value to the Embassy, although I thought I had been holding the whole operation together! There had been so much commercial work that they had appointed a new commercial counsellor under me, who had to justify his place. It did my career no good and was a lesson learned.

I doubt if the inspectors would have been very impressed anyway by the time I spent on amateur dramatics in Cairo. There had been so much good professional Japanese theatre, of all sorts, in Tokyo that I had not trod the boards there. In Cairo there was an active group of Cairo Players, of which I eventually became chairman. The couple running the local Christian school and helping the Anglican Church were the prime movers. At first they persuaded me to take part in a rather strange play by John Bowen, called *After the Rain*. I played the role of a man who takes the lead of a shipwrecked community at some time in the future, determined to create a new society of the elite and becoming like a god. There was a moment when I had a major argument with another character interrupted by my coming forward to the audience and saying dead-pan, 'I'm sorry I can't go on.' It was part of the play since I was a character playing a character, but the gasped reaction of the audience was satisfying. Eventually my character got killed. Reviewers were kind. I thoroughly enjoyed playing the main character, Garry Essendine, in Coward's *Present Laughter*. A review said that as the devastatingly charming lead (a role taken by Coward himself) it was difficult to know if Nicholas Barrington was acting or not! (If that's not self-promotion I don't know what is.)

I got particular pleasure by playing the role of Bottom in Shakespeare's *Midsummer Night's Dream* produced in my garden and directed by a keen but theatrically inexperienced young diplomat, Tony Brenton. I assisted him. I really enjoyed playing this character to the full, including the farcical Pyramus and Thisbe playlet at the end. It may have been the summit of my acting career. There are moments when Bottom has command of the audience when he wakes up from his dream on stage, remembering vaguely how he seemed to have had hairy ears but had been sleeping with a beautiful queen of the fairies.

The production was a great success, sold out for three performances, more than 300 for each night. So it covered costs. Everyone said how magically beautiful the garden looked. I put up a notice praising my gardener, Abdul Basith. My suffragi Amer spent a week of late nights watching the rehearsals and performances and cleaning up afterwards. He was entranced by it all. In contrast, Nabawi, the cook, thought it was quite crazy, and me too. The production was even given a good write-up for the BBC by Bob Jobbins in the *From Our Own Correspondent* series. He wrote that it would be 'very hard to imagine other countries producing such an uninhibited or, for that matter, such a professional performance as Bottom as the senior British diplomat who, shedding urbanity and self-consciousness, dominated the play.' I have been known to say that in Cairo my Bottom was much admired! I was less good, rather over-acting, as the butler in *Ring Round the Moon*.

At one time I agreed to take the small part of a prophet in a religious play for the local Anglican Church. It was one of those days. During my siesta I overslept, and realised to my horror that the performance was about to begin. I tore down the road in my car, threw myself into make-up and costume and just made it onto the stage in time. Coming back I found that I had forgotten my keys. The servants were away and I had to climb in through a window observed by sceptical bystanders. Then, in a rush upstairs to get a bath before an evening engagement, I caught the pocket of my jacket in the banisters and ripped it off! One of my rules now is always to touch my pocket to see that I have my keys before leaving the house.

There was another incident on the stairs when my family, mother, sister and brother-in-law were visiting. At the back of the large entrance hall there was a staircase mounting diagonally to the upper floors. Sitting in the study to the left of the front door I happened to look out and saw a creature scampering up the stairs. It was too far away and going too fast to identify. Bigger than a rat. The servants had gone home. Before going to sleep we searched every bedroom meticulously and stuffed blankets under the doors. Some appeared to have been nibbled in the morning. We never saw the beast, but found out what it had almost certainly been. A number of stoats live in the banks of the Nile. It had come in through a broken lattice window downstairs and presumably went out the same way. It must have been a traumatic evening for the stoat as well as for us!

In Cairo one got used to packs of noisy wild dogs in the streets, occasionally rounded up and disposed of, also constant hooting of car horns. On one occasion I found myself pressing the horn, stuck in traffic with a tight schedule. A policeman came up, asked me to wind down my window, and said 'Malesh', loosely translated as 'it doesn't really matter'! I realised he was right. There was nothing I could do. (I can't resist repeating at this point the story of a driver whose car was wandering all over the road. In this case also a British policeman came and stopped him and asked him to wind down the window: 'You're drunk,' he said. 'Thank God,' said the driver, 'I thought the steering had gone!') 'Malesh' was a popular word in Cairo. If someone bumped into your car they would say 'Malesh' even if there was damage. One-way streets were often not observed. One evening I was tired and when I found a car coming at me in a one-way street, instead of letting it pass, I positioned myself right in front of the bonnet so he couldn't proceed. He probably said 'Malesh', but I was angry and told him to go back since what he was doing was illegal. 'I'll take you to the law,' I said. 'I am a lawyer,' he replied. I gave up!

It was rather delightful that you would sometimes see sheep and goats walking through the centre of Cairo. Less pleasant was that all the cars were parked on the pavements so you could only walk on the streets. Later they installed kerbs of about nine inches high to stop the practice. After my time an underground system was installed which would no doubt have eased Cairo's traffic problems. Having said all this Cairo could be strangely beautiful. The Nile had a magic of its own at all hours of the day. It was of commanding size with swift flowing strength, bordered in those days by old eucalyptus trees, presumably at some stage brought over from Australia. I used to find the view from the terraces of the old Nile Hilton continuously fascinating. The great river seemed to have a life of its own, bearing its history along with it, a history that had touched millions of people for many thousands of years.

Close to the Hilton and the river was the Grand Egyptian Museum with an immense range of treasures, and many more in its basements, one of the great storehouses of the world. Some of the labelling in those days was also antique, but it didn't matter – the artefacts spoke for themselves. Each visitor would find their own favourite pieces, but the three galleries devoted to the Tutankhamun treasures were essential viewing. The craftsmanship, sophistication (there was a folding camp-bed) and bejewelled and golden brilliance of the prime pieces would take away the breath of the most hardened traveller. It was a pleasure to show people around.

The Giza pyramids and the Sphinx on the edge of the city and desert were also easy to get to, though one had to watch out for the centuries-old habits of the Egyptians. I had been in Egypt for some time when I drove a group of visitors to the Great Pyramid, parked my car in the sand nearby and took them up into the interior, that amazing stone tunnel built to give access to the principal tomb chamber in such a way that it could subsequently be blocked from potential robbers. On returning I found that I had parked my car badly over stones, but some locals offered to move them. I gave them a tip and drove away, appreciating their kindness. Until I realised, half-way down the road, that they must have put the stones under the vehicles themselves! One day, when visiting the Sphinx, which looked particularly dramatic illuminated, I was in the crowded chamber waiting to go through with other tourists when I saw that an American lady had accidentally stood on the bare feet of a little local urchin, who cried. She gave him something. On the way back I happened to notice the same little boy and watched him deliberately slip his foot under the shoe of another tourist. The subsequent crying was masterful acting, not overdone, and the reward was duly delivered. He was an expert! The basic rule when visiting Egyptian monuments in those days was to have plenty of small change with you. Egyptians setting themselves up as guides or caretakers would be content with small change, so long as it was something.

Further away from Cairo was Sakkara with the original step-pyramid, father of all the others, and a series of tombs with amazingly well-preserved reliefs depicting every aspect of the lives of ancient Egyptians. There was a string of lesser-known pyramids between Giza and Sakkara quite difficult to reach. I found a way to one of them where, providing you paid a village boy to look after your car, you could picnic undisturbed with your friends on slabs of ancient hieroglyphs, under palm trees, in the lee of a pyramid almost 4,000 years old. If you had a sharp eye (children were best) you could find ancient mummy beads in the sand, used for necklaces for ordinary burials in those days. Plenty of echoes of Ozymandias. To the west the lone and level sands would indeed stretch far away.

It was a privilege to get to know British Egyptologists. Henry James, Keeper at the British Museum, became a friend. I remember taking chubby little Professor Eothen Edwards, author of the classic Penguin book on the pyramids, to some lesser-known monuments. For some reason he was dressed in suit and waistcoat, looking like Mr Pickwick, but when he saw a gaping hole he plunged down inside, like the White Rabbit, despite my remonstrations. I would regularly visit Professor Harry Smith, who was working with a team at Sakkara based in a camp with a marvellous view over dunes, down to a sea of palms. As so often in archaeological digs, Smith's team, including students and experts on pottery, were paid practically nothing, but enjoyed the experience while they were fed and housed. Egyptology was so successful and popular in the early days in Britain that pioneer archaeologists hadn't felt the need to establish an academic institution based in Cairo, to compare for example, with the British Institution of Persian Studies in Tehran and British Institutes in Athens and Rome. The Egyptian Exploration Society suffered from having no local base. Other archaeological teams, especially the French, but including the Italians, Germans and Poles, seemed much better supported by their governments.

It is difficult to conceive that the pyramids were built about 500 years more before Christ than we are after Christ. Giza and Sakkara provided burial places for the great city of Memphis, near Sakkara, where Smith was working, though it was almost impossible to excavate because the site had been covered by villages and agricultural land and parts of it were regularly flooded. There was little to see in Memphis in my day except a dramatic statue of Ramesses II, which once stood 13 metres high and is now recumbent, protected in a small building (Plate 22).

In Egypt one always had the sense that there were more remarkable relics of the past to be discovered. There are pharaohs whose tombs have not yet been found. An event in Cairo that was still creating great excitement when I arrived was the assembly of a funerary boat found in a long trench beside the Great Pyramid. Clearing a pile of sand had revealed a series of stone blocks which were sealing a trench. Twenty-five years before a young archaeologist had cut through one block and discovered layers of wood, including oars, preserved intact for over 3,000 years. The sacred boat, almost certainly used to transport the bodies of dead pharaohs, had been carefully taken to pieces, and packed and buried. I met the local craftsman and boatman who had studied carefully all available evidence about the structure of ancient Egyptian boats and managed to fit the pieces together. It was a major achievement. Haj Ahmad Youssef Mustafa was now a local hero. The result of his efforts was a huge majestic structure with sharp prow and elegant lines, 150 feet long, made of dark, warm-coloured cedarwood. It was only then beginning to be available for VIPs and people with contacts with the Antiquities Department to see for the first time. A building had been constructed around the boat, so the temperature could be controlled. Other pits had been found empty. One still remained, probably containing the pieces of another boat which the antiquities people had decided should be left alone. There is a good archaeological argument for keeping some sites undisturbed for the benefit of future scholars, who might have better equipment.

The Antiquities Department was a powerful and important organisation. In those days its directors were cautious about allowing new excavations, particularly if previous work had not been written up. Together with the police they tried to stop illegal digging and the smuggling of artefacts overseas, but the scale of the problem made this almost impossible. There was a centuries-old tradition whereby Egyptians would dig into the ground, including under their own houses, hoping to find objects of value. The whole country is an archaeological site. Dr Zahi Hawass, Director of Antiquities, recently in office until the Arab Spring, differed from his predecessors. He was an extrovert buccaneer who encouraged further excavations. He was a good publicist for his country's historical heritage but for that very reason not universally admired by scholars. In mid-2013 he was apparently back in office according to one report and, true to character, engaged in opening at last the second boat pit.

I used to visit Luxor and Upper Egypt at least twice a year, sometimes with visitors and friends, sometimes alone. (It can be confusing that Upper Egypt, meaning up the river, is much further south than Lower Egypt.) It was a particular pleasure for me to take my mother, sister and brother-in-law along the traditional route for tourists. We started by flying to Abu Simbel where massive figures cut out of the rock had been raised by UNESCO to avoid them being flooded by the new lake created by the Aswan Dam. The dam had played a political role in Egypt. Designed to provide regulation for the waters of the Nile, which were the country's essential lifeblood, the project was not considered appropriate for funding by the USA because of the quantity of arms Nasser had been getting from the Soviet bloc. This then encouraged Nasser to turn to the Soviet Union to fund the dam – with all that followed. Just below the dam, the town of Aswan with traditional hotels looking over clear water, with little islets and many recreational boats, still seemed straight out of Agatha Christie. The form was to take a passenger vessel from there, going down the river to Luxor, stopping off at one or two temple sites. The boat would move at a gentle pace giving pastoral views of farmers on the banks. Most people felt that continuing down the river all the way to Cairo would take too long. One would need to be with exceptionally good company.

Just beyond, that is north of Luxor, was a special temple at Abydos, which was worth a visit by car. It was here that a remarkable English lady, born in Greenwich in 1904, spent the last years of her life working barefoot as a guide. She had become a local phenomenon given the name of Omm Seti. She had been obsessed since birth with Egypt, claiming to have dreams that showed she had been in past life a priestess of this temple. She had married an Egyptian in London and come with him to Cairo. After 20 years when the marriage had collapsed she came to Abydos, which she felt was her home. The stories she remembered or dreamt about life at the time of the Pharaoh Seti, 3,200 years ago, were so remarkably realistic and consonant with what experts knew about that time that many people thought she was indeed an example of reincarnation. Sadly she died just before I first went to Abydos, where I met her adopted son.

There was much to see at Luxor, with the benefit of a clear guidebook written by an English woman living in Cairo, Jill Kamil. She was an ideal picnic companion at any site. I had visited Egypt many years before, stopping off on the way home from Rawalpindi. In Luxor I had found myself with an ancient guide or 'dragoman' who was very knowledgeable but kept me away from certain places because of his own infirmity. He told me he had known Howard Carter. Eventually we reached an understanding whereby he stood at the entrance of some tunnel or tomb, told me what to expect, and left me to explore it alone. Now, knowing the country better, and with the benefit of Jill's guide, I was happy to wander alone among the great monuments.

Luxor temple itself, in the town, was accessible and striking, especially illuminated at night. The extensive temple complex of Karnak a tonga-ride away was mind-blowing, with stone columns reaching to the sky. My globe-trotting uncle Geoff thought it the most impressive monument in the ancient world. Then, across the Nile, where black and white pied kingfishers would hover in the yellow evening light, there were the tombs of the kings and of the queens and, best of all because more intimate with colours well-preserved, were the tombs of the nobles. That was where you needed plenty of small change. Less visited were the great silent courtyards of the funerary temples, the Ramesseum and Medinet Habu, where one could find oneself quite alone surrounded by ancient ghosts.

I never went to see the less spectacular antiquities in the Nile Delta, near the Mediterranean Sea. Alexandria itself, Egypt's second city, I had reason to visit diplomatically. It was a strange conurbation stretching for miles along the littoral with no real heart. Few remains of the metropolis of Greek, Roman and early Christian times have survived. Nothing is left of the famous library that was destroyed. The site of the Pharos lighthouse, one of the seven wonders of the ancient world, is clear. French archaeologists have found stones from the old structure under water. There are also columns and other remains of what may have been Cleopatra's tomb, also below the sea. But what happened to the tomb of Alexander the Great? After his premature death in Babylon, his body was being taken home for burial in Macedon when it was hijacked by Ptolemy, Alexander's commander in Egypt, who was making a new kingdom for himself as the empire split up. I have always found this an interesting period of history when Seleucus, cavalry commander and one of Alexander's lesser known companions, inherited the bulk of his Levantine and Persian Empire. Ptolemy brought Alexander's body to the city Alexander had founded, where it was said to have been exhibited in a tomb protected by a sort of early glass for over 200 years. It was visited by tourists and pilgrims from all over the Roman Empire. But in riots in Alexandria involving the Jewish community around the time of the first millennium it was apparently damaged, and disappeared to be heard of no more. How fascinating if it could be rediscovered! It is known that if you dig deep under many of the houses in Alexandria you will find remains of the old city.

Sadly I never got to the Siwa oasis, further west in the desert, famously visited by Alexander. I did go snorkelling in the Red Sea. With a small group I went to a spot 30 kilometres south of the Suez where the hills came close to a shingly beach. There were only five or six other cars spread along a wide expanse. About 30 yards out in the sea the sand changed to coral. With goggles and flippers one could glide slowly over the fascinating tropical world. The coral itself, brown, pink and blue in all shapes and contours, was like an underwater forest. Fish were of all sizes and all colours – electric blue, phosphorescent turquoise, blue and orange, brown and white stripes, yellow on green. It put me off slightly that there were some large jellyfish around. At one point looking at the multi-coloured seabed I noticed a few thin, shark-like fish alongside me, also enjoying the view. Not being a great swimmer this made me nervous, as did the warning that one shouldn't let one's feet land on the coral where there might be poisonous spiky creatures. I am not brave in the water. The only time when I really felt confident snorkelling was after retirement on holiday in the Seychelles. There the water was calm and I found myself swimming alongside turtles, such ungainly looking creatures, but clearly so happy in the water. I put my hand out and touched one and he turned his face to me as if to say, 'I don't think we have been introduced!'

President Sadat was the key figure in Egypt throughout my time there. I have recorded elsewhere some of the opportunities I had to meet him and get an impression of a remarkable man, who may have been autocratic but who had many bold achievements to his credit. The Egypt I knew was at times chaotic, but never violent. Sadly, the year after I left, Sadat was assassinated by Islamic extremists as he was attending a military parade.

I heard this news when in Tehran where I had been posted, after three years in Cairo. The Shah had fallen. I had represented the British government at his funeral in Cairo. American Embassy hostages had only recently been released. There was considerable tension and uncertainty in Iran as the revolution was settling down. Because we had withdrawn our staff at one stage my official title was the head of the British interests section of the Swedish Embassy, but I was treated in all respects, except protocol, as an ambassador and lived in the old historic British compound in the centre of the city.

It was in the main Residence dining-room that Churchill's famous birthday dinner took place during the Tehran conference in 1942 when he had Roosevelt on his right and Stalin on his left. Stalin had almost walked out on seeing a large portrait of George V, thinking that we were honouring the Tsar. They were so alike. A brass plaque on the wall recorded all those who had attended the dinner, a roll-call of political and military personalities of the three powers. In idler moments I researched this event. I was puzzled for a time by 'Flight Lieutenant Oliver', until I realised that Churchill's daughter Sarah (whom I had met in Spain) had at that time been married to the Austrian entertainer Vic Oliver. She had been a dancer in a troupe of which he was the star. At Churchill's insistence he had become a naturalised American before marrying Sarah. During the war she joined the Women's Royal Air Force (WRAF). I found that the cook who had prepared the food for this event was still alive and recorded his memories of the occasion.

My own hospitality was enhanced by the discovery of abandoned boxes of fine wine in the former military attaché's house. Many other such caches had been destroyed. I was permitted to use the wine for official entertaining and to pay an appropriate amount to charity.

At Christmas the Residence was perfect for traditional parties for staff and the British community. I went to town with all the trimmings. I recorded in my letter home that I personally made two-and-a-half-foot-high coloured cut-outs of the three kings to greet people as they arrived, at the foot of a sizable Christmas tree with lights in the 'oriental' hall. There were elegant paper chains in the drawing room. Constant log fires helped the atmosphere. Dinner on Christmas day was for 22 around a long table for Embassy members not on leave and a few outsiders who were close friends. We played the traditional Barrington family games. Over sherry we had a treasure hunt trying to find duplicates of items on a tray, which had been hidden with imagination. The menu was fish mousse with prawn and smoked salmon accompanied by a glass of white wine. Then roast turkey, sprouts, roast potatoes, beef sausages and stuffing, with a Margaux claret. Following a recipe sent by my mother I had helped the cook make a very successful Christmas pudding several days beforehand, served with mince pies, brandy butter and champagne Then there were cheese, nuts, dates and fruit, and coffee for everyone seated in the drawing room while we played the adjective game. (You write a story beforehand, bringing in all those present, leaving numerous gaps for adjectives. Then you ask guests sitting around the room, in order, to suggest adjectives of any sort, which you write into the text. It takes a bit of time but when you read it out at the end the result is usually hilarious.) We also did the special aeroplane game when people are taken away one by one and blindfolded. With the help of a plank and some books, and two lifters, they get the impression they are going up in an aeroplane to hit the ceiling and then are told to jump. People had to suffer these games in Cairo and in Islamabad too! My letter home recorded that this party had been preceded by a Christmas eve service with carols conducted by a German pastor, attended by 120 people. This account reminds me of the story of the little girl who prayed, 'Lord, forgive us our Christmasses as we forgive those who Christmas against us!' But of course such Christmas celebrations can be important for morale of staff and the British community in a potentially hostile environment.

One year a much appreciated Aladdin pantomime was put on in the lecture room of the British Institute of Persian Studies (BIPS) building, adjacent to the Gholhak compound. I was roped in to play a small role of the Sultan of Shemiran. Martin Charlesworth, the resident director of BIPS, gave a series of lectures there on Iranian history, which were much appreciated. The library was a valuable resource for a number of Iranian scholars. There was also a rehearsed playreading of *Midsummer Night's Dream* in the Golhak Residence garden, for which I played Oberon. I was rather proud of making an ass's head for Bottom out of numerous wire coathangers covered in papier mache.

The Gholhak Residence in the even larger rather wild embassy compound in the hills north of Tehran was more like a chalet, with a private garden surrounded by trees and a small circular pool. I fixed up a pingminton court. One had to go outside to climb the stairs to the main bedroom. There were magical moments listening to nightingales in the garden, the bird that features so often in Persian poetry as the desperately aspiring lover courting the rose. I found that I could learn and remember the work of Hafez and other poets. The rejection of Western culture under the Ayatollahs produced a revived local interest in Persian poetry.

It was at Golhak that I hosted a lunch on one occasion for a mixture of friends and, over the coffee, toasted myself, to everyone's astonishment. I told them it was because it had just been announced in London that I had been awarded a CMG! A CVO (Commander of the Victorian Order) had been practically automatic because of the state visit to Japan. Being a Commander of St Michael and St George was probably more of an achievement. Some people disparage honours but I consider (I would, wouldn't I?) that the sign of official recognition of one's work is good for morale, and good for one's friends and family. And, as one Oxford wit once remarked, it gives such distress to one's enemies! Since someone once refused an honour after it had been approved by the Queen, which was embarrassing (I believe it was the writer John Galsworthy), people are always asked in advance. You are not allowed to tell anyone, except a spouse in great confidence, but you know an honour is coming. It did not stop me always wanting to check with a *Times* reader in London that the announcement was actually in print and that nothing had gone wrong, before local celebrations. Sadly, the Golhak Residence was abandoned over the years and I was told recently it has deteriorated into a ruin. I did a reasonable sketch of what it looked like at the time.

The small embassy team worked closely together. I trusted my deputy Chris Rundle, who, with his wife, was also interested in Persian poetry. I also relied greatly on my two house servants and my driver. The man who kept the two residences clean and operative, and who served at meals, had been doing a junior job with former ambassadors. He was loyal and astute. When one of his young sons got caught up with people who persuaded him to join up with the Basij – a youthful volunteer army that were being used by the regime as cannon fodder in the war with Iraq – my servant went round to the recruiting depot and told them how happy he was that his very unstable, unreliable son was being taken off his hands by the military. After reflection, they said that they didn't need him! My cook, a cheerful character, produced good food under difficult circumstances. My driver, neat competent and intelligent, knew all of my movements. I never wanted to risk driving myself.

Reporting on the political and economic situation was difficult but we did manage to help a number of British companies doing business in Iran, as well as British subjects who found themselves in trouble.

Life was not all work in Tehran. There wasn't much to see in the city itself, an ugly metropolis that had grown too fast. There were a few old palaces preserved to demonstrate the Shah's sybaritic lifestyle. Some contained exquisite silk carpets. Farah Diba had helped organise some local museums worth visiting. There were items of modern sculpture she had collected as part of her controversial efforts to introduce Tehran to modern Western culture. (My Japanese actor friend, Yoshi Oida, had performed in an avant-garde Peter Brook production near Persepolis for one of her festivals.) I managed to visit in Tehran some local *zurkhanes* (houses of strength) where half-naked muscular body builders would exercise to the sound of drums and religious music, a tradition which it is believed goes back before Islam.

Best attraction of all was to visit the nation's crown jewels in the basement of the Central Bank on those occasions when it was open to diplomats, VIPs and their guests. Keys of three responsible officials were needed to be brought together before such an opening, not surprising considering that the hoard helped to provide backing for the nation's currency. There were heaps of diamonds on display, including some with a slight pinkish hue, and some slightly yellow. The uncut Darya-ye Noor (sea of light) was sitting there, once companion to its chiselled sister the Koh-i-Noor (mountain of light), now among the British crown jewels. A large globe had land and sea distinguished by different coloured precious stones. Alongside antique pieces of jewellery were some more modern designed for the Shah's queen, notably a tiara of large glowing emeralds. Finally there were two ceremonial chair/platforms covered in jewels, one of which was purported to be the Peacock Throne looted from the Moghul Emperor in Delhi by Nadir Shah, the Persian who was one of the world's last great conquerors.

I could travel a certain amount. When I visited Isfahan I made contact with the family of my old instructor from SOAS, Heidari, and was a little surprised to see that Reza Qoli Borumand, with whom I had smoked a pipe of opium many years before, was still alive at an advanced age. His habit didn't seem to have done him much harm. All the great mosques, madrassas, bazaars and bridges were well preserved and local guardians were only too happy to show you around. It wasn't long before tourists started coming again, with benefits for local people.

I made an ambitious journey with my driver to Shiraz where I found new friends among cultured Iranians who made sure I was entertained for every meal. I paid homage once again at the tombs of Hafez and Sa'di and I revisited Persepolis and Naqshe Rustom. I visited the site of the former British Council premises where I pointed out to a group of young Basij, who had made the place their headquarters, that the property belonged to Britain and should eventually revert to us. They were a little taken aback. Thinking about it afterwards it was rather an odd thing for me to do.

There were no clear restrictions on our travel in those days. With a group of Persian friends I went beyond Shiraz down the dramatic road to the ancient site of Bishapur, one of the capitals of the Sassanian empire. Stone ruins of palaces and a fire temple remained at the mouth of a gorge. Islamic iconoclasts had defaced some stones and painted over a few reliefs, but that had been stopped. Beyond some of these reliefs cut into the rock was the entrance to an enclosed D-shaped valley. We made a stiff climb, during which I wore out a pair of shoes, to a large cave near the rock summit on one side where there was a broken colossus statue of the Emperor Shapur I, reputed to have been carved originally from a stalactite. He had ruled over an extensive empire in the third century AD.

There was a fine view. The unexplored cave behind looked like something out of *Raiders of the Lost Ark*.

I also went 70 miles east of Shiraz to Firuzabad, the old winter headquarters of the Qashqai tribe, where could be seen the massive ruin of the palace of Ardeshir, Shapur's predecessor. Enjoying a picnic lunch on that trip I recorded that I was serenaded by a persistent cuckoo. At one point the road curved in a loop round a high hill topped by the ruins of a fortified palace called the 'Castle of the Daughters'. These Sassanian fortifications date back earlier than the mediaeval castles in Europe and the Levant. My driver thought that I was insane to climb up to the castle, but I was escorted by a helpful Qashqai tribesman in distinctive hat whose main interest seemed to be how much a wife cost where I came from! Throughout Iran it was expensive for bridegrooms. They had to pay a heavy sum to take someone's daughter as a wife. One of the jokes addressed to people with daughters was to say, 'how much did you sell them for?'!

The Iranians have the great quality of being able to laugh at themselves. I remember seeing a Persian verse written on the back of a car: 'I have suffered so much that I am fed up with this world. My face may be young but I am old!' (My favourite such notice is 'Undertakers love overtakers!') When driving over the mountainous road to the north of Tehran to the Caspian, on one occasion my companion told me the story of a bus containing 20 mullahs that had crashed into a ravine, killing them all. The driver had jumped out in time and was found weeping by the side of the road. 'You should be laughing,' said a passerby, 'there are now 20 less mullahs.' 'I am weeping,' said the driver, 'because it was a 40 seater bus'!

Some events that happened towards the end of my time in Tehran meant that a subsequent posting to Beirut was aborted for security reasons. Not knowing quite what to do with me the Foreign Office sent me to New York for a few months in the autumn of 1983. I was then chosen to organise the London G7 Summit for Mrs Thatcher before being given a serious new job as under-secretary in London.

9

UNDER-SECRETARY AT HOME, VIA NEW YORK

I was attached to the UK Mission to the United Nations (UN) as a supernumerary ambassador lobbyist for the General Assembly session. We were successful in trying to minimise a hostile vote which would have required Britain to negotiate with the Argentinians over the Falklands, from where we had expelled their invading forces. In general it was useful for me to learn about the workings of the UN, an often maligned body doing an essential job.

Meanwhile I much enjoyed living in New York. My well-appointed apartment, high up on First Avenue, had a little balcony which gave me splendid views of a forest of skyscrapers, made more magical as dusk arrived, displaying thousands of lighted windows. I could never tire of the bright lights of Broadway, nor of those immense towers of glass on Sixth Avenue. I would gaze up, imagining that set on their side among fields each would be like a small town. I was able to entertain in my apartment – for instance a group of visiting UK parliamentarians which it fell to me to organise. One of them was Lord James Douglas-Hamilton, relative of the Duke on whose lands Hess had landed unexpectedly during World War II. I had always been fascinated by this story about which Churchill had insisted no news should get out until the end of the war. Lord James gave me a book about Hess with his thank-you letter. For various parties I would mix up useful UN contacts, including old friends like the Egyptian and Japanese ambassadors (Moussa and Kuroda) with local New York friends, or with special visitors, such as Tetsuko Kuroyanagi from Japan.

When she visited I spent time with her friends the Romes at their large apartment on Fifth Avenue, which included a fine collection of African sculpture. I was privileged to go with the Romes to social events lorded over by the then queen of New York theatre, Mrs Richard Rodgers. I was able to enjoy the theatre, opera and ballet in the good company of Jackie, an hospitable friend of Ronnie Grierson, who was a professional Christies' wine expert, which was unusual for a lady, and whose family had regular seats booked at the Opera House. We saw Joan Sutherland in *La Fille du régiment*, a Peter Brook *Carmen* and the Béjart Ballet. She took me to her club, a ladies' institution where men were only allowed as guests, something that never, as far as I know, has been started in London.

I roamed through the Metropolitan Museum where I remember noticing for the first time among the mass of exhibits, an important display of fine old carpets, about which I felt I had now become knowledgeable. I revisited the Frick, also the Museum of Modern Art, the home of one of my most favourite paintings in the world: Rousseau's depicting the lion and the sleeping mandolin player. As you look at the picture, you hold your breath so that the man shouldn't wake up.

I enjoy music but find it hard to discriminate through lack of real knowledge. I recognise and enjoy well-known passages which I often cannot place. In contrast I have become much more familiar with the work of great artists. What other paintings are my favourites? I think immediately of the portrait of the doge of Venice by Bellini at the National Gallery in London – such a serene, wise, powerful man simply portrayed against blue. I have spent much time in front of the emotional *Descent from the Cross* by Van der Weyden in the Museo del Prado. I loved Rembrandt's representation of Abraham and Isaac from the Hermitage, at one time lent for showing in London. Then, of course, Van Gogh's landscapes with dominant brush strokes and his apple trees. Breugels. Vermeer's tranquil large view of Delft, in that city. Early Picasso. The ceiling of the Sistine Chapel … I had better not go on.

At an art exhibition in New York I met a very attractive young woman, Kay Hartenstein, who became a friend. She moved to London and visited me when I was in Pakistan. Her knowledge of the more extreme forms of modern art were slightly outside my range but coincided with the tastes of Charles Saatchi, whose wife she became before he met up with Nigella Lawson. Personally, I don't think he gained by the exchange. The new marriage sadly also collapsed. (I have just noticed that Saatchi hasn't mentioned Kay or their daughter in his latest *Who's Who* entry.) Cautious about crime I used to dress down when walking the streets of New York in the evening, occasionally consuming huge juicy steaks in Frankie and Johnnie's restaurant. What I loved about the city was the monumental architecture contrasted with the intimate scale of many restaurants and corner shops. A cobbler near my building unerringly picked out my repaired shoes from a great pile.

As for the G7 Summit in London it enabled me to see something of Mrs Thatcher in action. I didn't always agree with her but I admired her. I was in charge of all the physical arrangements, including handling security and thousands of press. I am happy to say it went well and the Prime Minister recorded her pleasure.

In the run-up to the Summit one of the bonuses for me was a meeting of senior officials I had to organise at Leeds Castle in Kent. This is a gem of a medieval fortified house on two islands in a lake surrounded by meadow and woods. It was fascinating to have the chance to get to know it well. Conveniently situated on the route from Dover to London it was associated with a succession of Queens of England in medieval times. The name appears to have nothing to do with the busy town in Yorkshire, which was probably no more than a village in those days. I liked the story that Leeds Castle played a role in the emergence of our Tudor dynasty. It had always seemed odd to me that Henry V's wife, the French princess depicted charmingly by Shakespeare learning English, should have married a Welsh squire after Henry's death. Apparently she was only in her early 20s when he died and she was given Leeds Castle as her dower house. Owen Tudor was her very handsome Clerk of the Wardrobe and one can only imagine how love blossomed in that romantic place. They married secretly and were arrested when it was discovered. She was soon released and he escaped from the tower. Their son, the Earl of Richmond, was the father of the first Tudor king, Henry VII. One would think this a good subject for a play! Henry VII's mother was, of course, the Lancastrian heiress, Lady Margaret Beaufort, who after pregnancy at age 13 could have no other children. A tiny lady of strong character, highly educated, she outlived her son into the reign of Henry VIII, interested in his marriage prospects. She was a great benefactor who founded two Cambridge colleges. The Earl of Richmond died young. Lady Margaret married twice more. Her third husband, a Stanley, held office and was trusted by Richard III, but it was he who swung the battle of Bosworth Field against that King in favour of his own wife's son. That was, at least, the subject of a Shakespeare play. History is interesting enough without having to make things up!

Expecting to stay for a period in London, I decided I needed a somewhat larger house, at least one that had two bathrooms, an essential requirement for civilised living. I put my little Alwyne Villas house, which had no central heating, on the market and found bigger accommodation around the corner which suited me much better. It had a master bedroom and bathroom at the top, and guestrooms and bathroom at the bottom, leading out to a little garden full of fruit trees and bushes: producing apples, pears, plums and quinces as well as raspberries and gooseberries. I used to irritate my sister by taking a basket of fruit down from London to her farm, when I went to stay! The house was pre-Victorian dating from about 1830. The last owner was an enthusiastic do-it-yourself man who had restored the house extensively, which meant it was never quite clear where all the various pipes and wires went. The drawing room on the first floor was a reasonable size once I had removed two large dividing doors.

The house was in Canonbury Grove, facing onto the New River Walk, a long narrow park full of trees and shrubs alongside a stretch of water, home to mallards and moorhens. Large trees hid the houses on the far side. When the population of London was rapidly increasing in the sixteenth and seventeenth centuries the main natural wells had become polluted. An enterprising gentlemen, Sir Hugh Myddleton, an MP and jeweller to the Crown, whose statue is on Islington Green, had the idea of tapping springs 30 miles to the north in Hertfordshire and bringing water in a surface aqueduct with a nicely calculated gradient to a round pond near Sadler's Wells, from where it was piped to houses in north London. It was quite an engineering feat. The company responsible, which almost went bankrupt until rescued by a loan from King James I, became the ancestor of London's first water boards. The water in the park followed the line of that aqueduct, though the flow had been diverted, years before, further up the chain. My sister generously persuaded my mother to release to me in advance some of the inheritance that I might have expected so that I could finance the purchase of my new house.

Many weekends I still used to visit my mother in Cambridge, staying there in the annex to my parent's house in Trumpington, and later when my mother moved to a flat nearby, in her spare room. It was always a pleasure also to visit my sister Sara's and my brother-in-law's farm near Woodbridge, which became the third point of a triangle, somewhat further from London than from Cambridge. John and Sara's three attractive and intelligent boys were growing up fast. It was wonderful for them being on the farm with its amazing views down to the Deben estuary. In the marshy fields bordering the sea-wall numerous birds were to be seen. I am essentially a city dweller but it is always a pleasure to stay at Hill Farm, walk around the fields with John, a knowledgeable countryman, and enjoy the family's warm hospitality. There was also a welcome at my aunt Freda's home in Cley in Norfolk, enjoying another great view, this time of the large ancient church across a green. Norfolk was the home of numerous fine churches from the days when it was one of the richest parts of the country, thanks to wool. On walks one could enjoy vast expanses of sky, sometimes under the flapping wings of overflying geese. Seals poked their noses up in the sea.

For three years I was now to be assistant under-secretary of state for the public departments, in effect the interface between the Foreign and Commonwealth Office and ministries and institutions at home. I was fully occupied with supervising eight departments or equivalent covering consular and immigration questions. Responsibility for cultural relations involved close liaison with the British Council. Relations with parliament, the church, universities and the arts also fell under my remit.

There was considerable parliamentary interest in our cultural policy overseas and a committee decided to make a thorough public examination of the Foreign Office's policies. We had to submit to them a paper on the subject beforehand. This led to the worst example of incompetence in my professional career. I had inherited an excellent head of cultural relations department, who soon left, with a parting lunch from me at the Athenaeum. To succeed him personnel put forward a man with cultural interests and contacts. He had something of drink problem and I was told it was under control. I was persuaded to accept him against my better judgement. It turned out that he was virtually an alcoholic, secreting bottles in his various cupboards, and consequently unreliable. The head of department was the key figure in the bureaucratic structure. There were some good people under this gentleman and normally we got by, but the drafting of the paper for parliament was primarily in his hands. I allowed the deadline to run too close. It was no excuse that I was heavily involved in other activities. I should have taken charge and drafted the paper myself at the expense of other work, since I had clear ideas what to say. It was a classic example of priorities. In the end I was forced to submit a wholly inadequate paper direct to ministers. For this I was rightly admonished by the permanent under-secretary whose hard-working private secretary came to me to try and cobble together something acceptable. Apologising to my boss, I rather pathetically pleaded in excuse the number of reviews that had been or were taking place in the departments for which I was responsible. Trawling them quickly I maintained they amounted to 48! I then carried on.

How one remembers mistakes. One just hopes that they don't hit the headlines! When I was Private Secretary a young note-taker submitted to me a wholly inadequate record of a bilateral meeting at which I had been present between Alec Douglas-Home and Home Secretary Leon Britton. I was swamped and had no time to redraft it, so I put it away into my box where it stayed. I still have it somewhere. There is no record of that important meeting, at least on Foreign Office files. There! I have admitted it at last. One also remembers uncalled for discourtesy, especially to one's juniors. In Pakistan I went once with house guests on a fascinating expedition to the countryside with local scholars, to see a range of little-known fossils and pottery shards (probably Kushan). When I returned, tired, I found a visiting MP with a group of his friends waiting to come to dinner. I was convinced that I had told a lady officer on my staff that I was only expecting the ex-minister and one other. She was convinced that I had asked her to invite them all. I was inexcusably angry with her. If she ever reads this I should like to apologise.

* * *

The past rolls out in fits and starts. Scraping the floors of memory there are loose ends to tie up. No matter how busy I was, close family was always important. My mother was nearing 80 now and my sister, her husband and I decided to make a special occasion of that event. My mother had stayed on in the neo-Georgian house in Trumpington, south of Cambridge, with its walled garden where she had lived with my father. We were determined that she should take her own time to move to somewhere smaller, which she eventually did, finding an apartment in a block nearby rather like a Cambridge court. We all thought it was better that she should stay in touch with her local friends. We decided to give her a big birthday lunch at the Garden House Hotel and invited a range of people including family, Hutton and Cambridge friends, but told them to say nothing so that it would be a surprise. (Some were so discreet that they were astonished to find members of their own family at the event.) In the run-up period mother noticed that some people looked at her oddly. We told her to expect a small lunch of a dozen or so family so she got herself looking nice (not difficult) in a pale blue and brown dress.

She was surprised and delighted when she found over 80 people there to greet her including some old friends she had not seen for years. How much better to have this sort of party when people are alive, rather than linked to funerals when they are gone. The guests sat in separate round tables of eight or nine, each headed by a close family member. At the end I made tribute in a speech mentioning father and referring not only to mother's loveable qualities but also her foibles: cutting bread crooked, using plenty of plastic bags, reducing everything, even a few peas to an eggcup, and preferring everything painted in white. She was generous but frugal, needing persuasion to buy something new for herself. Thank-you letters praised the warm family atmosphere which had been extended to all the guests and demonstrated the great affection in which mother was held. Amelie Boyd, widow of a Fellow of Clare and mother of my diplomatic colleague John, kindly quoted at the end of her letter a saying of Henry Thirkill, Master of Clare: 'Once I see the mother I know the quality of the son'!

It was not long after this happy occasion that mother was knocked down by a driver crossing the road in Trumpington. What caused me distress was that the police did not seem to appreciate that the driver had been in the wrong. The latter hadn't been allowed by his insurers to apologise of course. I wrote him a personal letter saying that I hoped that he was ashamed for what he had done to a vulnerable old lady. It did no good but made me feel better. It did not take long for mother's bones to be mended and she lived for another eight years.

Going through boxes of hoarded letters I began to find several from my sister's three sons now becoming individual personalities, as they had shown at their grandmother's 80th birthday party. They have always been meticulous in writing letters of thanks, a result of good training by their parents. I tried to keep in touch with them as well as my godchildren and honorary godchildren. I continued to take an interest in the wider family, including some individuals of special character like my great-uncle Donald Allen who wrote supportive notes to me in my various posts until he died. It was only after then that I obtained from his grandson the citation for his MC and Bar in World War I. His bravery had been remarkable. He had been a second lieutenant in the Royal Artillery. In September 1917 he had left his dugout during an intense bombardment to rescue his men, personally carrying two wounded to safety though shells were bursting around him all the time. He stayed at his post, eventually having to repair the communications line for the rest of the night. 'It is impossible,' said the citation, 'to speak too highly of the extreme gallantry and devotion to duty of this officer.' Again in January 1918 he was in a forward observation post where he continued to pass back valuable information while those around him were killed. Twice he took key messages back through a heavy hostile barrage. 'By his coolness and disregard of danger,' according to the citation, 'he not only set a good example to all ranks, but largely contributed to the success of the operations.' Donald had never spoken in detail of these events and we had never asked him, as we should. I even wonder if my father knew all the details of the exploits of the uncle he much admired because if so I think he would have told me.

Another remarkable relation of the older generation was my aunt Winifred. She had more years to live but her character didn't change. She had been a shy admiral's daughter who had worked as housekeeper for my uncle Jack Bill who had lost a leg in World War I. She was the first housekeeper of whom he became fond. Winifred lived for many years after uncle Jack died, latterly in a residential home in Eastbourne where my sister visited her often. She was lonely and yet self-contained, always trim, slim and smartly dressed, displaying on occasion a wicked sense of humour. I have a thank-you letter from her saying she was ashamed for not writing sooner, 'lazy old trout that I am!' In another she says of the fellow residents of her home, 'nearly everyone here is deaf, and several daft as well. I sometimes think I would prefer to live on a desert island.' When I visited her once she expressed these views quite loudly when walking through the hall with other residents sitting there!

More serious was the end of my special uncle and godfather Geoff who had been so generous to me over the years. Most of his life had been spent flying back and forth over the Atlantic but for years he had made a base in an attractive house with tennis court and big walled garden on the edge of an Essex village. There was a well-known story in the family that he and one of his cousins in the Bill family had visited a fortune-teller years before in Wales. This was a down-to-earth farmer's wife who had a great local reputation for prediction, even for the horses. She was very reluctant to exercise it but agreed to see the two young men. First in was my uncle's cousin who came out looking white. They never knew all that she told him, but one thing was that he had been working standing at a high desk that was hitting him in the stomach and that he should change his mode of work. He realised that this had been the cause of some of his health problems. To uncle Geoff she said, 'Take care of your father, he's getting old now.' He died shortly after. She also said that Geoff would spend a large part of his life travelling backwards and forth across the sea. She warned him about air travel which Geoff linked to a terrible storm in which his aircraft was involved years later in the USA, to such an extent that passengers doubted if they would survive. Geoff was convinced of that lady's gift.

He lived alone, now in his middle 80s. The priceless Belgian couple who used to look after him and his guests, Emile and Martha, had died. The giant antediluvian gardener, Padbury, was also no more. But the gardens still looked marvellous as did the mixed wood beyond, which Geoff had planted. His house was full of fine antiques and glass and a mixture of modern and classical paintings. He listened to music and read much, never watching television. But he was getting very forgetful and would not acknowledge this. One day returning with provisions from a local shop he crashed his car into a tree. He cooked not only food but some of his fine old plates in his oven. Local people began to take advantage of him. When the word got around to charities that he was good for a donation he was sent a lot more applications (which I found distasteful) and wouldn't take advice. Eventually there was no alternative to putting him in a home. He had some of his personal things with him and the nurses did their best but he deteriorated quickly. He would complain that he was not being looked after properly. One never knows the truth in such situations. The staff always appear kind when you visit. One answer is to make sure there are plenty of visits. There was one heart-rending occasion when I called and Geoff asked if I had my car with me. When I said yes, he said, 'please now take me away with you, otherwise I shall die in this place.' But he needed constant care. Did I do as much as I could to help him? I am not sure. His end was a release.

Only a few of his many friends worldwide were able to come to the little funeral service in the local church.

There are a couple of unforgettable experiences in this period in London which I must record: one bad, one good. A diplomatic colleague and friend kindly invited me to dinner at his home south of London and to stay for the night. I arrived in good time for a gossip and then went up to my spacious bedroom to change and to have a bath. A couple of my hosts' small children came up to talk. I got on with them well, following my usual practice of treating children in conversation like adults. When I realised it was time I had a bath I told them they must go, but they said they wanted to stay. I think that the little boys were about five or six years old. When I then said that they really must go one of them clung onto my leg and when I started gently to remove him his brother attacked me on the other side. They worked in unison biting, scratching and hurting me. It was very difficult to get rid of them without injuring them. They behaved like demonic children as though they were both having fits. What could I do? I couldn't shout for help. I'm not very fond of horror films. Give me detective stories, love stories or even cowboys. But these kids were behaving like satanic children who might well be depicted in a horror movie. Eventually, considerably shaken, I got them out of the door. There was nothing I could say to their parents downstairs, who were quite unaware that anything had happened. I couldn't say, 'your children have just attacked me' nor 'you have bred a couple of devils!' I said nothing but left early the next morning. I never saw these children again until they were grown up, now married, at their father's funeral. They seemed perfectly normal but I looked at them warily. I had no idea if they remembered the incident and I didn't care to ask.

The second unforgettable event I reported fully in a letter to my mother in December 1985. As head of department in the 1970s I had been roped in several times for the Queen's annual party at Buckingham Palace for the Diplomatic Corps. This time I was one of four under-secretaries chosen as escorts for the Royal Family. There were careful printed instructions and a briefing at the Palace a day before the event by the marshal of the Diplomatic Corps, a retired general. I had realised in time that my old set of tails were not smart enough, and, to hell with it, bought a new one. I discovered that I had been designated to escort

Princess Diana – the chance of a lifetime. I planned to wear miniature medals, which I have hardly worn since, and to wear the CVO around my neck rather than the more senior CMG since it was a royal occasion.

That morning I put everything ready on my bed before I went to the office. This was wise because I had to attend ministerial meetings during the day to discuss the extension of visa regimes. I also had to go to a drinks party in the early evening for contacts in parliament. I didn't leave the office until 7 p.m., getting home to my little house in Islington at 7.30 p.m. Bath, brush suit, shave (for most of my life I had to shave twice a day) and answer telephone calls. I was away by 8.20 p.m., slightly later than intended. Nowadays I should never run a thing so close. I had a clearish drive through town arriving at the Palace gates at 8.40 p.m. (note contrast to current traffic), parked with my special sticker and had my vehicle checked by a security man, who asked to see inside the bonnet and boot, a routine of which I approved. Then in at the door on the left as you face the Palace, along the household corridor, check coat, scarf, umbrella and make a quick cloakroom visit to see all was in place. Tying a white tie is never easy. About 20 Foreign Office ushers and escorts with their wives were gathering inside the entrance. We went up the grand staircase as the Palace flunkeys – footmen in red and gold, pages in black and gold uniforms, and gentlemen ushers in tails – were making last-minute preparations. Guests would not be let in until 8.50 p.m. After final briefing we received a vital crib: a booklet with the names of all ambassadors and High Commissioners listed in the right order and with the correct designation. Seniority depended on length of service in London. High Commissioners were marked in red. Some ambassadors liked to be called 'The French Ambassador', some 'The Ambassador of France', all in the book. There were late amendments for drop-outs and changes.

Then, as the diplomatic guests assembled, I went into the picture gallery and had a peek at the glorious paintings while greeting some ambassadors I knew, and some of the British guests. Harold Wilson was there in breeches to show off his Garter, as was Lord Carrington, flown in from NATO in Brussels where he was then secretary-general. I spoke to my boss, the Foreign Secretary Geoffrey Howe, and his wife, as well as his predecessors Francis Pym and Michael Stewart. I described the latter as ageing but still mentally alert. At 9.20 p.m. escorts got ready by the doorway where the Queen would enter. Two trumpeters on either side gave a fanfare and the Royal party emerged. All bowed or curtsied.

The ladies looked out of a picture book. I noticed the Queen's jewels but not what she was wearing except that it was full and richly embroidered. The Duchess of Kent was in elegant grey-green. For me, of course, it was the Princess of Wales who was important. The Queen moved off down the line accompanied by the Lord Chamberlain bearing his traditional long thin white wand – a splendid anachronism, though sometimes used, I was told, to tap the toes of intruding feet. Then the Duke. Next was Prince Charles.

Then it was my turn to greet Princess Diana, with a bow from the neck. 'Bad luck. What an awful chore to look after me.' 'On the contrary,' I replied, 'I am the envy of all my friends your Royal Highness.' She looked quite lovely close to. Her dress was of pale blue taffeta, fairly full with puff sleeves. It was wide in the shoulders and low at the back. She wore old Queen Mary's drop tiara, a twist of tiny pearls at the neck and other jewels. I noticed her beautiful skin and complexion and fine hair. She was very natural and smiley. 'I've got to keep up this time,' she said, 'I was ticked off last time for taking too long and getting behind.'

Then we were off past some more British VVIP's including, I noticed, Edward Heath, Lord Hailsham and the Thatchers. As I accompanied the Princess to present the first Heads of Mission others were all lined up through the state rooms, in order of precedence. Just the simple presentation, after checking the crib. Then moving to stand opposite the next ambassador so that the Princess knew where to move to. She was somewhat pushed for conversation with the first few but soon got into her stride. No political talk. Many of the ambassadors spoke about the Prince and Princess of Wales' recent trips to the USA and Australia. It was not my job to join in. I noticed how the ambassadors' eyes lit up and those of their wives and staff members they presented as they saw Diana in all her natural dazzling beauty. Several of the communist wives dropped neat curtseys. Even the Vietnamese and Nicaraguan were charmed. There was quite a bit of gay laughter. I made sure that the Princess heard the names of the countries clearly. I wasn't sure if she knew where half of them were or which were communists, who were not friends at the time, but it didn't matter. We progressed through the great rooms and sometimes I looked around and felt it was all like a film set. Except for the picture gallery, in faded terracotta with pictures individually lit, the other rooms were rather over-ornate with plenty of gilding and silk hangings. The final ballroom was something of an Edwardian monstrosity like a cinema or Mormon temple. But at least the whole place, I reported, looked like a palace. Flowers were magnificent. Human furniture was provided by ancient retired officers in uniform with helmets and pikes, standing at each doorway as if out of Gilbert and Sullivan, clanking when they moved.

As we walked between the rooms we exchanged some conversation. 'Oh dear, my feet,' she said at one point, 'I think my shoes are coming off.' Not to be outdone, 'I think my trousers are coming down,' I said. The braces had been attached too wide at the front and the straps were slipping over my shoulders. Nothing I could do, nowhere to go, I wrote. But fortunately the waistband of the trousers, tight round my too-plump tummy, prevented disaster, as the Princess expressed amused concern. There was a large crowd in the ballroom at the end and then I escorted the Princess with her lady in waiting, who had been keeping an eye on us a little behind, through the rooms back to take my leave formally. 'A lot of trouble for you.' 'It was a pleasure your Royal Highness.' Then off to the buffet.

It may have been on this occasion that we heard that the Canadian High Commissioner, when presenting, as permitted, a couple of members of his staff, said that only a few of his large mission were allowed to be presented. 'I know. I'm afraid that my house is just too small for my guests,' said the Queen, overheard by Canadian diplomats who were delighted at her deadpan sense of humour.

The Princess got to the end of the diplomatic line at 11.25 p.m., about 20 minutes after the Queen. She was tired, but I wrote that she was still as charming, relaxed and glamorous at the end as at the beginning. There was little time for me to get a drink and some indifferent snacks (I had wisely had a sandwich or two at the parliamentary drinks party). In the ballroom some people were dancing to the music of a Guards band on the balcony. *God Save the Queen* was played at midnight and we all drifted off. Little did I know that some years later the Princess of Wales would come to stay in my house in Pakistan, and that I would be back in the ballroom to rest my knee on a velvet cushion.

When the time came, after three years, for another posting abroad, I used what influence I could within the system to be chosen for Pakistan. The job made sense given my past experience. Visiting the sub-continent with an immigration hat I had noticed the fine new Residence that had been built for our man in Islamabad. Eventually the posting came through. Preparations and farewell parties started in the spring of 1987. I kissed hands with the Queen and there was loads of briefing in all areas of my future work.

I stocked up with new suits, tropical for the summers and warm for the winters, as well as plenty of shirts and underclothes. I needed less of the latter than I expected because I found that my efficient dhobi, laundryman at the Residence, washed ironed and returned shirts virtually on the same day. I resolved that as an ambassador I was going to maintain standards by wearing clean shirts, underclothes and socks everyday without fail. I did not always retain this tradition after retirement. Most of these items came from Marks and Spencer, rather than Turnbull and Asser. Apart from wearing decent shoes (polished – a National Service legacy) and having some good suits, including a few from Savile Row tailors, I paid little attention to clothes, certainly not to fashion, except perhaps owning hundreds of ties and matching colours with cufflinks.

I gave myself a treat by spending the inside of a week at Champneys Health Spa in Hertfordshire, building myself up for Pakistan. I recorded that the place was not as beautiful as Shrublands, the fine house and garden near Ipswich where I had gone during my leave from Tehran and the Ayatollahs (now sadly closed). Champneys was a rather ugly Victorian red brick building but there was a fine lawn with great trees, to be seen from a good swimming pool. Whereas at Shrublands I had been restricted to hot water and lemon with a small bowl of honey four times a day, here there was just a very low calorie diet with plenty of nutritional advice, as well as opportunities for sauna, exercises and massage. Best of all there was a small craft and leisure centre with painting materials where I spent two hours every day. It was a good break mentally as well as physically, though I am embarrassed to say that when I finally left I stopped off at the nearest hotel and had a full English breakfast!

10

AMBASSADOR IN ISLAMABAD

It was great to arrive in Islamabad on a fine day as a fully fledged ambassador. My immediate concern was about my nephew Rupert, my sister's middle son, who had been going around the world east to west with a friend and was due to arrive at any moment. He had crossed the border from India alone several days before. I had arranged for him to stay in Lahore with my old friends the Saigols, until I myself had arrived in Islamabad. Rupert was then aged 20, about to start his studies to be a vet. He soon turned up by bus and enjoyed a welcome warm bath. I discovered that he and his companion had met up on the journey with a group of young people from a sect founded by an eccentric clergyman in the USA. Rupert's friend decided to stay with these people. Rupert had wisely decided to carry on with his own programme, including a visit to Kashmir (which I have never succeeded in visiting, to my great regret). His ticket would take him back to Delhi, but I made sure that after a week with me he should fly straight home to London from Pakistan. I distrusted such cults. Over a weekend I went with Rupert for a night up in the hills, with another embassy couple, beyond Murree where the next morning we saw the spectacular view one could enjoy in those hill stations: layer upon layer of mountains, blue, purple and misty-white, topped by distant snow-capped peaks. We returned via the Buddhist temple ruins at Taxila. I gave a dinner party for Rupert on my birthday with some of my oldest Pakistani friends, including young members of the Shahid Hamid family, also the local BBC reporter.

I presented credentials soon to President Zia ul Haq and was thrown into a maelstrom of visitors including Princess Alexandra and her husband, the first royal visitors to Pakistan for years. Their visit went very well, coinciding with that of the English cricket team, which went less well thanks to an argument between Mike Gatting and an umpire on the pitch.

We always did our best to support visiting British teams. Helping prominent visitors from home is part of the consular and representative element of the work of the ambassador. Sometimes we can bask in their reflected glory. As a diplomat abroad you meet an interesting group of local people of course, but you also come into contact with prominent British people whom you would never normally get to know. They are usually grateful for any hospitality and kindness you can show them. A good example of this was the British component of an international team planning to make a winter assault on K2, the world's second highest mountain, in December 1987. I had a vague introduction to Roger Mear, one of our climbers. He and a few others came around for drinks. Roger stayed with me for a period of convalescence on his way back and we started a friendship that has lasted. He came out some years later to make, with a colleague, the first successful British assault on Nanga Parbat, that dangerous mountain that marks the western end of the Himalayan chain. I have several times visited Mear and his British-Pakistani wife at their home in the Peak district. His main claim to fame was having walked overland to the South Pole 'in the footsteps of Scott' with a couple of colleagues, about which he produced a book with marvellous photographs. Later he made an attempt to traverse Antarctica solo, on skis with a kite, but his equipment malfunctioned and he, being a sensible fellow, aborted the mission rather than trying to be too heroic. This required courage. I never forget Hemingway's account in *Death in the Afternoon* about a famous bullfighter taking part in a grand final benefit appearance not liking the expression of the bull that confronted him and deciding, despite the crowds and the hype, not to fight it, but to put down his sword for ever there and then.

It was a delight also to help family and friends who took the opportunity to come through Islamabad. Bamber Gascoigne was making a film about the Moghuls following up the book he had produced with his photographer wife. Julian Pettifer was making a film about missionaries. When my friends the Barbors made the first of two enjoyable visits they used part of the time to visit a hospital (Peter) and a prison (Tricia, who was a prison visitor). It was a new show prison but even then it was good they had allowed a visit. When my Japanese friend, the television star Tetsuko visited, it greatly increased the respect in which I was held by my Japanese ambassador colleague. Her visit coincided with that of my old friend Roger Berthoud and his wife, at that time a leader writer on *The Independent*. It was interesting to learn how leader writers had to operate. Roger's visit merited a reference in his autobiography, more literate than mine. I gave a big party for them all. We also had a visit by the editor and founder of *The Independent* newspaper, Andreas Whittam Smith and his wife, whom I much respected. Their visit was an excuse for a dinner in their honour. They came to visit their son who worked for a time for the English language *Friday Times* weekly in Lahore, owned and run by Najam Sethi, who had been an undergraduate at Clare, with his wife – a paper which I have continued to read and enjoy to keep me up to date with what is going on in Pakistan.

The rich green Margalla Hills that overlooked Islamabad were a constant source of pleasure. One could drive up in one or two places, mainly to the restaurant where the Princess of Wales later met scholars, as part of her programme, and further up near to a favourite picnic place of mine. But one could wander at will and explore many other routes on foot, always surrounded by varied vegetatian and wildlife. The prime minister's official house was high up on the city's edge. Beyond it, past groves of tall mango and lychee trees, were streams where I once saw a rare giant kingfisher splash into the water. Tricky to find was an irregular path leading up, if you were skilful, to a magical little rock pool, perfect for an intimate skinny-dip. Residents of Islamabad became keen to protect the hills from depredation. Regulations forbade buildings above a certain height. Quarrying firms that started to strip vegetation in certain areas were eventually stopped by command of Nawaz Sharif's government, after protests. This also applied to quarries near the Buddhist ruins of Taxila on the other side of the Margallas, to the relief of archaeologists.

Just off the road to Murree, close by a checkpoint, I discovered a road leading to the right which ended up where, after parking and a short walk through greenery, there was a perfect picnic place by a little river, with a rock face on the other side. In the heat of summer people would drive further up through the pine forests to Murree itself, where there were hotels and more walks. I loved it when old friends took the trouble to visit me in Pakistan, so that I could show them something of the beauty of the country and introduce them to my Pakistani friends. One such couple were Michael and Susan Williams, always good company, whom I had known since childhood in Hutton Mount. I remember taking them on a trip beyond Abbottabad along the scenic valley route towards the Indus where, as we rested for lunch, we caught a glimpse of a long-tailed paradise flycatcher. That was on the way to Swat. I also wanted to show them Murree. I had been taken once on the well-known 'pipeline walk', following a gentle gradient of four or five kilometres by the route where the British had sunk a pipe bringing water to Murree. On one side the hill climbed steeply; on the other there were glorious views of layers of distant purple hills and snow-capped mountains. I was confident that I could take my friends on the walk in the reverse direction. We were duly dropped off by my driver who would pick us up at the other end.

I must have started off at the wrong place, however, because instead of following a level course our path plunged into a valley with thick trees and bushes and soon almost disappeared. We forged ahead going in what at least I knew was the right direction, but I became completely lost. My friends were tolerant. It had become a real adventure. After considerable struggle we came at one point to a clearing where I was astonished to see a group of large red-flowering rhododendron bushes, rather trees, of a good height. These were the first I had ever seen, or heard of, in Pakistan though the plant was reputed to come from the Himalayan area. We collected cuttings, before ploughing on and eventually meeting up with my vehicle by what I thought was something of a miracle. My driver had been searching for us. I planted the cuttings but they never took. I tried to remember how to reach the hidden glade but never found it again. Nor did I hear of anyone else who had seen such giant rhododendron trees in the hills. People were sceptical when I told the story. If there had been no witnesses I might had thought it all a dream.

Among regular visitors it was a pleasure entertaining Sue Farrington, a young lady who had once served in the Embassy and had become fascinated by the historical record encapsulated in British cemeteries all over the country. These were not the carefully kept Imperial War Graves cemeteries for those killed during world wars, but the graves of other British citizens of all categories, including military men killed in skirmishes on the frontier. Sue Farrington had an excellent pedigree as the cousin and family friend of one of Britain's most distinguished governors of the Frontier Province, Sir George Cunningham. She had travelled all over the country seeking and recording British graves, and had published useful books on the cemeteries in three of the main Pakistani cities (and others on Bangladesh). Her records were such that if you knew, for example, that your great-uncle had been buried at Quetta, she would tell you where the grave was, and the inscription. As a result several people went out to visit. (The classic inscription, almost certainly apocryphal, is of a grave recording the assassination of a British officer by an Islamic fanatic with the words 'Well done, thou good and faithful servant'! An authentic inscription dated 1888 in the Peshawar Cemetery read 'Remember men, as you pass by, as you are now so once was I. As I am now so you will be. Prepare yourself to follow me.') Sue illuminated history through her lectures. In retirement I became a council member of the British Association for Cemeteries for South Asia (BACSA) in which Sue was a key figure. With minimal overheads it brought together British people with a variety of family connections with the sub-continent to keep memories alive and provided funds to maintain British graves.

Another local expert who gave good lectures was a young man called Guy Duke, who worked for a time in the remote valleys just off the highway north to Gilgit, trying to record and preserve the environment of the rare and elusive tragopan pheasant. He achieved good relations with local villagers who had little contact with the outside world. He was supported by Keith Howman, founder and president of the World Pheasant Association, who was a welcome and fairly frequent visitor with his wife. It was Keith who got me involved, again after retirement, in an organisation to support the work of Maureen Lines, an intrepid lady who lived with the Kalash people in Chitral and who met the Princess of Wales there.

In Taxila, so easy of access from Islamabad, there were the principal ruins with a few tourists, but plenty of lesser known places of great charm and interest tucked into the further green valleys, with no tourists at all, such as Giri and Bhamala. They were perfect for picnics, at which my staff became skilled, combined with culture. Quite early on I met Drs Raymond and Bridget Allchin, archaeologists and historians of the sub-continent, who were excavating a pre-historic site down towards Lahore, which I later visited. It was a pleasure getting to know and sometimes entertain the Allchins with their wide understanding of local history. They eventually invited me to become a trustee of the Ancient India and Iran Trust in Cambridge, which they had helped found. It was a good institution with which to be associated after retirement. Dr David MacDowall, a numismatist and educationalist who had recruited me after I had first returned from Kabul as a founder member of the Society of Afghan Studies was another interesting scholarly visitor. I took him to the the local Friday market in Islamabad where mixtures of antiquities and junk from Afghanistan, India, Iran, Russia and China, as well as from Pakistan, were offered for bargaining and sale, mainly by Afghan traders. Equipment taken from Russian soldiers fighting in Afghanistan, including fine fur hats, was on sale. I asked MacDowall which of the ancient coins, heaped in piles, were genuine and which were fakes. He told me that the large silver coins purporting to be of Alexander the Great were forgeries. The rest were all genuine!

The dramatic circumstances of the death of President Zia and the successive elections as prime minister of Benazir Bhutto, Nawaz Sharif and Benazir again are covered elsewhere. I knew all those concerned well. The main foreign policy issues with which we had continually to deal were Kashmir and Afghanistan.

Understanding Afghan problems meant fairly frequent visits to Peshawar, the base for combatants, observers and healers of the fighting over the border. It had become a frontier town with echoes of the wild west. The road from Rawalpindi, part of the old Grand Trunk road coming from Delhi, cut through the Margalla Hills near Islamabad by an obelisk dedicated to Brigadier John Nicholson, one of the British heroes of what we called 'the Mutiny'. Further on beyond Taxila it passed the arms production city of Wah, near which there was a road off the other side to an old Moghul garden, deemed so beautiful that one of the emperors had exclaimed 'wah!' in delighted surprise. Still further on, the main road crossed the Indus near the impressive fort of Attock, occupied by the army. One could stop off just below to visit an old caravanserai in the shadow of the fort. It was one of the best preserved of such buildings once to be found on all routes in that part of Asia, affording overnight protection for merchant caravans. Beyond the Indus the road went through the garrison town of Nowshera and on to Peshawar. There was an attractive diversion to the north, crossing various arms of the Kabul river where one could see one of the greatest archaeological mounds in the country, marking centuries of human habitation, at Charsadda.

As you approached Peshawar by road from Islamabad its bulky fort loomed up on the horizon. This had been mostly built by the Sikhs, who had won the city from the Afghans and then lost it, after the Sikh wars, to the British. The old city of Peshawar was centred round a bustling colourful bazaar where I could wander freely, perhaps watched a few paces behind by the discreet plain-clothed policeman allotted for my protection by the Pakistan government. Muslims in all sorts of dress from all parts of the area would be seen in the bazaar. I would be greeted warmly, particularly if there was a purchase in prospect.

There was a group of merchant houses in the old city known as the Sethi houses, belonging to families who had traded up into Russia, which had survived with all their details, including carvings. To avoid rigours of climate principal rooms were situated underground with a system of tunnels to allow cool air to flow freely. Efforts continued to be needed to ensure that these unique buildings were preserved. On the other side of town was the cantonment residential area in typical Indian-style grid pattern, where officials and politicians lived; here I rented a villa to use as my base and where I could entertain (also used by the staff for recreation). The landlord next door, the redoubtable Begum Saifullah, sister of Aslam Khattak the former Pakistan ambassador whom I had known from Kabul days, had elegant grey cranes in her garden.

I would drive up a curved road through green lawns to the portico of the imposing Governor's House, redolent of the Raj. The governor had a special role in relation to the tribal areas, which were not part of the province for election and administration purposes. When I first called on the chief minister – each province had a governor, chief minister and cabinet, provincial assembly and judiciary – he was concerned, as so often, about votes. There were so many people sitting everywhere in his house and garden that it was quite impossible to have a private conversation!

Peshawar boasted a good hospital still named after the wife of a former viceroy, and a lively university. I had great respect for the judgement and wide historical knowledge of the archaeologist who was then vice-chancellor, Professor Durrani. Two of the most interesting archaeological sites in the whole of the Indian sub-continent happened to be in Pakistan: the Indus valley sites in Sindh, also extending into Indian Gujarat, and the Gandhara remains in the North-West Frontier area centered around Peshawar and including Taxila. Several of

Pakistan's most active and internationally respected archaeologists were based in Peshawar. Gandhara is a hybrid culture arising from the merger of descendants of Alexander's armies, cut off in Central Asia, with Kushan tribesmen from the north who became converted to Buddhism. Distinctive stone sculptures of the area show the influence of both cultures.

In Peshawar there was also Edwardes College, a highly regarded educational institution linked to the local Church of Pakistan (Anglican) diocese. During most of my time in Islamabad the director was a medical missionary Dr Ron Pont, whose wife was a surgeon. She was recovering from multiple sclerosis, which was so unusual that many thought this a genuine miracle. The Ponts had been missionaries in Iran which they had left just before the church there had been attacked, shortly before my time. Ron and his wife, who both had well-earned OBEs, continued to work in the Frontier for 20 years, latterly in the Christian hospital at Quetta while that area was a centre of Taliban activity. It is difficult to exaggerate the respect I had for the Ponts and their work. It was no surprise that their two sons devoted themselves to aid work in difficult places.

During my time in Islamabad we had significant visits not only from senior service officers, civil servants and cabinet ministers, but the Speaker and the Archbishop of Canterbury. I have described separately the visit of Diana Princess of Wales who stayed with me for three days and who took the country by storm.

All this meant that the Residence, my home for six years, needed to look good and work efficiently. When I first arrived the house had seemed bare. My own pictures, carefully arranged, livened up the rooms, accompanied by a few of the modern prints that went with the house. (There was one good Victor Passmore.) Some of my pictures had been inherited from my uncle Geoff, some I had found and purchased myself mostly from galleries in London's Cork Street or from antique shops in East Anglia. I thought of them as an investment which provided greater pleasure, and less anxiety, than stocks and shares. During Princess Alexandra's visit furnishings had been set off by fine flower arrangements by the wife of our naval and air attaché. Later my chief bearer Lall himself developed a flair for bold flower arranging.

Thanks to Lall Khan and his staff the Residence ran smoothly. It had to, given the volume of entertaining. There was a small office inside the front door for an invaluable household comptroller, at first the wife of a member of my staff, latterly an Australian diplomat's wife. They budgeted for the shopping, kept the accounts, sent out invitations and made sure the place was in immaculate order before guests arrived. They would help a guest to settle in, sometimes receiving them if I was delayed. Some of this work would normally be done by the ambassador's wife. People thought it surprising that I coped without one. I used to say that 'a good wife is better than no wife, but that no wife is better than a bad wife!' There were practical examples of this in the diplomatic service.

The modern Residence made entertaining easy. From the entrance hall a wide staircase led to the public rooms on the first floor, spacious drawing and dining rooms, with balconies and good views. The dining table could seat 20. I would sit in the middle of the long side facing the windows with my principal guests opposite and on either side of me, so there were at least three VIP places.

I made a point of having opposition as well as government representatives at my functions, sometimes providing them with a rare opportunity to meet in a civilised environment. I have a letter from a friend from the secretariat of Benazir Bhutto's People's Party saying that my hospitality was a welcome change from his recent dwelling (prison), thanking me for concern for his welfare and appreciating the dignity and respect with which I had treated opposition members in a mixed group. Sometimes the senior Pakistani guest would fail to turn up at the last moment, thus completely upsetting the placement. I got into the habit of laying out name cards in my study and disappearing for ten minutes before the meal was served to arrange and distribute them.

Lall was superb, running the household efficiently with two younger bearers as well as a 'sweeper' who came in the daytime to clean kitchen and floors. Unique in my experience the wine and store cupboards were not locked; nothing ever went missing. Nor was I nervous about Pakistani security agencies being allowed to install swooping microphones. Random checks found nothing. One of my successors was not so lucky. Of course, nothing seriously confidential was said away from the office or perhaps only in the garden. For large receptions and functions on the terrace and lawn, Lall would muster extra bearers from other embassies and private houses. Kerosene torches on poles created a special atmosphere.

If it rained, as sometimes it did, the house, even with the addition of a tented 'shamiana', was not big enough for an event such as the annual Queen's birthday party. Only once in five years did it rain on that occasion. We knew it was coming and, rather than cancel, I decided to move the whole operation into the embassy's underground garage. We asked people to evacuate their cars, imported loads of carpets which we ranged under foot and to decorate walls and brought in as much greenery from outside as we could collect. Guests were at first taken aback, but then agreed it was all rather fun!

Though I say it myself, my cook produced delicious food for all these events. It was Napoleon whose advice to his ambassadors was 'tenez bonne table et soignez les femmes'. For a dinner in honour of a special visitor the dessert would often be rich fruit salad in one of the cook's spun sugar confections. Rahim was something of a sculptor. For our army chief he produced a tank, for the admiral a boat and for an air marshall a fighter aircraft. Archbishop Runcie got a mitre and crook. I have a photo of only one of the cook's inventive creations. For a dinner party in honour of the Queen Mother's 90th birthday he produced a fine crown, duly reported home to Princess Margaret by one of her ladies-in-waiting whose husband was serving at the Pakistan staff college. (We had a suitably framed photograph of the Queen Mother, black-bordered note paper and a visitor's book, all ready for her demise, but that robust lady effortlessly outlasted my professional career.)

I always served alcohol no matter who was present. If a senior Pakistani declined, others more junior, if they were on his or her sight-line or anxious about their careers, would also refuse. Otherwise often not. At a reception one of my well-connected lady friends chose orange juice but indicated that if a little vodka could be incorporated she would be grateful! On the other hand I never served pork to Muslims.

Even in winter the garden was fine for functions so long as the sun was shining, as it usually was. Storms came mostly in spring. Generally speaking the climate was perfect so long as there were air conditioners in the bedrooms for the high summer. Insects were not a major problem. In summer it was too hot for mosquitoes and in winter at night, too cold. One had to be more careful outside in spring and autumn, using anti-insect cream and keeping up anti-malaria tablets.

The garden was dominated by the distant view of the Margalla Hills. I spent a good deal of time there performing simple tasks such as cutting deadheads and eliminating old wood from the trees and shrubs – leaving debris for the gardeners to take away! The main part of the garden was a flat lawn below the ample terrace suitable for major receptions and other events. There were a few beds for roses and others for seasonal flowers such as zinnias and sweetpeas. Hiding the surrounding wall was a mixture of trees and shrubs which I soon arranged to have floodlit at night from lights in front and below. This was good for security and looked dramatic in the evenings. There were oleanders, hibiscus, bottlebrush and citrus trees in the garden as well as qumquats. There were two fine jacaranda trees with their delicate blue-mauve blossom, one by the terrace and one in front of the Residence. There was an avocado that never bore fruit. Perhaps it needed more time. Avocados were rare because local people had not yet developed a taste for them. There were strong-smelling frangipanis and a number of other shrubs with white blossom that in the evenings seemed to be pumping out fragrance. In one of my letters home I wrote of the garden being 'awash with the scent of honeysuckle'.

I improved the garden where I could. For example, introducing bouganvillea, which blossomed over the archway down to the pool, and bananas which I persuaded the gardeners to import from Peshawar. The bananas flourished in one or two places protected by the wall, their grand, clean, boat-shaped leaves contrasting with other plants. It was exciting when large brown buds appeared, on a curved stem like the handle of an umbrella, developing into a stack of mini bananas. When grown we would cut them and keep them wrapped indoors for a time to ripen. They tasted delicious.

My predecessor and his wife had a small child so the swimming pool had been fenced and a formal water feature stretching in front of the terrace to a large flower-filled urn was left empty. I added water, got a little fountain going, imported water lilies and added a few goldfish bought in the market in plastic bags. Some grew to be large and feathery. Kingfishers appeared on occasion which gave me pleasure – there were plenty to be seen in the country around. Also the occasional heron, which I liked less. Once when interrupted it dropped a fish from its beak which lay dead on the side. It looked a lost cause and began to sink when I threw it back in but suddenly, with a flip, it was alive and active again. Frogs by the little stretch of formal water would croak quite loudly at night in certain seasons, sometimes squatting on the water lily leaves. Once I saw two giant frogs sitting by the side of the water, but never again. I also saw a cobra one afternoon on the terrace, which gave me a bit of a shock, but it soon disappeared. I know not how nor where. More common and dangerous were little krait snakes. Once we found a nest of them which had to be eliminated. We would catch sight of a couple of charming mongooses (mongeese?), who presumably kept most snakes away.

The lower part of the garden, down steps to the right around the swimming pool, was less formally arranged and more private. I had direct access to it from my bedroom one floor below the entrance hall. Three family bedrooms were there, with bathrooms, which seemed a strange idea but worked well. (My bedroom had two linked bathrooms, one each for an ambassador and spouse so they could have dolled themselves up at short notice at the same time.) After only a short time in post I wrote home that there were quiet afternoons when I would swim in the pool as the sun went down, with birds twittering in the bushes. I learned gradually to identify them. Several of my diplomatic colleagues were serious birdwatchers. I was keen to learn partly for my own pleasure and partly to be able to respond to questions from guests. There were stonechats, white-cheeked bulbuls, purple sunbirds and black drongos with long forked tails. Occasionally an eagle would fly overhead. Some birds were rare and gave particular joy. We might see colourful bee-eaters, and elegant ivory-coloured paradise flycatchers, with their looping flight. Once I saw a powder-blue verditer flycatcher. Occasionally I would glimpse a golden oriole or a group of scarlet avadavats. I recorded once hearing myna birds making a great racket in a corner of the garden and saw a salamander about two foot six inches long slink away. That was a rare occurrence. Bigger animals could not get into the garden over the wall. But at night after dinner watching from the terrace one could hear jackals howling from only just beyond the compound. I used to remind guests that this showed that we were in Central Asia, not in Milton Keynes!

Before entertaining guests a tour of the garden was usually on the menu. We would pass a couple of trees whose delicate leaves rubbed between fingers would astonish visitors by smelling strongly of pepper. At some seasons a guava tree would be heavy with large flying-fox bats. I encouraged bamboos of all sorts, including one magnificent specimen in a corner near where I created a pingminton court. The shoots of this dark green polished tubular plant, about a couple of inches in diameter, would grow I swear, a foot a day. Eventually it got so large that I am told it had to be removed after I left.

I must mention here that one December I was presented with a handsome live female turkey with Christmas in mind. It arrived with a card from the admirable chief secretary of the North-West Frontier Province. (Chief secretaries knew everything that was important going on in their provinces so I made a point of getting to know them.) The bird looked so decorative in the garden and did so little damage (the cook fed it I think) that I decided not to sacrifice it for the table but to keep it. For a time it gave pleasure to me and especially to visiting children. Then one day it disappeared and we realised that it could have flown over the garden wall, food we feared for some local fox or jackal.

Some weeks later, however, it suddenly reappeared with a baby turkey in tow! It had found a nesting place in a corner of the garden which we had deliberately allowed to run wild. Since it was some months since the turkey would have seen a mate we wondered if she had been granted some form of virgin birth! For a time there were two turkeys decorating the garden. Then one died. The survivor, whom we called Cleo, liked to roost at night on one of the low walls in the servants' quarters. She began to treat the whole compound as her territory. One day my PA told me, with embarrassment, that some members of the staff were unhappy that the High Commissioner's turkey was sitting on the bonnets of their cars; not very good for the paintwork! Oh dear. I apologised profusely to all concerned. We had to try and restrict her movements from then on.

Sometime later members of the Residence staff presented me out of the blue with a magnificent male turkey. The female is attractive close up but the male is, of course, more spectacular. My staff had felt that Cleo had been lonely and psychologically disturbed since she used to sit outside the front door or different rooms looking sadly into the glass. Life improved with the new male displaying his colourful fan tail and doing the occasional 'gobble gobble'! I called him Prospero. The pair of birds was passed on to my successor, with the hope that he would not eat them. I never enquired. If any progeny eventually resulted I never heard. Now I think about it perhaps the servants were harvesting eggs! It is worth recording that my Muslim servants were genuinely kind to birds and other living things, except snakes.

In the wider compound I brought in an abandoned statue of the young Queen Victoria which looked good, erected in front of our flagpole. I saw looking after the estate as one of my responsibilities. Down behind the statue, by the side entrance to the lower Residence garden, was a large square empty basin surrounded by shrubs clearly designed for water. Encouraged by my artist cousin Susan who made a design during her visit, and helped by a friend of long standing Bim Riggall on another visit, I turned the basin into a water-garden. We established little islands linked by curved lines of stepping stones made of logs of wood cut to the right height (I was influenced by the garden of the Heian shrine in Kyoto). We got fountains working, installed water lilies and other plants, and imported goldfish. Gradually a variety of marine life developed, including tadpoles, dragonflies and other strange creatures, creating a new ecology that gave me considerable delight. As the poet said 'What is this life if, full of care, we have no time to stop and stare?' I would insist on showing the new water-garden to guests. My successors made further improvements.

Partly to learn about the birds and plants in my garden and those seen on walks in the neighbourhood, including up in the nearby hills, I was a keen member of an admirable organisation that had existed in Islamabad for some time, the Asian Study Group. Once a month, except in summer heat, a bird expert would take a group of residents to search for and identify interesting birds. Amateur ornithologists on my own staff were extremely knowledgeable. Once a month too, a young Pakistani lady from the National Herbarium would take a group out to nearby woods to look at wild plants, not only those that were attractive in flower, but those which had medicinal value, were possible to eat or were poisonous. One of my first secretaries was astonishingly well informed about local plants. He produced a booklet recording all those he had identified. Books were published under Asian Study Group auspices on local birds and butterflies for both of which I wrote introductions. Mammals were more difficult to see. We knew there were porcupines because we saw the holes where they lived and the occasional abandoned spine. We heard the jackals. Tribes of monkeys would cross the road when we were driving up to the hills. On one occasion I encountered a group of about 60, young and old. Small barking deer like our muntjacs were seen rarely, wild cats almost never, though there were leopards ranging over large areas in the hills. These were all nocturnal creatures. Some Pakistani friends used to hunt elusive wild boar but I never saw any.

The great authority on birds and other wildlife in Pakistan was an Englishman, Tom Roberts, who had been brought up in Pakistan. His father had been principal of the first agricultural college in the sub-continent near the present-day textile city of Faisalabad. Finding further preferment barred because he was not a member of the ICS (Indian Civil Service), he resigned around 1920 and started to buy land which he farmed. At one time he owned some 32,000 acres in different places in southern Punjab, mostly producing cotton. Much of this remained in the family, locally managed. (It was rare for Britons to own land in the sub-continent, unlike for instance in East Africa.) Tom, the only son, had had to keep an eye on the farms, but had concentrated on becoming a naturalist. He had worked for a time for the Food and Agriculture Organization (FAO) in Karachi. He had already written a pioneering book on the mammals of Pakistan and then started to produce comprehensive works on birds and butterflies. In 1984 he retired to live with his wife in Anglesey, where I later visited them. On his occasional visits to Pakistan it was a privilege to make an expedition in his company. He needed only to hear a few notes to identify an unseen bird. Tom lectured well, illustrated by his own photographs. He was modest about his immense reservoir of knowledge which he was always happy to share.

The Asian Study Group brought together diplomats and other expatriates as well as Pakistanis in Islamabad. Besides birds and plants there were groups learning about local antiquities, different religions, carpets, gardens and other subjects where there was interest and local expertise available. One of my defence attachés started a popular group visiting historic battlefields. Hikes were organised in the hills. I remember a visit to a snake farm, where we clung to children as the staff flicked snakes out of three large containers into which they had been divided, on the hook of a stick, then pinched them hard behind the head with their fingers so that drops of poisonous serum could fall into a glass to be used for making antidotes. Snakes were not considered a problem for foreigners or tourists, but occasionally for farmers in the countryside.

My predecessor's wife, Gabriele Fyjis-Walker, had been president of the Asian Study Group. When I arrived the wife of the Canadian High Commissioner was in charge. Then a lady connected with the UN who had been lined up to take over had to leave Pakistan because her husband was ill. I was happy to be asked to become president and took considerable pains over succeeding years to keep the organisation flourishing, with regular committee meetings in my drawing room. I wished there had been a similar organisation in other posts I had served. Each season was launched with an interesting talk in a hall where various experts behind stalls encouraged people to take an interest in their particular activities. There was usually a big end-of-season party with an Asian theme, sometimes in my garden. Once this was a Moghul event with classical Indian dance, an art which was under threat in modern Pakistan.

The committee operated harmoniously. Tension only arose when a small group had to decide which photographs had to be included in the annual calendar! A brilliant variety of images produced a reasonable income. When my time came to leave there were no obvious diplomatic candidates to take over as president, so I was succeeded by my good friend Parvin Malek who kept the organisation going for many years. I had known her and her husband, Shaukat, the first doctor established in Islamabad, since my Rawalpindi days almost 30 years before. It was rewarding to have such continuity of friendship.

Another thriving organisation bringing the expatriate community together with Pakistani participation was RATS, the Rawalpindi Amateur Theatrical Society, of which I had been a member in my Pindi days. More of that later.

One of the pleasures of being a diplomat is that you can devote time to areas of local activity that interest you, performing at the same time a representative function. As head of mission you are never really off duty. I became particularly interested in the thriving art world in Pakistan, never missing an opportunity to visit or open an exhibition. There were lively artistic communities, particularly in Lahore and Karachi. I bought some of their paintings. Some prominent individuals were fine artists. Ejaz ul Hassan was a PPP politician, ex Cambridge, as well as a professional artist. Hanif Ramay was another politician who painted professionally. Zubeida Agha, a fragile lady of good family, produced pioneering abstract paintings. Lady Noon was a keen amateur artist.

When my cousin Susan Bird visited, it was an excuse to bring together a number of local painters whose work I had admired. The quality and range of the work produced was, I thought, impressive. In Lahore I had become friends with the painter Salima Hashmi, former director of the progressive College of Art near the museum which had been headed once by Kipling's father, where students of both sexes mixed in an enlightened atmosphere. Salima was the daughter of the great left-wing Urdu poet, Faiz Ahmad Faiz, whom I regret I never met. Her mother was an old-fashioned English radical who, with a sister, had come out to India in the 1930s. They had both married prominent

Indian intellectuals. Alys Faiz committed herself to support her husband including when he was in prison. (It is interesting that although Pakistanis universally admire Faiz and people like the parents of Tariq Ali, there has so far been no significant support in Pakistan for ideological leftist parties.) I liked the story of when Alys Faiz was taken into police custody during a women's demonstration in my time on some issue. Her concerned son-in-law had asked the police where the elderly lady was. They told him please to come and take her away quickly. She had berated them loudly and publically for not having a police van with a low enough step for her to climb aboard!

Another visitor from the art world at home was Kay Hartenstein. This was long before she got married to Charles Saatchi. We had a great evening at Salima's house in Lahore, sitting around on cushions and talking about all aspects of the art world and many other things. I met all Pakistan's major artists except for the reclusive Jamil Naqsh in Karachi who played hard to get, though my friend John Cowasjee, member of a well-known Parsee family and an old Reptonian, gave me one of Naqsh's nudes as a present. I finally met him after my retirement.

I also got to know a number of Pakistanis who wrote poems and novels in English. Quite a few of my Pakistani friends had a better command of my own language than I did myself. Some would beat me at word games, which was extremely irritating. The quality of writing in English was good in everyday journalism. Some novelists in English such as Bapsi Sidwa, a Parsee, were already well known. A growing tradition of good Pakistani novelists followed the lead of Indian counterparts. Several of my friends, like Shahid Hosain and Kalim Omar, were amateur poets. One evening I invited them, together with Pakistan's most respected poet in English, Toufiq Rifat, to an event where people around the room recited their own poems or poems of which they were particularly fond. I took the opportunity to read some of my own favourites from Donne, Matthew Arnold and Robert Graves.

In all such cultural activity I worked closely with my good friend Les Phillips, the local British Council representative, a man of energy who made things happen, and whose son is now my godson. Besides supporting visiting theatre and local theatre groups I had considerable respect for the two Rafi Peer brothers who were keeping puppetry alive, maintaining a tradition of periodic festivals attracting puppeteers from around the world. I met one or two Pakistani actors and directors in the film industry including another Rafi Peer brother, but it was always a struggle for them to compete with Hollywood and Bollywood. I was lucky enough one day to entertain the admired filmmakers Merchant and Ivory for a private lunch, when they were passing through.

I was less involved in local music. There were lively pop bands thriving in Islamic Pakistan, notably 'Junoon'. Adnan Sami Khan, the portly young son of Pakistan Foreign Office friends, had been to Rugby school. He had an amazing self-taught gift of synthesising Western pop and Eastern classical music. Music poured out of him. He soon outlived the innocent youngster I knew, becoming a celebrity with a film-star wife. In some ways the most attractive local music was Kawwali, the traditional Sufi instrumental and vocal music, performed sitting on the ground, which often contained subtle and witty political comment in Urdu which was inaccessible to me. My main problem with Eastern music, and I know it is a deficiency on my part, is the lack of any time structure. If the mood is right and the performers have command of their audience they may go on for ever.

I probably didn't do as much as I should for charities, for which I felt ladies were better equipped. I gave a reception once for a worthy local Catholic hospice and was astonished at the number of women that turned up and the way they piled their plates high with the snacks that I had provided. One children's charity which I permitted to take over my house left behind as a present a large stuffed toy camel which I called 'Godolphin' for some reason. I still have it. I was a strong supporter of SOS villages, some of which I visited, where orphans were looked after in an enlightened way.

The charity that I and my staff particularly admired was the Layton Rahmatullah Trust. This had been set up by Graham Layton, an Englishman who had stayed in Pakistan after partition and had made money in the construction business with a Pakistan partner. Having no children he decided to devote all his money to setting up hospitals treating the eye diseases which were so prevalent in the sub-continent. Often modest treatment or surgery could transform people's lives. Layton, now an old man and weak, was still around and much cherished by honest public-spirited Pakistanis who got together to ensure that his good work was carried on. Princess Alexandra met Layton and visited his Trust's main hospital in Karachi. She had a special link with international charities dealing with eye health. As well as establishing state-of-the-art hospitals in major towns, the Layton Rahmatullah Trust equipped mobile clinics to carry the curing operation to more remote areas.

As far as sport was concerned I had my regular swim. I used to play tennis at the High Commission Club. One year a letter home recorded that I was runner-up in the singles and winner in the doubles, but the staff may have been polite. (George Bush senior was asked how things had changed for him after retirement. 'I win less often at golf,' he said.) The Club was later greatly expanded, providing a safe and familiar haven for the young British officers and their families. There was a busy bar, reasonable basic food and a shop nearby, all in a compound ringed by houses for junior staff. It was important for morale, though I always encouraged staff to explore and learn about the country and make local friends.

In my garden the pingminton court was quite often used. Readers may already have been puzzled by this word. Thinking that the game I had invented might be given some publicity by one of the pack of journalists accompanying the Princess of Wales, I had tried to patent the game before the visit. Since I had played it over the years in various places I was told that a patent was not possible. Too many people already knew about it. But I could, and did, register the name as a trademark. Pingminton, for the uninitiated, is a mixture of ping pong and badminton, which clearly could not be called 'bad pong'! We had played different versions of it in the Barrington family for years and I had gradually refined specifications and rules. Players use ping pong bats and a shuttlecock. It provides excellent enjoyment and exercise once you get the hang of it. I was world champion! I doubt if my dreams of making the game widely known and practised – who knows, at the Olympics? – were in any way realistic. But I haven't given up hope. Only I know the best dimensions of the court and height of the net (oh well! Net should be six foot six inches high and 13 foot wide. The court should extend 17 foot each side of the net). Those setting up the game are advised to use string and large hair-pins to mark the court on grass. Other markings are of course needed on solid surfaces. Ping pong bats and shuttlecocks are easy to obtain.

The scoring, ping pong style, is much simpler than badminton scoring. The first side to win 21 points wins the game. Service moves first from the right hand and then the left, changing sides every five points. At 20 all, the winner must be two ahead, with service changing at every point. Servers stand with their back foot on the line like in squash, firing across to the opposing diagonal court. Drop-shots, lobs to the back of the court, drives and smashes are all deployed. Since you need the movement of the whole arm to hit the shuttlecock with the bat as opposed to a stringed weapon, the game is very energetic. It works well in doubles too, with service rotating among the four players. Like tennis the server must be received by the diagonally opposite player after which it is free for all. Sometimes one player goes forward and the other stays back. Only one serve is allowed, but beginners may need to practice to make sure that they can get the shuttlecock across without it being too easy to smash back. Since the middle line is not usually marked some trust has to be placed on recipients. If the serve does not end in their quadrant they may chose to return it or to let it fall and secure the point. The whole game is great fun, I promise. If someone else makes a fortune from it please give credit to me and the Barrington family! The only problem is that it mustn't be too windy. One of my visitors suggested in that case that players should change ends every ten points.

11

TRAVEL IN PAKISTAN

In those days when travel was easy and secure, I made a point of visiting all the provincial cities regularly, especially Karachi, the country's commercial and financial centre where lived a reasonably large expatriate community.

One of my early visits to Karachi coincided with the Caledonian ball for the local British community. I was invited to be chief guest and took trouble to lard my speech with digs at the Scots (heart-rending pleas from Scottish sinners in hell fire: 'Dear lord we dinna ken, we dinna ken'. Firm voice from above: 'Well you ken noo!'). The Scots have, of course, a great record of service overseas as loyal Britons. The thought of Scottish independence appalls me after the centuries of close cooperation. Scots are invariably better organised as a community overseas than other UK elements. After several years, however, I got fed up with Burns' night dinners, where one learned more about that poet than one wanted to know, and had to stare at a revolting looking haggis knowing that one would be required to eat some of it!

I loved Lahore. With Delhi it was one of the two great cities of northern India. It is mentioned in *Paradise Lost* as 'Lahor of Great Mughal'. Beside the famous landmarks such as the fort, the mosque, the Shalimar Gardens and the tomb of Jahangir (with its exquisitely beautiful inlaid marble sarcophagus) there were fine British period imperial buildings to admire, such as the High Court, the Post Office and Government House, the latter built around an old Islamic tomb. The Anglican cathedral had been completed in 1887, the second in India after Calcutta. In between calling on various dignitaries I took particular interest in the city's minor Moghul monuments which were little known even by educated Pakistanis. There were many interesting buildings tucked away in the old walled city. I wandered the back streets to find them. I hoped at one time to produce a booklet on the subject but never had time to finish it. Once again, going beyond my responsibilities, I would urge Pakistani politicians to preserve their historic buildings, several of which were collapsing, or under threat from local encroachment. The Department of Antiquities had neither the funds nor the clout to do what was needed.

A classic case was the Cypress Tomb of a late Moghul princess in a dirty courtyard not far from the Shalimar Gardens. The tiled panelling high up on the brick tower was strikingly beautiful. Few people had seen it. I suggested to the authorities that the rectangular ground on which it was placed might be cleaned up and turned into a little park to set off the monument. Grateful for my interest, the Antiquities Department welcomed my idea and handed the site over to the Lahore Development Authority. Then the Auqaf department, responsible for the finances of the shrines in Lahore, took it over. They allocated the land to three religious leaders who immediately started construction of houses where the park should have been and tried to sell the land. It was reported in the press that the British High Commissioner had expressed shock over this development (quite right) and written to Prime Minister Nawaz Sharif who instituted an enquiry. The local inhabitants wanted a park. I have recently discovered that houses were built so that the tomb is now boxed in to a small compound, perhaps because of my intervention. At least it is protected by a fence and enjoys an explanatory notice.

Nawaz Sharif listened when I spoke to him of such things when he was prime minister. I even wrote a letter to him suggesting a legislative framework for conservation along the lines that my old friend Shahid Hosain continued to advocate when he was permanent secretary of the culture department under Benazir. It continued to make me angry to see how Pakistan's heritage was being eroded or forgotten, though there were so many monuments which should be a resource for future tourism. One elegant ruined pavilion in a field outside Lahore city which I had been taken to see earlier during my time had been demolished on the authority of a junior official when I tried to visit again.

Further south at Rahimyar Khan I visited a Unilever factory and stayed nearby at the professionally run farm estate owned by Daniyal Mueenuddin. He was the son of my old friends from Pindi days, the Election Commissioner and his American wife. Danny had studied in the USA but had become at home in both cultures. He was now learning how to be a Pakistani landowner, depending, at first, on a good local manager. We discussed his labour difficulties. At my request Danny took me on an expedition across the featureless Cholistan desert to the fort of the Amirs of Bahawalpur, rulers of the largest of the semi-independent Indian states that joined Pakistan. The fort was a massive brick pile surrounded by bulbous bastions, but with little inside. Nearby was an elegant mosque and a building containing immaculately kept tiled tombs of the Amirs. I had asked my host if on the desert journey, where we had been led by a sort of Pakistani bedouin, we could pass near some of the old sites of Indus Valley cities that I knew were dotted over the desert. We stopped in two places, walked across the sand and collected a few of the extensive pottery shards on the surface. They were 3,000 years old. I gave references for Danny who was applying to study law in the USA but it was only 15 years later that I heard of him again. He had practised law then given it up to try his hand as a writer while still caring for his Pakistan estate. Out of the blue he published a highly acclaimed book of short stories of Pakistan in which his farm and the family rock house near Murree featured. He depicted with acute observation some of the poorest elements in Punjab rural society.

Having family visitors from home was a good excuse to explore different parts of Pakistan. Some of the stories are worth telling. The first is typical of Pakistani hospitality. My mother and sister came to visit in the spring of 1989 and I drove with them to Swat. We returned a different way, over the Ambela pass. Coming down to the plains near Swabi we missed one or two places where it would have been suitable to stop and have a picnic, deciding to drive on. Suddenly quiet areas were no longer to be seen. There were people everywhere. Eventually the ladies in the back of the car said they really did need to attend the call of nature. But what to do? Getting desperate, I asked driver Yusuf to slow down so that I could try and talk to a young man walking by the road. Did he by any chance know of a spot where lady visitors could rest? 'I can help you,' he said, in good English, 'Our family home is just over the other side of the road.'

Following his directions we turned aside and drove into a walled compound. There, in a grass courtyard, the young man said we could set up our picnic. He took the ladies off to wash. He and the rest of the family were sensitive enough to let us enjoy our food undisturbed. They later came out and talked. It seemed that the father of the family had died. There were three sons, who had all studied English. My mother and sister were introduced to the boys' mother in the house. We thought the family had been immensely kind and considerate, typical, as I found, of much Pakistani hospitality. I kept up with the brothers subsequently. Life was never easy for them, but they studied and worked hard, maintained high principles, and earned themselves worthwhile jobs, in one case serving the community in the Frontier Province.

We were more adventurous when my sister came with her husband and I took them on a trip up to Gilgit and Hunza in the north. After flying to stay in the comfortable hotel in Gilgit built by the Aga Khan, we drove up the Karakoram highway, constructed by the Chinese with great effort and some loss of life. We passed the magnificent mountain of Rakaposhi on our right, always a glorious sight. We stayed in Hunza with the Mir and his wife and explored the old fort from which his independent ancestors used to rob caravans going into China. His father, who had acceded to Pakistan, had been a character much lauded, but the son was also shrewd and in touch with his people. The status of the Northern Areas was anomalous. They had not been completely integrated into Pakistan because they were once technically part of the State of Kashmir, which Pakistan had unrealistically dreamed of retaining as a whole unit. So they had, at that time, no elected Assembly members. The Hunza people were Ismaili Muslims, liberal and tolerant, living healthy lives, often to a great age. Hunza has reasonable claims to be the Shangri-la of legend. It was cold bucket and showers in the bathroom but the Mir and his wife were very hospitable. We tasted some of the famous alcoholic 'hunza water'. The snow-capped peaks visible in different directions were awe-inspiring. The Mir pointed out that as we had driven up the new highway, dug out of the mountainside, we might have spotted, on the other side of the valley, the traces of the little footpath over which as a child he had taken several days to walk to school in Gilgit.

I also took Sara and John on a trip to the central Salt Range in the Punjab. ICI had a soda factory at Khewra near one of the biggest salt mines in the world. I think only one in Poland topped it. We stayed with the hospitable manager and trundled into a tunnel on an antiquated rail trolley. Inside the walls were of opaque pinkish glassy salt, reflecting the lights of many lamps. Eventually we reached a vast cavern extending hundreds of feet up into the mountain. It had been hacked out by generations of workers. Our host lit a candle below a balloon contraption which sailed serenely up into the void until it was lost from sight. My dear sister, like many visitors from home, had lived something of a charmed life. When in the morning, before departure, she said she had seen a fascinating large insect in her room, I expected to find something like a praying mantis, that amazing brown or bright green insect that would sit up on furniture peering round with its triangular head. They were slow moving so not scary, though one had landed on my neck, years before, and given me a fright. However, what Sara had been looking at was a very large cockroach! Embarrassing for our kind host.

When my eldest nephew Andrew came to Pakistan I took him on one of my visits to the Christian missionary hospital at Bannu at the edge of tribal territory in the North-West Frontier Province. There was a tradition for people from the embassy to take supplies down to Dr Ruth Coggon and the small group of European and antipodean nurses who helped her. The hospital had been founded by one of the great missionary names from the Frontier, Dr Pennell. The doctor who ran the men's side was the son of a boy converted by Pennell. He was not easy to get on with. The women's side, led in inspiring fashion by Ruth, had a reputation for treating women's obstetric gynaecological problems from a wide area including inside Afghanistan. I was told they treated women's problems 'between neck and knees'. On one occasion Archbishop Coggon, who had preceded Runcie, came with his wife to Islamabad on his way back from visiting his daughter. I gave them supper to meet a few friends. He had the reputation of being modest and scholarly. I wrote home that he had displayed much more intellectual sparkle than I had expected from such a gentle character.

On the subject of family visits I should mention that my youngest nephew Crispin came towards the end of my time in Islamabad. We made an adventurous trip by helicopter all the way north to Gilgit accompanied by Jamshid Burki, one of the best sort of senior civil servant, then (permanent) secretary of the Interior Ministry. He was a cousin of Imran. As we traversed dramatic mountain scenery with deep valleys it was pointed out to us how helpless a helicopter was if there was no level place on which to land! We were also reminded that several years before a Pakistan International Airways domestic flight had gone off course in the high mountain area and completely disappeared. There was still no trace of the machine or its passengers by the time that I left Pakistan.

We had grand views of Nanga Parbat and, in the distance, the distinctive cone of K2, the second highest mountain in the world. Cris and I stayed in a hotel by a lake surrounded by mountains and then went east to Skardu when we embarked on a precarious climb up to the ruins of the fort, rewarded with more great views. We saw the old wooden palaces around Khaplu, not far from the line of Pakistan/Indian confrontation by the Siachen glacier. We only got a brief impression of the Deosai plains near Skardu, snow-covered in winter but bursting with wild flowers in summer. Some years later a group from the Cambridge Botanical Gardens, led by Superintendent Tim Upson, collected a number of these special high-altitude plants now to be seen in their glasshouses.

Finally my middle nephew, Rupert, came out for a proper stay nearer the end of my tour. He and a friend of mine, Jenny from the Hermon Taylor family, drove with me down an unfrequented route along the west side of the Indus to rarely visited Dera Ismail Khan. On the way we stopped near the town of Kalabagh on the Indus at a point where, after joining with the Kabul river at Attock, the river erupts from a long rocky gorge. When I had first been in Pakistan the Nawab of Kalabagh had been a powerful figure as governor of West Pakistan under Ayub Khan. I had been friends with his eldest son Malik Muzaffar, who had been a member of the National Assembly.

While I was away from Pakistan the old Nawab, then retired, had died mysteriously at his family home. The rumour was that he may have done something to offend his wife and had been killed by his three sons with her knowledge. Another story was that he had planned to leave a large part of his estate to a favourite factor who was not a family member. Once back in Pakistan as ambassador I was invited by Malik Muzaffar to visit his home. He was now the senior member of the family. I didn't dare ask him about his father's death. He indicated that a rival local politician had been responsible. Kalabagh was interesting because it was a classic example of thriving feudalism in Pakistan. The family were chiefs of the Awan group, one could almost say tribal group, of Punjabis. They lodged me in an elegant guesthouse with a wide terrace overlooking the river. All around were attendants with guns and crossed belts of ammunition like something out of the Mexican Revolution. They were powerfully built men, with great black moustaches. The horses and cattle they showed me were immaculately kept. Hospitality was generous.

Some months later I heard that my friend had been shot and killed by a neighbouring Afghan tribesman. It made me realise that the armed men had not been just for show. I was sad but who knows the rights and wrongs of such affairs. The story was that an Afghan shepherd boy had been killed while the Kalabagh family had been hunting, and this was revenge. But there had always been tension between the Kalabaghs and their neighbouring Pushtun tribes to the west. Local loyalties were fierce.

Another example of the feudalism which had survived in so many ways was visible nearer to Islamabad at the somewhat bare mansion of Atta Mohammad Khan, almost a caricature of a feudal landowner, tall with massive turban and handlebar moustaches. Cheerful and generous he invited me and some friends to watch bull-racing and tent-pegging, which is pricking with a lance a wooden block set in the ground while galloping at speed on horseback. He and others would show off their skills at the annual horseshow in Lahore, which I saw twice, once with John Hermon Taylor and his wife who were visiting. I am told it has now been discontinued. What a pity! The President's bodyguard and other military units not only looked magnificent in uniforms but showed great equestrian skill. There were musical rides and horse dancing with many types of sport and displays. At one of these horse shows they staged the Afghan game of Bozkeshi, as a tribute to their Afghan refugee guests. As usual it was exciting and barely under control, not designed for the confined space of a stadium. The persistence of feudalism with its good and bad aspects showed that any efforts at land reform had had little effect.

I continued to travel around the country right up till the end of my time, most notably in Sindh. Tourist sites there were less well known than in the north even though some were perfectly accessible from Karachi. Not far east of the city was a mysterious collection of decorated brick tombs, the Chowkundi tombs. It was here that I first met the remarkable German lady scholar, Anne-Marie Schimmel, who was a mine of information about Pakistan and all things Islamic, particularly Islamic mysticism. I was fortunate enough to see a good deal of her, including after retirement, since we had several mutual Pakistani and Iranian friends. I attended some of her lectures where, head down, she would speak with great rapidity and without a note. I was at St James's Piccadilly for her well-attended memorial service.

Further away from Karachi near Thatta was the long string of Makli tombs with coloured tiles, Persian style. Archaeological sites in southern Sindh were connected with the first Arabs who brought Islam to the sub-continent. The province was littered with colourful shrines of local saints, some of which were visited by itinerant malangs, comparable to India's sadhus, who would make music and dance at festivals in religious ecstasy. It was common for both Hindus and Muslims to worship at some of these shrines, a practice severely frowned upon by Muslims of Wahabi inclination. There were little-visited tombs of the former rulers of Sindh, the Kalhoras, to be seen in Hyderabad, a major city not to be confused with Hyderabad in Indian Deccan. I particularly admired the elegant mosque and tombs further north at Khudabad, where, as in many places, time and neglect were eroding beautiful buildings to a heartbreaking extent. I toured the Indus Valley site at Mohenjo-daro, centre of one of the great ancient civilisations.

I finally achieved a visit to a place of mystery that I had long hoped to see. This was Ranikot Fort. I was taken with a small group by the doyen of Sindhi culture, Hamid Akhund, including police protection. We followed in convoy the main road up the west side of the Indus beyond Hyderabad, and then turned left and drove on a dusty track until we came to a range of dry hills. We noticed signs of brick battlements on the hilltops. Substantial walls, wide enough for a walkway above, curved up over the ridges, punctuated by fat towers. In one or two places they gave way to a precipitous crest of rock that served as its own protection. The walls came down to let a small stream through a disguised gap, once a proper gateway, where we entered. There was little vegetation and only a few shepherds' huts. Miles away in the distance we could see further stretches of the wall at various points. We drove up to a citadel type of fort with a better view, but sparse inside. It was perfectly believable that the outside walls up and down were as many as 18 miles round, enclosing about 20 square kilometres, reputedly the largest fort enclave in Asia. I learned that there were four entrances and a spring inside the territory. A seasonal river was dry when we were there. We had to leave in the late afternoon, being advised by our guides and police that the area could become a haven for dacoits (local brigands) after dark.

Distinguished scholars are at odds about the origin of this extraordinary phenomenon, which must have taken years to construct and surprisingly is not mentioned in early guidebooks. To me the walls and crenellations looked as if they were of a similar period to Rohtas fort near Lahore, namely the sixteenth or seventeenth century. Some think that they are much older. Others maintain they only date just before the British period when Sindh was ruled by the Talpur dynasty. But the latter were not all that prosperous and why should they have constructed such a vast length of wall when fertile lands were not far away? It is true that the Talpurs were originally a Baluch tribe and probably came down from what is modern Iran. Perhaps there were other nameless groups on the move before them who decided to spend time in a protected area short of the Indus. Large armies and numerous followers could have been accommodated in the defended area, but unless the climate has completely changed how would they have been fed and found enough water in that mainly barren landscape? It is good that there are historical mysteries still to be solved.

Travelling in Sindh was made more comfortable by the hospitality of local landlords, some of whom owned whole groups of villages. In the north of the province there were several towns which I visited including Sukkar, Larkana (home of the Bhuttos), Shekarpur (formerly a centre of Hindu traders now the base of the influential Soomro family, some of whom were friends). Further on the road to Quetta is Jacobabad, one of the two towns in Pakistan, together with Abbottabad, where the local people have so far insisted on keeping names linked with past British administrators. The remarkable clock built by Jacob was still to be seen in the Deputy Commissioner's house. Jacob's tomb was well maintained as was the tomb at Las Bela, west of Karachi, of another of the legendary British political officers working in that part of the world, Sir Robert Sandeman. He it was who had united the unruly Baluch tribes and earned their respect. In Islamabad I had given a special dinner for Baluch friends to mark the centenary of Sandeman's death.

Sometimes consular problems involved travel. The most difficult consular case which I inherited from my predecessor was the situation of Mrs Hazel Taylor in her run-down estate south of Lahore, where she and her former husband had been breeding horses for years. It is worth recording as a symbolic 'end of Empire' story. This lady had complained to us about being dragged around and injured during a local hospital visit. In 1991 we also had to remonstrate strongly in writing to the Pakistan government after a woman friend of Mrs Taylor was manhandled and forced away from visiting her by army people in civilian clothes. We complained that Mrs Taylor was being kept, at that time, like a prisoner in her own house, without a telephone. Part of the house was sealed off. This was not the way to treat an elderly lady who had spent years living and working in Pakistan breeding fine horses. I protested personally to the chief secretary of the Punjab. The civilian authorities were embarrassed but it appeared that they had the army on their backs, who were waiting for the day when they could eject Mrs Taylor from her property and take it over themselves. It was an example of the ugly side of what could happen in Pakistan if you did not have friends in high places.

Things were slightly improved after the fuss we made. Mrs Taylor was given full access to her house but she complained that numbers of her breeding mares had been taken away. When I think back about the visit I made to her, the scene had elements of a spooky film. She was of advanced age and did not look after herself very well. The large rambling house was full of dust, dark to keep the sun out and in bad disrepair. It looked as if servants had been purloining items of porcelain and furniture (she had probably paid them little). I was entertained in a small clear area where one loyal bearer offered me tea in a fine cracked cup. I imagined cobwebs, bats, Miss Haversham in the next room. However, when Mrs Taylor asked one of her staff to take me on a tour of the extensive surrounding huts and paddocks I saw well over 50 healthy looking horses.

It was later that I found about more about Hazel Taylor's history. She was one of the daughters of a wealthy South African of German origin, Denis Vanrenen, who had bought a long lease of a large area of fertile land in Renala, southern Punjab, before World War I. He had farmed there and bred horses that had a high reputation. Hazel's English mother, returning to her home by train from Karachi in 1948, had been attacked in her carriage by brigands. Her dead body was found beside the line. Among those at her funeral were prominent Pakistanis such as Firoz Khan Noon and his wife Vicky and one of the Leghari family. Hazel married Colonel Taylor, an army vet, and after her parents' death bought out her brothers and carried on managing the land, which included now the largest and highest quality stud in Pakistan. She claimed that Jinnah had asked the family to stay on after

Independence. The stud's breeding mares, with some fine stallions, produced prize-winning racehorses for meets at Lahore and as far away as Poona.

At one point Mrs Taylor also bought a farm in Kenya and lived there for a period while her husband ran Renala. During that time she became friendly with other British farmers in Kenya including an uncle and much-loved aunt of my brother-in-law John Symes. They had gone out to try farming in Kenya during the Depression. I had, therefore, a personal connection. Hazel was in fact the second cousin of John's aunt. A website created by John's cousin Peter Symes, a documentary filmmaker, based on his grandmother's copious diaries (www.wynnesdiary.com) gives an impression of the life in India of the intrepid ladies of that era.

When Hazel's husband had died she arranged for a retired Pakistani army officer to look after the Renala estate but she found out he was making too much money for himself and was persuaded to come back and take over. She sold the Kenyan farm (she was also the owner of a small stud in Swaziland). Because she and her husband had never taken the chance to buy the lease, and apparently never paid rent for some reason, she became involved in numerous lawsuits. I can imagine that she was stubborn and difficult. Neighbours encroached on her property. The Pakistan army 'remount' people needed horses for cavalry and ceremonial purposes, and good breeding mares. They had always expected to take the estate over and so continually made difficulties for Mrs Taylor, including planting hostile articles in the local press.

Mrs Taylor had some loyal Pakistani friends particularly an admirable couple, the Mohsins, who ran a successful horticultural business, Mitchells Fruit Farms (another business started by British people), not far away. I stayed with them in comfort. I remember rare hornbills nesting in the garden. Setwat Mohsin made a point of visiting Mrs Taylor regularly but she could not persuade her to sell up and buy a smaller property which would have been more easy to manage. The old lady feared being evicted, but was determined not to move. She had one eccentric son who came and went in an unpredictable way and did little to help her. She had alienated the rest of the family. Our protests alleviated Mrs Taylor's living conditions but the battle over the estate mired in lawsuits was not something she was likely to win.

I discovered later that though the army did eventually take over the stud after I had left Pakistan she had been allowed to stay on in the old house for her lifetime, coping with health difficulties and awkward domestic arrangements. She had survived until about 2000, latterly bedridden, when she died and was buried at Renala. She had managed to pass some of her best horses to the Leghari family and to sell off the timber of some of the trees she had planted. Her friends believed that she must have died a wealthy woman, with money in Switzerland, Ireland and elsewhere. All this presumably came to her son John whose 'elevator did not stop at every floor' as the Americans might say. He was not married and when last heard of was living poorly in a shack on the estate. It was a strange, sad story.

Part of my responsibilities involved encouraging the Pakistanis to control production of drugs and to inhibit their export to the UK. I had specialised Customs officers on my staff. They did good work. Unfortunately one of them crossed the Afghan border with a group of colleagues to peek at some abandoned Soviet equipment and was kidnapped by a minor Afghan warlord, who kept them in a hole in the ground. I deployed what contacts and influence I possessed on either side of the border to achieve the group's release, in conjunction with Dutch and German colleagues. Hamid Karzai, then deputy foreign minister in the Afghan government, was helpful. One difficulty for me was that I had been planning for some time to take a week's local leave to go with my friendly Italian ambassador colleague and a small group to visit Samarkand and Bokhara, places that I had heard and read about so much ever since my first days in Kabul but never visited. (I had acquired a series of rare travel books about the area. For example, the story of the English vicar Joseph Wolff. He had travelled all the way to Central Asia to try and discover what had happened to two British officers, Colonel Stoddart and Captain Connelly, who had gone to visit the Amir of Bokhara. He found out that they had been cast into a pit and eventually executed for not having treated the Amir with sufficient respect. The eccentric Wolff managed to return unscathed. It was after having bought a copy of his account published in 1846 that I discovered that it had been inscribed by Wolff himself.)

When I informed the Foreign Office of my plans, instructions came back that so long as the member of my staff had not been released it was imperative that I should not leave Pakistan. Everyone in London relied heavily (they said) on my knowledge, advice and contacts in both Pakistan and Afghanistan. Ministers were quoted. The popular press would slaughter the government if something went wrong – clearly for them a key point. There followed a free and frank exchange of telegrams! I explained that I needed a break and had not taken the decision to leave for a week lightly. Everything was in the expert hands of my staff. Local Afghan commanders were about to put pressure on the individual concerned.

Of course this did no good. Ministers said that after careful consideration I could not be spared. I had to cancel Samarkand. It was only a few days later that the hostages were released and reached Quetta. I noted wryly that in a 'seminal' speech about the British Foreign Service made shortly afterwards at Chatham House and circulated to all posts, Foreign Secretary Douglas Hurd had made a point of praising the way that the High Commissioner in Pakistan and his mission had handled this kidnapping!

I reckon that being a bachelor and so not having to worry about school fees meant that I was sometimes more frank than was prudent in dealing with headquarters. I had protested strongly about some of the new management theory procedures that I felt were a waste of time and diverted effort from essential work. For example, I thought that performance pay, a sort of mini-bonus, was insulting because I would do the best I could in any job without needing any incentive.

I became known in Pakistan not only for taking an interest in all aspects of local history and culture but also for discarding dignity and treading the boards. It was a pleasure to be associated again, after 20 years, with the Rawalpindi Amateur Theatrical Society (RATS), of which I became patron. I started by playing the doddery Reverend Chasuble in *The Importance of Being Earnest* put on at the American school. In a *Peter Pan* pantomime I was roped in to play the sad Mr Darling who is seen in the last act living in a dog kennel, doing penance for having allowed his children to fly away with Peter.

In 1990 I played the dignified Duke Theseus in an enjoyable production of *Midsummer Night's Dream*, which took place by the swimming pool in my garden. There was a convenient separate entrance for members of the public who didn't have to go through the house. The audience sat on two angles of the pool in a suitably leafy setting. Reflections enhanced the spectacle. As in Cairo, we built a structure behind a bush so that Puck could appear suddenly on occasion as if suspended in air. It was a great collaborative effort by RATS, well appreciated by the local Pakistani and expat community. A kind local review said that the beautiful garden added a dreamy atmosphere to the production, made more exotic by the water.

It was only a few weeks later it was announced in the June Queen's Birthday Honours that I had been made a knight. I had been told several months before, of course, so had probably been going around looking particularly smug. Such honours were by no means automatic in those days; today they are awarded even more sparingly. I was delighted that the powers that be in London had considered my hard work, which I reckoned often beyond the call of duty, worthy of recognition. I told no one beforehand except my mother, by letter to be opened the day before, so that she shouldn't suffer shock. I knew she would be delighted. I wished my father had been alive. His sister, my aunt Freda, wrote a warm letter saying that she had not imagined that the baby that she had once held in her arms would end up this way. It was my last communication from this remarkable woman, since she died soon after. My cousin Sue, her daughter, arranged to give me a present of a splendid pen and ink drawing by a friend of hers called Gino d'Achille, to be seen among the illustrations of this book. It depicts me with helmet and shield being dubbed by the Queen while surrounded by courtiers and many corgis, including one sniffing the trunk of an attendant elephant.

Some local comment expressed disorientation: 'Who is this man, who is a duke one day and a knight the next?!' I gave a supper party for old friends on the day the honours were announced but before the news reached Islamabad. John Harrison my deputy had heard through London contacts but I swore him to secrecy until I announced the news, proposing another toast to myself. Some of those present I had known for 20 and 30 years, including Afghan friends the Sherzois, who had recently got out of Afghanistan on their way to go to the USA. I cannot resist recording something written by a respected liberal scholar and theatre director, Shoaib Hashmi, Salima's husband, because it was probably the nicest thing said about me or that I would liked to have been said:

> A friend has recently received a signal honour. Plain Mr Barrington has been created a Knight of the Realm: This entitles him to be addressed as Sir Nicholas and to have his name followed by KCMG which stands for Knight Commander of Michael and Saint George and if I haven't got that exactly right remember that the purpose of this is to tide you over the mid-

week blues and not to qualify you to edit Debrett's Peerage. Anyway it couldn't have happened to a nicer man. The new knight takes his work just seriously enough to make a stir and himself just not seriously enough to make many friends ...

It was even more important now to avoid pomposity. I still cherish the gift of a picture drawn by Jasmine, the young daughter of my friends Micheline and Benon Sevan (the UN representative dealing with Afghanistan), showing the Queen dressed in pink with a crown, standing on a podium and wielding a huge Claymore sword which seems more likely to decapitate me than to tap my shoulder! Besides adding to my own prestige and that of the High Commission within Pakistan, the knighthood would have been useful if I had been planning to make money after retirement. I never pursued this idea. It did help, however, in the various charitable and fundraising activities with which I became involved. And it reinforced my aim to give something back to the community.

The volume of letters of congratulations, some from unexpected quarters, was good for morale. There was confusion about exactly how I should be addressed. I have envelopes describing me as an MP and a Lord, as a Fellow of the Royal Society and as a professor. In one case I was addressed as 'His Excell J On', which seemed more suitable for some Chinese mandarin. Perhaps my favourite is a letter that was sent to 'His Excelency, Mr Necklace Brinton'!

Three small parts in RATS' productions had been fun, but directing and taking a lead role in *The Tempest* in the autumn of 1993, six months before my retirement, was an experience of a different order. I was only patron of RATS but they agreed that I could co-direct the play with the wife of a member of my staff who had some professional experience. There was nothing democratic about the casting of Prospero! I had not had much to do with *The Tempest* before and thoroughly enjoyed researching the play's background and writing notes for the programme. Shakespeare seems to have got his idea from a shipwreck that had taken place on the island of Bermuda. Christopher Columbus' discoveries in the Caribbean are likely to have had an influence, as well as the word cannibal, on the name and character of Caliban.

I had plenty of time during a caretaker government the preceding summer to learn what was a very long part, often while swimming up and down my pool. If you are directing and acting you must know your lines. The play was to be staged in my garden, as in the case of the previous *Midsummer Night's Dream*. We used all areas, including the distant balcony of the house, to keep the audiences on their toes. We selected and rehearsed school children to be sprites and hobgoblins who had to bring food for the shipwrecked courtiers out of the bushes and then spirit it away. Music was carefully planned and incorporated. We created out of cardboard the prow of a boat for the first rather muddled shipwreck scene in semi-darkness (a battery of lights was erected behind the audience). Prospero's cave among the vegetation was easy. I acquired a fetching beard in a theatrical store in London, and enjoyed supervising everyone's make-up. (Current undergraduate theatre never seems to use make-up sufficiently.)

I wore a dark blue ankle-length gown with sandals, embellished, at the end of the play, with a cloak glittering with gold as the Duke of Milan began to assert his rightful status. I asked Lall Khan to find outside the compound a piece of wood which could serve as a magic staff. As so often, he excelled himself. He cut down a branch with multiple spikes at the top, all stripped bare to white wood. My magic book was one of the volumes of an eighteenth-century edition of *Paradise Lost*. You can see how much I was enjoying myself.

Ariel was the bright young wife of the US assistant naval attaché who himself became Prince Ferdinand. Grim, powerful and pathetic Caliban and comic Trincolo were played by two of our visa officers. The latter is now a vicar in the east of London. The drunken butler Stefano was the Pakistani chairman of RATS.

Prospero is a wordy part particularly in the earlier scenes of exposition which I had to try and make lively and interesting. But there were, of course, great speeches including 'Our revels now are ended', concluding: 'We are such stuff as dreams are made on; and our little life is rounded with a sleep.' Also the commanding 'Ye elves of hills, brooks, standing lakes and groves', going on to 'This rough magic I here abjure', when Prospero gives up his magical powers, breaks his staff and drowns his book. This imagery was all very appropriate as I was about to give up my own diplomatic powers and privileges.

As a bonus, Prospero speaks a final epilogue directly to the audience asking for their approval. That was great fun to do, finding yourself holding the attention of an audience which would hopefully erupt into applause. Beside the spectacle and the enjoyment of performing with friends, I hoped that the play made those present – full houses of Pakistanis and foreigners – enjoy Shakespeare in traditional dress and even contemplate the concepts of use of power, nature and nurture, forgiveness and reconciliation that emerge from the play. I have an inadequate video of this minor triumph. To cap it all I designed the poster of which I was rather proud. Reviews were complimentary about the production as a whole and about the performance of Prospero. Letters were kind. For example Mr Alexeyev, the new-style ambassador of the Russian Federation wrote that *The Tempest* was not his most favourite play of the 'Great Master' and he could never have imagined that he could enjoy it so much! (Who would have thought that all references to Shakespeare in the Olympic ceremonies in London in 2012 would relate to *The Tempest*?!)

My mother came out on her last visit while I was rehearsing for *The Tempest*, frail now, accompanied gamely by my cousin Jane. The Residence staff called her 'mother' and looked after her so well that Jane and I could even get away to Lahore. Another spectator was Jill Freud, wife of Clement. I had always organised good parties after the productions of her Suffolk theatre group that she had brought to Pakistan. On the basis of my Prospero Jill was rash enough to invite me to take a part after my retirement in a production by her company of *Hay Fever*. That was recognition! I did not take the offer up but at least I was able to help for some years as chairman of her company's management committee in Suffolk. I might have stayed longer if I could have persuaded her to risk a Shakespeare. But she knew her audiences. Summer productions in Southwold and Aldeburgh were usually sold out.

When the time came to retire I had been so long in Islamabad that there were a plethora of farewells. I was especially sorry to say goodbye to my loyal household servants.

An embarrassing gift was handed to me when I made my farewell call on the head of the Pakistan Air Force. It looked like a large elaborate walking stick but on examination I saw that it doubled as a gun! I took it home out of courtesy but then quickly wrote a polite letter saying I was obliged to return it since the British Customs were not keen on people importing guns and would probably delay my baggage. But if my friend could present me with a fine local ordinary stick with a horn handle I would much appreciate it and remember what it might have been. The local stick arrived and is well used. Another present I valued was an ancient bottle, possibly dating back 1,000 years, which had been discovered cleverly by one of the Embassy local staff and presented to me at a rather emotional farewell with all of them gathered. They knew my tastes.

PART III

12

HOME AT LAST, CAMBRIDGE

David Gillmore, old Cambridge friend, now permanent under-secretary, who would be retiring shortly after me, had been asking me for years what I planned to do after retirement. I had always replied that I was still concentrating on my job and would only start thinking seriously about the future after I had returned home. I had plenty of energy left but was not sorry to retire. Although fixed retirement ages were being questioned and have now in theory disappeared I thought it reasonable to require diplomats to go at 60 so that others could enjoy senior responsibility when they were best equipped in their 50s. If their children had come late in the day there was a chance for them to earn a little more money. Whatever one chose to do, one should now have enough time and good health to make it worthwhile.

Anyway, I was home for good at last after a career of 37 years. There was washing up to be done in the form of farewell calls on Hurd, Gillmore, and other people in business and government. Also a farewell audience with the Queen at Buckingham Palace, together with a few other colleagues and their wives. It was clear that the monarch continued to keep herself well informed about the issues with which we had been involved. My immediate problem was to buy a new car. For the first time this could be a foreign make. I had considered it impossible to promote British exports while driving a foreign car. In the end, however, I chose a Rover hatchback which came to be called Raina and lasted me for over a dozen years, before giving way to a nippy little Honda called Harriet. Both automatic of course. I consider devotion to gears a form of snobbery. I had to settle into my Islington house and start to get my Cambridge house, also evacuated by tenants, properly furnished and equipped. I was to become familiar with the M11. A journey of one and a quarter hours carried me from door to door provided I avoided rush hour. I was in for a busy period of life with many options ahead and I used to say that I could keep going as long as I maintained two modest houses, one car and one body in reasonable condition.

When asked about regrets at what I had left behind I would reply, as I still do, that I was not in the business for regrets. It was true that it had been a pleasure to be able to say to my chief bearer that there would be 50 for lunch tomorrow and to know with his 'OK Sahib' that all would be arranged smoothly. I had to get used to the fact that I could no longer slip into the back of a car and expect it to drive off. What I missed most of all, however, as I continued to find over the years, was when something went wrong with my houses and repairs were needed I could no longer call someone and ask them to fix it. Dealing with builders, plumbers, electricians and so on was one of the least attractive aspects of coming home.

My retirement was, of course, my 60th birthday. I gave one of my large drinks parties at the Athenaeum, a tradition that has since been continued every five years. Princess Alexandra and her husband were kind enough to attend. Among friends from all walks of life was Anna Cropper, the actress sister of my old school friend Max, who brought with her uninvited Bert Kwok of the Pink Panther films, though he attacked no-one. My sister and her husband also gave me a special birthday party in the garden of Hill Farm, their home in Suffolk. Childhood friends from Hutton were there as well as Max Cropper himself and his latest fiancée, soon to be his third wife. (That also ended badly. I could write a book about the problems of my mercurial friend and his family!) People came up to talk to our mother who sat in a chair on the lawn looking at the magnificent view of the Deben estuary, with sailing boats and distant Woodbridge. She was now aged 88 and frail.

Mother had come through a serious colon cancer operation the autumn before, after her visit to Islamabad, but had since become unstable on her legs and fallen from time to time, requiring visits by my sister from Suffolk to Cambridge. Her Trumpington flat was too small to have a permanent carer *in situ* so eventually Sara decided, with my agreement, that our mother would have to go into a home, though I had always said I would never allow this to happen. I was very much aware that such treatment of an elderly relative would have been unthinkable in the families of my Asian friends. But they, of course, had servants. Sara found a home nearby in Woodbridge where mother was surrounded by familiar things. My priority was to visit her regularly, which I did most weekends.

By an extraordinary coincidence (though we are told they are never as extraordinary as they seem) two doors away from my mother's room was another elderly lady who the people at the home told me had a connection with Pakistan. It turned out to be the former Molly Ellis, married name now Molly Wade, the young girl who had been kidnapped from Kohat by Afridi tribesmen in a notorious incident in 1923. I knew others involved with that story. She did not have long to live but I had several good conversations with her. She told me that her ordeal had been physically tough. She had been carried through rough terrain, mostly by night, with inadequate clothes and shoes, but never been sexually molested. I met her ex-army son Peter.

Mother had always loved the sea and I would take her out in the car to Felixstowe, Southwold and other Suffolk towns, where we would indulge ourselves with illicit chocolate ice-creams. I did a couple of successful sketches of her. She was beginning to lose the will to live, and in the late autumn she died. It was not, of course, unexpected but it was a sad break with the past. As I find myself saying when I write condolence letters to others, losing one's last parent wipes the sheet clean of all childhood and early history, which one can no longer ask about from the best source.

I had never persuaded mother to write about her own childhood, nor about mine. She had been a sportswoman and artist, keen to build on her limited education. She was a loyal wife, beautiful in her youth and graceful in her old age. (To ward off worry she came to be attracted by an old axiom learned from me: 'Nothing matters very much and most things don't matter at all!') She was full of consideration for other people and loved by everyone who came into contact with her. It was only after her death that we found out about a number of people to whom she had given time and provided comfort. She would often send to people apposite and comforting pieces of poetry. I read out some of her favourite poems in her crowded thanksgiving service at Trumpington. They included Kipling's verse which we both liked about the Norman baron giving advice to his son that 'When the Saxon stands like an ox in the furrow and grumbles this isn't fair dealing – my son leave the Saxon alone!' One of the themes in the letters of condolence which I received, and have re-read with some emotion, is how my mother made all who were with her feel good about themselves.

In her early married life mother had been happy to let the men in the family take the lead over decisions, as well as in political discussions. She confided to me that women had their own ways of getting what they wanted. After father's death she had become more assertive in her views and more right-wing, finding it hard, for instance, to accept the way England was developing into a multi-racial society. It never stopped her treating people equally on an individual level, whatever their background or colour. She was of the generation that rarely considered the need for a wife to earn money on her own, so that her artistic ability remained undeveloped except as a hobby. She did charity work but eventually gave up 'meals on wheels' when she found that many of the people she was helping were younger than she was and were little assisted by their own children. She could be resolute on occasion. I shall never forget a party in Essex where coats were left in an upstairs room. My mother noticed another woman guest coming down the stairs about to leave wearing a black Persian lamb coat (not uncommon in those days). 'She's wearing my coat,' mother said. We tried to prevent her creating a scene but she insisted on accosting the woman and persuaded her, from the contents of the pockets, that she had indeed got the wrong coat!

When I was overseas we would exchange letters almost weekly as I had done when my father was alive. They kept my letters; I retained only a few of theirs. I had always felt secure, as had my sister, in my mother's love. Included in the inscription on the plaque where her ashes are buried in Trumpington churchyard, next to my father, is 'Love is like that. The more you give out the more you have left.' This was taken from one of her letters to me.

Her death was the end of a generation. A couple of years later my sweet uncle Arthur, the last of the Bill children, died just short of reaching 100. I had been in touch with friends in the Palace to make sure a letter from the Queen would be on its way but it was not needed. With the increase in general longevity the staff at the Palace dealing with these letters had greatly expanded.

Part of the furniture for my Cambridge house came from material I had inherited from my uncle Geoff and kept in store. He had left his estate to my sister, my cousin Jane and me, and his possessions had been divided up entirely amicably, with items going to other family members. After the death of aunt Winifred uncle Jack's estate was left to his two sisters, some of which came down to Sara and myself. With money saved from a reasonably abstemious life and few expensive tastes (no yachts nor fast cars!) I had no financial concerns, so that I was able to give a certain amount away over the years, particularly for the education of relations and godchildren.

I did not therefore need a job, though at one time I thought it might be convenient to have an office base. Tim Renton, a former junior Foreign Office minister with whom I had worked, nobly invited me to join him at a meal with the directors of Flemings but nothing came of it. They could not have been impressed. A number of senior business men had written warmly about my contribution to their interests in Pakistan but no one queued up to give me a job and I showed no particularly keenness to get employed. Flies were cast over me about becoming an MP (the assumption was Tory but I was a confirmed floating voter) and master of a college. But I never put my hat in the ring and would probably not have succeeded. I did not want to commit myself to any one activity or organisation – a classic dilettante.

I soon enjoyed getting to know Clare College properly. As a bachelor with a house in Cambridge I became more involved than other Honorary Fellows. It was like being part of a new family. Professor Bob Hepple, who was taking over as master, invited me to join a development committee, mainly to secure funds for the construction of an addition to Memorial Court with a proper lecture theatre. Fundraising at Cambridge was in its infancy. Academics tended to turn up their noses at the idea of asking for donations. It was not easy for the University's first director of development, my friend and former colleague Bill Squire. His wife, who later became a successful principal of Hughes Hall College, was then still serving in the Foreign Office. The British had a lot to learn from their American cousins on establishing a practice of regular giving immediately after graduation.

The modest development team at Clare had as their first task to organise proper records of alumni, which were far from complete. The next task was to keep former Clare students informed of what was going on in the college, through newsletters and reunion dinners, making them feel that they were always welcome back at Cambridge. I was one who pushed for the tradition of holding a special Alumni Day every summer at Clare where several of the current Fellows could talk about the sort of work they were doing. In those days most alumni had little idea about what the college and its Fellows were up to. Research was then needed to identify potential substantial donors, to whom the approach had to be carefully prepared, involving the master himself. I was asked to be joint president, with David Attenborough, of the college's first development campaign which was launched at a splendid concert in St Johns, Smith Square, London in November 1998.

Hepple, now Professor Sir Bob QC, FBA, had been a liberal South African lawyer involved with Mandela in the early days. After the latter had been arrested the authorities came after his anti-apartheid associates and Hepple had to get out. He had been a Fellow of Clare in 1960s and then professor of law in London. He took me with him on a promotional visit to the east coast of the USA where we met former Clare students. I was particularly glad to go for the first time to Boston and Harvard where arrangements for a dinner were made by Professor Jim Thomson, an authority on China, whom I had admired when he was a student contemporary at Clare years before. The few Americans studying among us at that time on different grants and exchanges had had a disproportionate influence in the student body. Jim had seemed very sophisticated and wise; he was now showing his age, however, and died not long after. The money raised in that first campaign was destined to shore up college finances in the face of a change in government policy, rather than for a new building. It was 12 years later, after the college had tempted from elsewhere an able young development director (and Egyptologist in his spare time) that we were able to build an admirably designed annex to the Memorial Court. By this time Professor Tony Badger, historian of the USA, was master, another popular figure.

I have felt welcome at Clare where I look in for the occasional free lunch and, more rarely, dinner. Contact with scholars in a variety of disciplines, including the sciences, has been invigorating. But I noticed that there seemed to be less social interaction between senior and junior members of the college than I had enjoyed as an undergraduate. There were fewer bachelor dons living in college. Most academics seemed under pressure to produce quotas of articles and research papers under new government management policies with their objectives and targets. Those academics who were directors of studies would entertain their students occasionally but there was little cross-discipline social activity. I discovered that the three general college societies of which I had been a member 40 years before had all vanished. I was told that there had been a period when all organisations that might have been considered elite became unfashionable and had faded away. Tutors also seemed nervous about allowing undergraduates to hold parties, fearing that these might result in too much drinking and even destruction of college property. Junior members of the college hardly ever seemed to invite dons to their rooms for parties, as I used to do. Though I have got to know plenty of undergraduates in recent years, I have only once been invited to a party in undergraduate rooms. I find that sad.

I decided to try and revive the college Dilettante Society. I cleared my lines with my old friend and tutor Professor John Northam, now back in retirement at Clare after his period of teaching drama at Bristol. I kept the senior tutor, Simon Franklin, informed and invited three bright undergraduates to become the first president, secretary and treasurer of the revived society. The idea was that someone would present a paper not on their own specialised subject, thus 'dilettante', which would be followed by a discussion in which undergraduates, graduates and dons would all take part on an equal basis. Bob Hepple spoke on 'Is Mandela a great man?' Our first treasurer, Gagan Sood, did research in the college archives and corresponded with former students, producing a brief history of the society. It had been founded in the college in 1882, had flourished in the 1930s and had existed under Northam in the 1950s in my time. As I write, the revived society has now kept going for 16 years. I have finally handed over my responsibility as unofficial patron to another Fellow of the college. I insisted on a record being kept of meetings. A tradition in the society started of an annual dinner, with a prominent guest. My main achievement has been to ensure that a new team of undergraduates take over at the end of each year. It is too easy for such societies to expire when organisers move on. I have given talks myself, sometimes filling in for someone who had to pull out, on: 'The history of Afghanistan' (that was after 9/11); 'What novels students read and what they should read' (deliberately provocative); and 'The fascination of numbers in world cultural and religious history'.

Among other college societies Clare Actors survives from year to year as an undergraduate group, traditionally performing Shakespeare in the sunken garden at the end of the summer term. (I had performed for them several times when an undergraduate.) In general I have found that amateur theatre in Cambridge has become much more fragmented than when I was a student. Meaning that there are a greater number of independent productions mounted, many of which are of uneven quality. Less reliance can be placed on the long-established groups such as the Marlowe Society and the ADC. The Mummers have virtually disappeared.

In Clare the Picture Guild of which I had been a keen member in my day barely survives. Gone are the days when undergraduates would organise significant exhibitions in the college. The college is still poorly off for pictures. For many years now, however, it has been in the forefront in music. It was one of the first three men's colleges to admit women. The mixed choir soon had a high reputation. The composer John Rutter was director of music for a time and his successor, Tim Brown, served the college in that capacity for over 30 years, only retiring in 2010. The college is so well known for music that aspiring Cambridge undergraduates with musical talent are keen to gain admittance even though they may be biochemists, philosophers, or language scholars. Evensong at Clare, with a well-planned service, is usually inspiring. Around the table at a farewell lunch I gave for Brown at the Athenaeum were conductors Roger Norrington and Ivor Bolton. John Rutter had to leave a little early to sort out the music for the marriage of Prince William, for which he not only wrote the anthem but adapted (unpaid!) all of the Parry music for the restricted orchestra. A couple of the brilliant young college organ scholars were also present, together with my old Reptonian friend and former organ scholar Martin How, plus Tim's worthy young successor.

At Clare I felt proud to be part of a tradition that went back for centuries. Older Fellows of distinction whom I came to know and admire included Professor Nick Hammond, the Greek historian, who had been an influential senior tutor at Clare before going off to be headmaster of Clifton College. He had parachuted bravely into Greece during World War II. I used to sit next to him in chapel. He was proud of his Jersey ancestry. King Edward VII's mistress Lily Langtry, the 'Jersey Lily', was a relation. He told me that his grandfather's prestige would rise when Lily came to visit him in his college rooms. Then there was Kurt Lipstein. He came from a well-known German-Jewish banking family, managing to get out of Germany before World War II. He never saw his parents again. He was a man of encylopaedic knowledge of law as it was practised around the world, revered by lawyers Europe-wide, where he spoke all the languages. He was the sort of man, as I remember

Arnold Toynbee whom I had got to know when he visited Kabul, who was always interested in what you had to say. He continued supervising students until a few weeks before his death in his late 90s! I joined the procession of Fellows to the service in chapel in his honour.

Honorary Fellows made periodic visits. David Attenborough is as impressive, and yet modest, as might be expected from one of the most admired people in British public life. Professor Jim Watson, co-discoverer with Crick of the double-helix key to life, I found amusing and interesting, rather than abrasive as some have found. He told me he was convinced that DNA would eventually explain all human attributes. It was a privilege to sit at dinner next to one of the great men of the last century and to be present when he gave the college a double-helix sculpture erected on the lawns of the Memorial Court. Rosalin Franklin, who was not given the Nobel Prize because they are never given posthumously, was recorded on the plinth and was represented by her sister, as well as by her nephew Clare Fellow now Professor of Russian Simon Franklin.

Rowan Williams, appointed Archbishop of Canterbury, was made an Honorary Fellow (not surprisingly) and kept in touch with the college where he had been dean. I have already mentioned how much respect I had for another former dean, the Rev Professor Charlie Moule. When I retired he was in a nursing home for clergymen in Somerset near where my friend Peter Barbor lived. We went to visit him on a couple of occasions. He was adored by everyone around him – alert, bright and emanating cheerful sanctity. He asked me at one point whether I was still interested in drawing since he remembered that I had told him about a picture that I was doing of my sister. That was 50 years before!

One special service in the chapel every year was in honour of benefactors, of whom the greatest was, of course, Lady Clare herself, the granddaughter of Edward I. She had started to rescue the college financially ten years after its foundation in 1326 and eventually gave it her name and statutes. She had lost three husbands, thus the tears around her distinctive shield. Having inherited great estates she took a vow of chastity to prevent her being married off again by her uncle the King. In maturity she became a benign and respected royal family member looked up to by her juniors. Everyone enjoyed the phrase she had used in the college statutes saying that her purpose had been for students to 'discover and acquire the precious pearl of learning'. This was

at the time of the Black Death when many scholars had been swept away
by the plague, especially in East Anglia.

Professor Hepple asked me to give the address at the Benefactors
Service one year, which gave me an opportunity to talk about my beliefs,
with advice for the young, not dissimilar to some of the ideas I had used
in speech day addresses in Pakistan. When I sent a copy of the text to
my old friend Donald Reeves, rector of St James's Church, Piccadilly, he
insisted that I should give a sermon in his church. I enjoyed giving my
first and last sermon in that friendly liberal environment (text is at the
appendix). I sent copies to one or two people. Those expressing
approval included Lord Runcie, Donald Maitland, who had been my
first boss in the Private Office, and David Manning (then ambassador at
Tel Aviv). Bishop Malek of Lahore said that on the basis of the sermon
he would be happy to have me as an ordained member of his diocese!
My evangelical nephew was critical. A passage from the sermon about
the moderation and humanity of most Muslims world-wide was quoted
in a seminal Runnymede Trust paper on Islamophobia. It was typical of
Donald's regime that there were questions after the sermon which led to
discussion. He had started the service by taking the communion wafer
and waving it as a gesture to welcome Hindu and Muslim and Jewish
friends, an approach with which I sympathised.

Readers may think that I am a conventional middle-of-the-road
Anglican but I have to admit that I espouse what may be thought of as
dangerously radical theological ideas! Traditional Christian concepts are,
in my view, unnecessarily complex, starting with the Trinity. My
Muslim friends accept that the words of the Qur'an – illogically arranged
in order of the length of chapters rather than period of inspiration –
came directly from God when given to his (probably illiterate) prophet.
But God as they know him, Allah, is one and indivisible. That is a
simple concept, easy to grasp, like that of the Jewish God. The
Egyptians, Greeks and Hindus in contrast had multiple gods, though
some were more important than others. The Trinity confuses our
Muslim friends, many of whom think it must consist of God, Mary and
Jesus. It also confuses me. I believe in one God, the creator of the
cosmos, who is Allah and Buddha, and maybe Shiva and even Zeus. He
is also Jesus, who is God incarnate. I am happy to accept that God is
unknowable to puny mortals, unlikely to be a white-bearded gentlemen
sitting on a cloud. I believe, with little evidence I confess, that God takes

a personal interest in this world and in me individually. In order to show the world something of what he/she is like he came to earth in human form at a certain point in time, as Christ. What does not make sense to me is that Jesus is portrayed by the Church as going up to Heaven and sitting on the right hand of his father. But he is the incarnation of God! How can God sit beside himself?

I know this is dangerous theological territory about the human or divine nature of Christ and I am not just trying to be clever. When I was an undergraduate, admiring old books, I bought from a second-hand bookshop a two-volume edition of *Paradise Lost*, with clear print and exquisite illustrations, printed in 1749 (one of them was wielded by Prospero in Islamabad). For the Milton anniversary in 2009 the library at Christ College Cambridge, where Milton was an undergraduate, included two similar editions in a special exhibition. The University's English faculty put on a reading that year of the whole of *Paradise Lost*. One day, from morning till late in the evening, members of the faculty took it in turns to read right through the story. I was able with my nephew Andrew and others to go along and listen, following the text in my book. For the first time I had the feeling that I grasped the essence of Milton's story.

In some ways Satan is the hero. At least he is the principal character. He felt betrayed because he had thought that he was God's favoured deputy, only to find God announcing that Jesus was henceforth to be his right hand. Full of resentment and jealousy Satan took his diabolical troops away into Hell. The story certainly suggests that God and Jesus were separate identities. In getting back at God by trying to damage his new project, the earth, Satan, in serpent form, is very plausible in saying to Eve, who had wandered off out of Adam's view, that the tree of knowledge should not be forbidden to anyone, since knowledge must be a good thing. I like the bit where Eve, having realised her mistake in taking the apple, urges Adam to save himself and disown her but Adam refuses, saying that they have been loving partners since the beginning and he will not abandon her.

And what is the need, frankly, for the Holy Spirit? (I cringe, fearing a bolt from the blue!) In my view, if God wants to do something on earth, he can do it; he does not need an amorphous separate entity called the Holy Spirit as his agent. I cannot myself conceive of the Holy Spirit as visually separate from God, for instance as a dove, as he, she or it is sometimes depicted. I used to be amused by a French verse about a bonhomme de Dijon 'qui n'aimait pas beaucoup la religion – ni le pere, ni le fils, ni le pigeon'! For me therefore, the Holy Spirit is again confusing. Perhaps it is something to do with the special number three? What anyway was Jesus doing for three days after his crucifixion before going up to Heaven? I am told that not believing in the Holy Spirit as a separate entity from God I may be called not a unitarian but a bi-nitarian, but it does not appear in my dictionaries.

Finally, having already offended many of my friends, I must say that though I love christenings as a Christian family commitment to the church, and I deplore the way too many children are not christened these days, I cannot accept that little children are inherently sinful until they are christened. My Muslim friends can't understand this doctrine either. Little children are surely the essence of innocence. Someone once said that they should immediately start suing their parents for bringing them into this wicked and corrupt world! The reader will appreciate that I would welcome it if the basics of Christian belief could be simplified so that they have a better chance of being understood and followed in an increasingly secular world.

On the clerical theme I should mention the pleasure that I have enjoyed in Cambridge through association with the cathedral at Ely. The services there are comparatively High Church in that majestic ancient building, only half an hour's drive from Cambridge. It stands on an island in the Fens, surrounded by a modest town. If the cathedral had only been half the size it would still have been an amazing achievement for those craftsmen of the twelfth century. I first got involved with Ely through the grandson of friends of my parents, who was in the choir. I went on a 'son et lumière' music tour during which a group of about 50 people moved between different parts of the cathedral, in each case with an historical explanation and a different choral presentation. After that experience I was easy game to join up as a member of the Order of St Etheldreda, a brilliant fundraising concept by Dean Michael Higgins, based on the name of the Saxon princess who founded the original building. Committing themselves to pay a certain amount of money every year enables members of the Order to feel that they are part of the cathedral family.

Functions are arranged including topical talks. I gave a talk there about 'A Diplomat's Experience of Christianity and other Faiths', similar to a talk I had given in Islington. At my suggestion David Ramsbotham, my old army and university friend, retired senior general who became an admired chief inspector of prisons, came and spoke eloquently about the need to rehabilitate prisoners. Field Marshal Peter Inge, cousin of one of the canons whose installation as bishop of Worcester I later attended, made a memorable remark in a talk he gave about Western alliances. He said he had been told that on joining the army there were three things to avoid: (1) never march to Moscow, (2) never get involved in the Balkans, and (3) never trust your baggage to the RAF! The cathedral is now in excellent repair. I attended a remarkable millenium banquet in year 2000 for 400 people seated down the nave to mark the completion of a major stage of the development programme. It was presided over by the Duke of Edinburgh who had been patron of the appeal. I remember something he said in his speech too. Talking about the repair of Windsor Castle after the fire, he said that one of the workmen would point up at the ceiling and ask visitors to admire the 'embezzlement'! Compare a new preacher being shown the microphone in a church pulpit and being warned that 'The agnostics here are terrible'!

More recently Ely has been concerned to raise money for music. I suggested that John Rutter be involved. On a special occasion he gave a talk about his interest in and devotion to choral music, including a delightful reference to continuity with the past. As a child he had met the composer Howells, responsible for much fine choral music, who had himself as a child met another of the great church composers, Stanford. Stanford as a child had met Brahms, and Brahms as a child had met Beethoven. John pointed out that he was therefore only four handshakes away from the great composer!

My own idea was to try and encourage better relations between music at Ely, inevitably restricted because of the modest size of the local community, and the outstanding music available in the Cambridge colleges. At my instigation an event was staged in which the Ely choir performed with choirs from Clare and Trinity, the first time this had happened with two colleges for over 50 years. Funds were raised. I hoped that the successful occasion would be repeated as an annual event, with different college choirs each time. That plan faltered in subsequent years but it looks as if it is being revived.

Involvement with Ely brought me into contact with a group of people whom one might call the Cambridgeshire county set, headed by the Lord Lieutenant, a man of quiet distinction. It has helped enlarge my horizons in Cambridge and enhanced my pleasure of living in the city.

Probably my most significant achievement after retirement was linked with Cambridge. I had kept up with Archbishop Runcie, who had paid a successful visit to Islamabad when I was there, had retired in 1991 and was now Lord Runcie. He got me involved in a committee to raise money for the Divinity Faculty in Cambridge, which needed to move from its old Victorian building in the centre of town to a new site alongside other arts faculties west of the Cam. He asked if I would chair the committee but I demurred. I wasn't sure what my commitments might be but said I would be happy to help. Runcie then chaired the committee himself working closely with the senior Professor of Divinity, the Regius Professor, David Ford. The latter was an Irish Anglican, the first holder of this ancient post who was not ordained. He had a consistent vision for expanding the work of the faculty to embrace studies of other world religions. This was an objective which I fully supported, examining what these religions have in common as well as what divides them. There were a few businessmen on the committee. Also Susan Howatch, a successful novelist of stories with a religious theme who had already given a million pounds to the university to create a post combining science and theology. Another member was Michael McCrum, former headmaster of Eton and master of Corpus Christi College, who became a good friend, cemented when we had similar prostate problems. I sat in on discussions about plans for the new building, noting how important it was in such projects for the architect personally to convince clients of the value of his design. The structure was duly completed and suits its purpose well. I can take no credit for that.

My contribution was in finding a source of money for a new post as lecturer in Islamic studies. I was determined it should be from a mainstream Islamic source, that is not from Saudi Wahabis, nor from Shias. Following contacts I identified a likely source as the Sheikh Zaid Foundation in Abu Dhabi. I cultivated the admirable Egyptian director Dr Ezzuddin Ibrahim, who was delighted to have a way of supporting Islamic studies in the UK. It helped that Runcie visited Abu Dhabi on a tour of the Gulf. At one point over lunch at the Athenaeum Dr Ezzuddin told me that a substantial donation was being lined up but that to clinch the matter it would be a great help if the Duke of Edinburgh, as Chancellor of the University, could write to Sheikh Zaid himself.

In bureaucratic mode I duly sent a letter to the Vice-Chancellor, Sir David Williams, Cambridge's first permanent vice-chancellor (i.e. not a master of a college taking turns in rotation) who couldn't have been more helpful. I enclosed a draft letter for him to send to the Duke and another draft for the latter to send to the Sheikh. Prince Philip made his letter more personal but it did the trick. It was a good example of how he took his role at Cambridge seriously and achieved results. Enough money was forthcoming to fund a lectureship in Islamic studies in perpetuity. In fact the Foundation had been prepared to pay more for a full professorship, but the University only wanted a lectureship at this stage. Details were finalised during a visit by Dr Ezzuddin to Cambridge, where we made a fuss of him: special Islamic exhibits on display at the Fitzwilliam Museum and the University Library and dinner with the Bishop of Ely.

One issue had been delicate. The Sheikh Zaid Foundation naturally wanted a say in the choice of candidate, to assure themselves that money had been well spent. On its part the University insisted on their academic autonomy, to ensure the requisite academic standard. The solution was for the Foundation to nominate someone to sit on the Faculty's selection board. It helped that an academic at Cambridge who liked to argue against the historic validity of the Qur'an moved elsewhere at this time. Even within the university there were difficulties: The Oriental Faculty were inclined to think that the post should lie with them. The candidate should of course know good Arabic. At one point I had said that unless the various faculties could reach agreement I was going to give up trying to raise money. Eventually the Oriental Faculty also had a hand in the selection process.

Tim Winter, a good Arabist who had been educated at Westminster and converted to Islam, was chosen to fill the post, to everyone's satisfaction. He has proved to be a source of sound and balanced Islamic scholarship for the University and wider in Britain. In due course he initiated an admirable project to establish the first Muslim college at the University, a theological college at Cambridge for qualified British imams, teaching them how to operate pastorally in a British environment. I was invited to give a talk there about my experience as a diplomat. They were a small lively group, mostly young British Pakistanis, including ladies, who knew more about Britain than about their families' country of origin.

It was natural that I had contacts with the Oriental Faculty, since I got to know those teaching Persian. At one stage someone in the University's management structure decided that 'oriental' was an old-fashioned perjorative term and that the Faculty should be restructured, including Near-East and Far-East elements, leaving a gap in the middle where the study of south Asia, Afghanistan and Central Asia should have been. It was already disgraceful that in a university such as Cambridge there was no longer a professor of Sanskrit. As far as nomenclature was concerned the School of Oriental and African Studies operated without problems in London. Along with many academics and scholars I found that as a MA I could put on a gown and protest at the proposed change at a formal session in the Senate House. But it did no good. There was a centre of South Asian Studies, mainly dealing with modern post-colonial history, but it was not part of the formal Faculty structure. I still believe that given the importance of India and the rest of south Asia, including Afghanistan, as well as the size of the British Asian community in the UK, more efforts should have been made to develop a range of South Asian Studies including history, language and art history, at Cambridge University.

The institution in Cambridge with which I became most involved, as a trustee, fulfilled some of these functions but was not formally part of the university structure. This was the Ancient India and Iran Trust, housed in an old Victorian building on Brooklands Avenue in a spacious garden. I have already mentioned my contacts with the archaeologists Drs Raymond and Bridget Allchin, who had invited me to become a trustee. They were two of the five co-founders of the Trust. Its area of activities covered the Indian subcontinent, Iran and Central Asia, places where I had served. The Trust receives no public money, since the founders were determined to preserve their independence. It operates economically on a minimum budget. I was fortunate enough to see something of Sir Harold Bailey, the senior of the co-founders, during the years before he died in his 90s, still working on Caucasian languages. He had been Professor of Sanskrit, with an encyclopaedic knowledge of the languages of Asia, ancient and modern – a gentle character, generous in sharing his knowledge. His unique collection of books and manuscripts was the core of the library in the old house, where he had lived himself until he died.

A programme of lectures and seminars, all in an hospitable, informal atmosphere, covers the early history and archaeology of the area, Indian and Islamic art history, religions such as Zoroastrianism, Buddhism and Manichaeism as well as early Iranian languages. Few of these subjects, if any, are included in the regular university syllabus. I have found many of the topics fascinating and enjoyed meeting the scholars concerned, including a number who came from abroad such was the Trust's reputation. In due course planning and fundraising for an extension to the library with an up-to-date lecture room which could seat more than 40 has taken a great deal of time in discussion with fellow trustees. There has been no real success so far. On this issue, as on others, I have valued the advice and friendship of one of the most prominent and respected members of the British-Pakistani community, Sir Anwar Pervez.

In 2003 I myself organised a seminar at the Trust on 'The Hindu Kush, a strange mixture of peoples and languages', which allowed me to invite specialists on Nuristan, including my surviving companion on the Nuristan journey in 1960, the German diplomat Reinhard Schlagintweit. Some time before J.T. Kendrick, our American diplomat colleague, had come for a year's study in Cambridge after retirement. The three of us had kept in contact and, at Kendrick's prompting, decided to pool our records and photographs to put an account of our remarkable journey of 1960, inside what had become a lost world, into the public domain. It was agreed that my narrative, the report to London that my ambassador in Kabul had instructed me to sit down and write after my return, should be the heart of the book. It gave some colour to the story and I did not change it. An old friend of my sister had helped preserve it by typing the faded flimsy copy in my possession. The Foreign Office, when consulted, didn't object; in fact they admitted that their copy was missing!

Since Reinhardt and I were busy, it was at first left to J.T. to produce an introduction, history and bibliography, but corrections were needed to his draft. I felt it necessary to fly out to Vail, Colorado and stay with him for a few days to sort it out. His house had a good view of wooded hills and ski slopes. There was little food in the kitchen. He operated on an eccentric limited diet. I took him for shopping in the local supermarket. On return he found that he had locked himself out. Friends got us inside. In long sessions we agreed on all the main elements in the book. Since J.T. had no success in finding a US publisher, it was agreed that I should continue to ask my friend Iradj Bagherzade of I.B.Tauris in London to have a look at it. Eventually he was persuaded, categorising the material, quite reasonably, as a 'pot pourri'. He was reluctant to list three authors, but I felt at least I had to share that role with Kendrick. Reinhard left all the drafting to us, but the three of us each produced a passage looking back on our experience. I worked hard at the essential maps and much of the rest of the text, including a condensed summary of 2,500 years of Afghan history in 11 sides of print! I enjoyed the research involved. A cousin of J.T. who lived not far from Cambridge acted as liaison with the Kendrick family and helped greatly in setting out the clean copy to be provided to the publisher.

Schlagintweit's black and white photographs were the best. One of my own colour photographs of a village *malek* (headman) set against an area of wild flowers high up in the Hindu Kush was chosen as the cover picture. This was at the far side of a difficult snow and ice col that we reckoned had been traversed by no Europeans before. I.B.Tauris chose the clever title: *A Passage to Nuristan*. The book was dedicated to Kendrick who sadly died in 1993, three years before publication. He had locked himself out once more and fallen trying to climb in. I wish he had seen the final version. Sandy Gall kindly wrote a preface.

I still find people who say that they have read and enjoyed the book. As it happened, years later, when going through a series of old boxes in my garage I discovered a bundle of old slides that included some photographs that would have been in the book if we had had access to them. This has been an opportunity to reproduce a few of them.

13

ACTIVITIES IN LONDON

In London I put out feelers to a number of charitable organisations. In view of my thespian background and links with a couple of their trustees, I offered to become involved with the Almeida Theatre, which was acquiring a good reputation in Islington. They stonewalled my letter, probably thinking I was pushy. As a result I was happy to let them know that I was giving a reasonably generous donation to Sadler's Wells down the road who were about to reconstruct the old theatre! It was a pleasure having contact with Ian Albery, leading the project, son of the well-known theatre owner, and to a lesser extent with Valerie Solti, widow of the conductor. My contribution was limited. I argued for the need to follow Lilian Baylis's concept of providing affordable theatrical entertainment for areas of London outside the West End. We had some success in keeping prices low and in attracting local Islington support. I tried to use my knowledge of and contacts with Japanese theatre to make Sadler's Wells the main base for all types of Japanese theatre coming to London. It didn't quite take off – a more sustained effort would have been needed with Tokyo and local Japanese firms in London. But Kabuki comes to Sadler's Wells, which I have much enjoyed and taken parties of friends to see. Also the minimalist Japanese theatre 'Butoh'. The new Sadler's Wells building may not be beautiful but it works well and flourishes.

I also became an early supporter of the Globe, helped by meeting the great Sam Wanamaker on one of my visits to the site. What an achievement it was for him, battling through bureaucratic regulations in another country. It is a pity that the building is so authentic that the seats are uncomfortable, but it is a great arena for theatre, a tribute to traditional Shakespeare that London needs.

I took an interest in several societies dealing with Asia. It was natural that I should resume contact with the Pakistan Society, of which I was a life member. (My father had given me the economically judicious advice, years before, to become a life member of organisations where possible while you are young.) The Society was chaired by my predecessor but one in Islamabad, Sir Oliver Forster, a popular figure who was also involved with aid to Afghanistan. It staged a successful annual dinner every year in Lincolns Inn, where Jinnah and Iqbal had studied, but was otherwise rather moribund. It consisted mainly of old hands reaching back to Empire days. The secretary, Mary Stafford, whom I had known as the wife of the war-wounded deputy High Commissioner in Lahore when I was in Rawalpindi in the 1960s, treated it as a gathering of her personal friends. She did not even allow members of the committee, which I joined, to have lists of members 'in case they got into wrong hands and were exploited commercially'! An extreme example of the theory behind the wretched Data Protection Act which prevents organisations disseminating perfectly harmless information. There were few lectures and little attempt to reach out to the increasingly important British-Pakistani community. A main objective became to persuade Mary to retire. Eventually we found a good successor ready to take the job on. I helped organise a farewell lunch at the Athenaeum at which we presented a print to Mary as a retirement gift. But her words of thanks indicated, to our dismay, that she looked forward to staying on! I am afraid that we had to change the locks in the little office and try to recover the papers at Mary's home, all the time saying how genuinely grateful we were for all her work over the years. Not a nice business. I have never been good at dismissing people, which may suggest a kind disposition, but certainly indicates a management weakness.

When Forster died I was reluctant to commit myself to spending more time on the society. The Pakistan High Commissioner at the time, Akbar Ahmad, persuaded Richard Fyjis-Walker (my predecessor in Islamabad) to be chairman, which he said he would do for a year, after which I agreed to take over for a limited period until I could find a successor. My assumption of office coincided with President Musharraf's military takeover in Pakistan in 1999, of which I disapproved. As a rather pathetic unpublicised protest I said I would therefore become only the acting chairman. We stepped up the lectures and other activities and livened up the committee. One of my achievements was to give more responsibility to one of the committee members who became treasurer and has provided the backbone of the society ever since. We organised a major seminar on investment in Pakistan and a successful event promoting tourism to Pakistan, but we probably overran ourselves: some excellent talks on managing international cricket, on plant collection in the Deosai planes and on the Brook Hospital for sick animals, a great success in Pakistan, attracted a disappointing response. Numbers of talks had to be scaled down.

I was in charge for two significant annual dinners: One where the Duke of Edinburgh, our British patron, had agreed to be the chief guest but was held up by an overrunning royal visit to Canada. The Duke of York nobly agreed to come at short notice and filled in well. The next year Prince Philip did come, arrived in good time, and was able to talk to almost all those present. His speech, loosely based on our draft, was well received. In winding up the speeches I was able to pay him tribute, attending the dinner as he was in the middle of his 80th birthday celebrations. I praised his contributions to public life over the years in pioneering such causes as playing fields for schools, science and the environment – often ahead of the time.

I believe there is still a need for a national Pakistan Society, a mother organisation linking the other Pakistan societies around the country, which should work with the Pakistan High Commission but should be independent of it. It should be run by a committee balanced between members of the British-Pakistani community and other British people who are not of Pakistan origin but who have academic, commercial, diplomatic or personal connections with Pakistan, including those who have travelled there.

My own support for Pakistan, after my retirement, was appreciated by most Pakistan High Commissioners in London. It was not unconditional; I did not always agree with Pakistan government policy. But there was, I felt, a continuing need to remind decision-makers in Britain that Pakistan, though not as large nor as important as India, was still a very significant country. Press coverage of Pakistan was not as good as it should be, given the country's strategic position and the numbers of people in the UK who have links with Pakistan. Coverage by journalists based in Delhi could never be entirely satisfactory. I persuaded the Pakistan Society to institute an annual award presented at the dinner for someone who had advanced public knowledge and understanding of Pakistan in the UK, an idea I borrowed from the Japan Society, of which I was also a member. Among worthy recipients were my writer friends Isabel Shaw and Victoria Schofield, and, before he died, birdman Tom Roberts. I was usually consulted about candidates even after I had given up the chairmanship. In 2009 they didn't contact me. I thought this was because I was past history. They surprised me by giving the award to me, which I found embarrassing. I had never had that outcome in mind.

More embarrassing was the suggestion made to me in the years after my retirement that I might be given a Pakistan national award. If the subject was mentioned I had always said that I was grateful for the thought but not interested. I did not want to be beholden to the Pakistan government in any way. I needed to be able to criticise them in public if necessary. I did reproach Pakistan for allowing Afghan Taliban leaders to use Quetta as a base and I have never hidden my disgust at the way Bin Laden must have obtained some high-level sanction to live in Pakistan. In any case I would point out that British diplomats were not allowed to accept foreign decorations (except, rather strangely, during state visits) on the principle enunciated by Queen Elizabeth I that 'I will not allow my dogs to wear other people's collars.' One normally responsible Pakistan envoy in London, however, recommended to Islamabad that I should be given the award of the Sitara-e-Qaid-e-Azam, without consulting me. It was announced in Islamabad and subsequently, to my surprise, I received congratulations. It was then pointed out to the Pakistanis that the British government had to be consulted through the protocol section of the Foreign Office before awards could be given to British subjects. On instructions I had to decline it formally. A frustrating episode, but it had been conceived in kindness.

One link with Pakistan that I have valued after retirement has been as trustee of the Noon Educational Foundation, undertaken at the personal request of its founder, Lady Vicky Noon. She was a larger than life character whom I met during my first tour in Pakistan and found rather formidable. She was married to the wheelchair-bound former prime minister, Sir Firoz Khan Noon. I got to know her later, as a widow, in the 1980s when I began to appreciate that under the sparkle and social charm, Vicky Noon was completely committed to helping her adopted country of Pakistan in many ways. Noon himself, a Punjabi landowner of impeccable reputation, had been High Commissioner for the Government of India in London before World War II, at times a member of the Viceroy's Council and of Churchill's Commonwealth War Cabinet. He had married the beautiful young Vicky, who had been born in Austria but had been educated and grown up in England, before independence, when he was already knighted. She continued her activities with educational and social charities after Firoz's death. For many years she was a widely admired chair of Pakistan's Red Crescent (Red Cross) organisation. President Zia subsequently asked her to become head of Pakistan's Tourist Development Corporation, in which post she made a considerable impact. For a time she was also ambassador to Portugal.

When her only relative, her sister, had died in England without children and left her money, Vicky, who had no children of her own, used the money to found the Noon Trust, to encourage Pakistanis to go to Oxford and Cambridge, as her husband and his friends had been able to do. She added more money of her own, in her will. Her aim was to counter, in a small way, the growing trend for Pakistanis to go to US universities. Noon trustees met once a year to decide how to allocate funds to the most deserving and needy candidates. These have to have secured admission beforehand. Criteria include that they should not have had the chance to study abroad before and that they plan to return to work in Pakistan. When I joined, Dr Homayun Khan, former Pakistan High Commissioner in London, was chairman. (He was the director then of the Commonwealth Foundation, the most senior Pakistani to hold a Commonwealth post.) He was succeeded by Dr Paul Flather, son of Baroness Shreila, whom I had enjoyed meeting in Islamabad. Paul had an office in Oxford (I had no such backing). It was a pleasure to be associated with a select group of British and Pakistani individuals who gave up some of their time voluntarily to carry on Vicky's work. She died in 2000. Trustees included a member of the Noon family and two distinguished academics: Professor Harun Ahmed, Professor of Microelectronics in Cambridge and Master of Corpus Christi College, who had come to Britain as a child, and Dame Louise Johnson, Professor of Molecular Biophysics at Oxford, widow of Pakistan's famous Nobel-winning scientist, Abdus Salam. A new trustee who gave us useful financial advice was a Pakistani businessman Ehsan Mani, from a Rawalpindi family that I had known since earlier times. From 2003 to 2006 he was the respected president of the International Cricket Council.

Some retired diplomats prefer to cut themselves off from their past. One friend spent most of his time going to the opera. It is natural that some become deeply involved in family affairs. These were not options for me.

I am a life member of the Iran Society which continues to thrive, though naturally avoiding politics. There remains plenty of cultural and historical interest in Iran. Lectures are well attended. I gave a talk there on my experience of 'The pleasures of Persian poetry' for which I put together a number of my favourite verses collected over a period of years, with a brief account of a few of the best-known Persian poets. It was a chance to parade for public consumption some of the telling expressions encapsulated in Persian, which I have loved to quote, for instance the line: 'Karshtand ta khorim. Karim ta khorand', translated as 'They sowed so we should eat. We must sow so that they (in the future) can eat.' A very succinct ecological statement. Also plenty of philosophical and lyrical poetry, much of which I know by heart. For this event I was glad to see in the audience my old respected mentor Sir Denis Wright. He was a classic example of a retired diplomat who had engaged in worthwhile historical research.

It was partly at his suggestion and that of my former teacher Professor Lambton, who also approved of my poetry paper in her undemonstrative way, that I joined the council of the British Institute of Persian Studies (BIPS). They thought it important that this organisation, linked to the British Academy, was not entirely run by academics. BIPS was the beneficiary of a modest government subsidy to encourage academic exchanges with Iran. It had a building in Tehran next to the Embassy compound at Golhak, with a library and accommodation facilities. In 1994 the chairman was my close friend and former fellow Persian student Desmond Harney who had retired both from government service and from Morgan Grenfall, and had become active in local government politics in London. He and his wife now lived in a tiny Cotswold village with a view over a lush green valley, where it was always a pleasure to stay. Sadly, Desmond wrote to me in 2000 saying he had 'hit the buffers'. He died of an incurable brain tumour at 71. I gave the memorial address at a crowded Kensington church talking about his background and career in government. He had made a mark in Iran. I reminded the congregation of his important book which had been a diary of the Iranian revolution of which he had been a well-informed firsthand observer. It had pleased Desmond that his book had also been published in Iran with only minor excisions. No payment of course to the author! I praised his brilliant photography which merited a book on its own. Desmond and his wife Judy had also served with great distinction in Kenya in the early days of independence, at the time of Kenyatta. It was there that two of his children had settled, including my godson Richard, who became a successful local lawyer.

I postponed joining the council of BIPS because I had been invited, for a year or so after retirement, to sit on the British Academy's Standing Committee on Schools and Institutes (i.e., the academic institutes around the world supported by the Academy). Our chairman was the strong-minded former director of the British Museum, Sir David Wilson, expert on the Vikings and resident in the Isle of Man (and the Athenaeum). The influential secretary of the Academy must have discovered that I was a retired ambassador interested in archaeology. Most of the funds were spent on the substantial British schools in Athens and Rome. In view of the political situation in Iraq and Iran it was tempting to starve archaeological work in those countries. I did my best to inject common sense into the debate and to allow the institute in Tehran, at least, to survive. Academic links with Iran prospered in succeeding years although the British government's close support of our US ally's anti-Iranian policies eventually led to the closure of the British Council in Iran. In the absence of any US representation in Tehran, British activities were always vulnerable to explosions of anti-Western sentiment.

Through BIPS I got to see something of the wider activities of the British Academy, which moved from a site near Regents Park to the much more accessible Carlton House Terrace, taking over the property which had been subsidised by the Foreign Office for the Foreign Press Association. The Academy, which covers arts subjects, was now sited near its much better known sister, the Royal Society, the temple of science. At BIPS council meetings I was sometimes a lone voice arguing for more attention to be given to the study of Persian literature as well as archaeological and historical projects. The pre-eminent British scholar in this field, my old friend, Peter Avery, whom I had known since 1958, was not an institution man and now rarely moved from his rooms at King's College, Cambridge across the path from the chapel. He was still producing books about Persian poetry. For a time I used to join a group of people sitting at his feet on Sunday mornings while he worked through poems of Hafez. Peter drank and smoked too much for his health. I was one of the last people to visit him before he died in 2008.

He was given a magnificent send-off by the Fellows of Kings in their great chapel, which he would have enjoyed. Unfortunately his special library was split up.

On the subject of Persian literature I must record an event which took place in Woodbridge in 1995 near the home in Suffolk of my sister and brother-in-law. I have already mentioned that close friends of theirs lived in a fine house and garden which had once been the home of Edward Fitzgerald, the gentleman scholar who was author of *The Rubaiyat*, his free translation of the poetry of Omar Khayyam. With Martin and Penelope Bartlett I organised a party sitting on carpets over their lawn at which I spoke about the Persian poet and Penelope about Fitzgerald. We tried to serve Persian type food and some of us were in Persian attire. Among those who attended were Clement and Jill Freud. It was good to get to know the genial side of the sardonic wit who was Clement Freud and to be entertained and cooked for occasionally by that well-known gourmet.

Among others at the Woodbridge party was Dr Briscoe, over 90 years of age, who was a member of the Omar Khayyam Club in London. He subsequently invited me to one of their dinners, where I knew nobody. The poet John Heath-Stubbs, who had collaborated with Avery and had written a poem for the occasion, was sitting nearby. Most of the 40 people present looked to me like prosperous city executives, though several were writers and publishers. I was taken aback by the tradition, of which I had not been warned, that speakers, as well as toasting 'The Master', successively insulted the various guests! I wished afterwards that I had got up and quoted some of Khayyam in the original, which I doubt that any others present could have done. There was a good seminar about Khayyam and Fitzgerald in Cambridge in 2009 attracting those interested in Victorian as well as Persian literature. It was timed to coincide with the bicentenary of Fitzgerald's birth and 150 years after the publication of *The Rubaiyat*. My old Persophile friend Roger Cooper, former prisoner of the Ayatollahs, came and enjoyed himself. At a reception at the Ancient and Indian Trust linked with the seminar I was caught by a hidden television camera quoting the master in the original Persian, which pleased some of my Iranian friends.

Both in Cambridge and London one can spend hours attending interesting talks and lectures. A few years after retirement I saw myself in London as the main link between three academic societies dealing with Asia. Since returning from my first posting in Afghanistan I had been a member of the Royal Central Asian Society which developed into the Royal Society for Asian Affairs. High-quality talks, mostly illustrated, took place after an optional sandwich lunch and a glass of wine, first in a room at Burlington House and subsequently at premises in Belgrave Square. The audience was always well informed and ready with pertinent questions. Many were friends and former colleagues. I was asked to join the Council and enjoyed the experience. I gave a couple of talks myself on Iran and Afghanistan. By the time I was privately sounded out about becoming chairman, however, I had already served on the Council for a good period and was not very well. So I felt unable to make the full commitment that would have been necessary. It is no good doing such things in a half-hearted way. Instead I presented the Society with a display cabinet.

I became a Fellow of the Royal Asiatic Society, with a long pedigree originating in India where the lectures tended to be more academic and specialised. They were wealthy with art treasures but were reluctant to dispose of them.

The third organisation was Asia House, newly established in London. The idea of a cultural organisation dealing with Asia had been kicking around for many years, floated by the eccentric Hungarian collector Edmund de Unger in association with a group of people with background in museums, auction houses and trade in antiquities. The project only got off the ground, however, when they persuaded my old friend, counsellor in the embassy in Tokyo, Peter Wakefield, to become chairman of trustees in 1993. A Foreign Office Arabist, Sir Peter had served as ambassador to Lebanon, to Belgium and after retirement as head of the National Art Collections Fund. He had always had a wide interest in cultural matters – one of the reasons we got on so well.

The concept of Asia House, modelled on the Asia Society of New York, headed at this time by one of the best of my US colleagues from Islamabad, Ambassador Nicholas Platt, was that major commercial firms would be ready to subscribe to an organisation which could arrange high-level, off-the-record meetings with influential Asian leaders. These in turn would welcome such an audience. The money would help fund cultural activities including lectures and exhibitions. At Peter's invitation I joined the Executive and Cultural Committees only a few months after my retirement. I could provide some contacts and ideas especially on south Asia and give Peter support. It wasn't easy for him at the beginning. He was criticised for being too close to government and for choosing an ex-diplomat as director, although the need for such a post was vital. At that time the organisation operated from temporary offices in Piccadilly. A cultural programme began to get underway when a good cultural director was appointed. The 50th anniversary of Indian and Pakistan independence was soon upon us. I was able to help, on the Pakistan side, with fundraising for an ambitious dinner event in the Albert Hall in the presence of the Prince of Wales and the Aga Khan. There was good musical entertainment. Everything worked well and Asia House made a profit.

I was also closely involved with an Asia House book about Pakistan to coincide with the anniversary. I proposed Victoria Schofield as the editor. She was an authority on Kashmir, a friend of Benazir whom I had entertained in Islamabad. Together we commissioned different articles on aspects of the 50 years of Pakistan. I wrote a substantial foreword which reasonably stands the test of time. Victoria chose the good title *Old Roads, New Highways* and the cover design. A comparable book on India never got off the ground.

My main subsequent contribution for Asia House was to plan and bring to fruition an exhibition of 50 years of Pakistan art, based on knowledge of many artists and sculptors in Pakistan and my conviction that there was much outstanding work that was being done there that should be better known. Having first persuaded the Asia House committee, I then managed to convince the Director of SOAS (Tim Lancaster) that the Brunei Gallery would be the right venue. Their first reaction had been that Pakistan art was not of sufficient quality, which had made me angry! Working with contacts and fellow enthusiasts in the arts, business and museum world a professional curator was chosen and initial sponsorship obtained. In February 1999 I visited Pakistan mainly to accompany Tim Wilcox the curator and introduce him to artists and collectors. The landscape painter Ghulam Rasul, director of the National Council of the Arts, was very ready to facilitate but not to try and control, since several volatile Pakistani painters distrusted anything to do with the government. Everyone was helpful and generous with hospitality, including Pakistani friends who define what it is to be erudite. I finally met the elusive star painter, Jamil Naqsh.

We obtained pictures from the North-West Frontier Province and Baluchistan, as well as from the main cultural hubs of Lahore and Karachi. I had to leave selection to the curator. I would have preferred even more paintings by earlier masters but the experimental work was in tune with current taste – including calligraphic items and modern miniatures, a field pioneered by Pakistani artists. Wilcox's attractive illustrated catalogue with the appropriate title 'Pakistan, Another Vision', carried an arresting cover of a figure plunging downwards, hopefully not into debt! In fact sponsorship covered costs.

In the spring of 2000 a crowded private view was opened with a splash by Princess Alexandra. The Pakistan High Commissioner was there with a visiting minister and representatives of sponsoring organisations. The rooms on two floors were full of colour and interest, popular with visitors and acclaimed by word of mouth. There was an associated seminar and a children's event. National press coverage was disappointing. Perhaps people found it difficult to believe that something modern and positive was coming out of Pakistan. Indian art had taken off in preceding years thanks to a healthy domestic market. Art also sold well inside Pakistan, so much so that artists kept little stock and collectors were reluctant to lend. It may be too much to claim that our exhibition was a major breakthrough but at least it did help to make Pakistani art better known internationally.

To continue the Asia House story Wakefield, with the help of high-level banking contacts, eventually managed to secure sizeable interest-free loans to purchase the long lease of a building with fine rooms to the north of Oxford Circus, where the organisation has been active. (After a fallow period following Peter Wakefield's funeral in south London snow, Asia House seemed to be embarking on a new lease of life in 2012 under the chairmanship of my friend John Boyd.) I had hoped at one time that the three main institutions dealing with Asia could be co-located, with coordinated activities and economies of scale, but it was not to happen. The Royal Asiatic Society moved from Paddington to a more convenient site near Euston and the Royal Society for Asian Affairs moved from Belgrave Square to near Victoria.

A few years after the Brunei exhibition I found myself organising a more modest collection of paintings for a local audience which gave me great satisfaction. The first professional painter that I had come across in childhood was Harry Webster, who looked the part – a contrast with the conventional social circle of my parents in Essex. He and his family remained my friends as they moved around the country where he had teaching jobs. The vibrant colours and dense textures of Webster's oil paintings were good to live with and I acquired a few.

Knowing he was over 80 I suggested to Harry one day that we should organise a retrospective exhibition, perhaps for his 85th birthday. When he told me he was already 86 I decided there was no time to lose! My brother-in-law had created a fine exhibition space in the upper storey of one of his Suffolk barns. After some effort, over 80 of Harry's works, some for sale but mostly borrowed from happy owners, were arranged chronologically. They glowed against the warm brick and were much admired. I produced a catalogue.

Celebrations included a cello piece by one of Harry's three exceptionally talented musical grandsons (whom, thanks to a friend with contacts with the Rayne Foundation, I had been able to help over tuition fees). The painter and his wife did not long outlive the event, proving the value of doing something in time. Webster might have had more commercial success if he had not so much enjoyed experimenting with different styles of painting, but I believe that his abstracted still lifes and landscapes, scattered now in private homes, will stand the test of time.

Not all the organisations with which I became involved after retirement were a success. The British Empire and Commonwealth Museum developed into a disaster. The idea of such an institution had been that of John Letts some 15 years before, which he had pursued doggedly. Thanks to the generosity of Jack Hayward, who had made money in the Bahamas, a large building complex next to Bristol Station, part of the terminus of Brunel's Great Western Railway, was purchased on long lease, later converted to freehold. Apart from a boardroom with a jumbo painting of the Delhi Darbar there was only a committee of trustees and plans on paper. Having heard about the project from the museum's legal adviser who had been visiting Islamabad, I promised to consider becoming head of a Friend's Organisation although I was reluctant to do this until the Bristol City Council, whose attitude to the museum had been equivocal, gave it support, which they did. Left-inclined, they had originally been reluctant to endorse anything which included the word 'Empire'. My experience in Pakistan had led me to believe that there was as much to be proud of as ashamed in our Empire history.

I was happy, therefore, to become the first president of the Friends and also a trustee. I believed that there were a large number of people throughout Britain who cherished personal links with the Empire and Commonwealth, directly or through relatives, and would welcome an objective story to be told for current and future generations. The problem was to reach out to them. Some would have artefacts to leave to the museum; others might be potential financial donors. We had several good Friends meetings, with increasing numbers. The first speaker was Jan Morris whom I had not met since I had known her as James Morris, *The Times* correspondent on Everest many years before. He had visited me in Kabul and I had entertained him and his wife when I was a Resident Clerk in London. When he had changed sex I was abroad. I had written saying that I had found it difficult to understand, but much admired his/her courage. In 1979 Jan had sent me a copy of her successful trilogy on the British Empire (published in 1973) since when she had been a supporter of the museum project. She gave an encouraging speech. On another occasion David Cannadine, the distinguished historian and Clare alumnus, spoke about the Empire's judicious use of ceremonial. He later became a trustee. I had dreams of appointing regional representatives and holding meetings in provincial cities. Also in Scotland where there was a strong Empire heritage.

But discussion among trustees got more and more bogged down with difficulties of funding, since the museum received no government money. The chairman when I joined was John Hemming, the South American explorer closely associated with the Royal Geographical Society. After a time he retired in favour of Dame Margaret Weston, the respected former director of the National Science Museum. She made considerable efforts to secure core funding from the Ministry of Arts and Culture, but in vain. The project had received new impetus on the appointment of a director, Gareth Griffiths, who eventually put together a worthwhile permanent display, telling the Empire and Commonwealth story in summary form, which was mounted in the Brunel building. I lent one of my Afghan Jezails for a section devoted to the Indian Empire. Researchers had tracked down the original soldier in the East India Company from whom the Afghans had stolen the firing mechanism. The exhibition was opened by Princess Anne, who typically took trouble to pay attention when shown round the exhibits and changed some of her pre-drafted speech accordingly to take account of what she had seen.

By this time I had handed over the presidency of the Friends to John Raisman, former head of UK Shell, whom I had known back in Tokyo and who had begun to take an interest in the project. In fact, at the time of the opening of this exhibition he took over the chairmanship. No one could have been better qualified. He had been born in Lahore and brought up in Simla. His father, Sir Jeremy Raisman, was one of those legendary ICS (Indian Civil Service) men of probity and dedication who had been promoted on merit. He had become finance member of the Viceroy's Council during World War II, in effect finance minister of the Indian empire. Some Indian academics, often touchy about the colonial period, began to recognise what he had achieved, which was gratifying for John.

It had seemed to me vital to develop close relations with the Royal Commonwealth Society of which I had been a member since childhood. I persuaded Sir Michael McWilliam, its chairman, to become a trustee, for which he was ideally suited with his early experience as a banker, as Director of SOAS, and as chairman of the Royal African Society. He eventually succeeded Raisman. It was a pleasure to sit around the table with trustees such as those and Lord Younger, former Conservative cabinet minister and chairman of a major Scottish bank, who was initially responsible for fundraising. (One could hardly imagine a more modest and decent politician. The only time I have been to Winchester School was to attend his funeral, just as the only time I have been to Eton was for Thesiger's funeral, attended by a Masai in full fig.)

The museum earned money from letting the premises for functions and attracted some donations, but none of massive scale to follow that of Jack Hayward. At one of the trustees meetings we were all gloomy about the Micawberite bad news that income was insufficient for costs, when Hayward himself, who rarely attended, scribbled on the table before him and asked if this would help. He passed around a slip of paper which went from hand to hand, causing the jaws of each trustee in turn to gape. It was a cheque for a million pounds! There were plans to develop the whole museum site, perhaps with an additional education building. But approaches to the Lottery cost money and still didn't work. Raisman brought in valuable funds and contributed himself but the sums didn't add up.

I wasn't myself too happy with the first exhibition which I felt, following academic advice, concentrated too much on the worst aspects of Empire at the expense of the positive. I thought it typical that there was no mention of Kipling. I was invited to give the annual talk of the Kipling Society in London in 2003, over which I took some trouble, also promoting the museum. My sister and her husband came as guests. It had been fun re-reading Kipling's poetry and briefing myself on his family connections. Through his mother he was related both to Baldwin and Burne-Jones. I had visited his old home, 'Batemans' in Kent, where some of his books, including on Nuristan, were still on the shelves (inspiration for *The Man Who Would Be King*). Thanks to Hayward his old Rolls Royce was preserved and exhibited there. I particularly liked the inscription on the bench at the far end of the formal lawn: 'It is later than you think', a nice hint to lingering guests! One of my imaginative ideas (I thought) which I couldn't persuade others to adopt was to invigorate the low-earning café that was part of the Brunel building, by calling it the Kipling Café, with vivid murals of my old friends from *The Jungle Book*, Mowgli, Baloo and Bagheera, that would attract children, and some poems, not only the popular *If*, that would appeal to older generations.

In any case, the project was soon to run into the ground to my deep regret. Without core funding, it seemed clear that a national museum in Bristol would never be financially viable, despite bank loan and overdraft. The exhibition was closed and artefacts put into store. Trustees, now under the chairmanship of Neil Cossons, former director of English Heritage, inheriting something of a poisoned chalice, concentrated on trying to secure a new site near Tower Bridge in London. Staff were reduced to the minimum to save costs. It then emerged that despite trustees' warnings about the need to preserve the collections carefully our director, Gareth Griffiths, whom we all trusted and who had worked hard to put the museum on the map, started to sell off individual items in the collection, denying to us that he was doing so. A successful temporary exhibition had been mounted under his supervision on the anniversary of the ending of the slave trade. A further temporary exhibition was scheduled to deal with the Palestine mandate, the curator of which was Gareth's partner, though few of the trustees were aware of the relationship. It may have been to obtain finance for this project that Gareth started to betray all his curatorial instincts by disposing of selected items from the collection to the antiques trade. Some pieces of New Zealand provenance first attracted the attention of people in that country and alerted us to search for other examples of things that had gone missing. The stores turned out to be in disarray.

I felt deeply embarrassed about obligations to people I had encouraged in the early days to present their personal treasures to the museum. We could now have no confidence that these had been properly cared for. Even items donated by trustees had been marketed (but I got my jezail back!). The museum which had once received awards for its exhibitions and activities was now disgraced, as more people in the know began to appreciate what had happened. After a couple of difficult trustee meetings Griffiths was sacked and went to ground. Police were brought in but eventually decided that there was insufficient evidence that they could take to the public prosecutors. The task now became to try and organise a proper audit of the collection, to pass it on to a reputable organisation – the most promising candidate was the Bristol City Museum – and to sell the building to cover the museum's debts. This was finally achieved thanks to hard work by several people.

It was a sad story, deeply depressing for me personally and for many of the distinguished group of fellow trustees. The reason for the museum's demise was not just of course the unauthorised actions of the director, but the refusal of the government or Lottery to provide core funding for a museum which filled a gap in British recorded history, despite the large amount of private funds and donations it had attracted over the years. It was a reflection of the fact that the whole concept had not gained sufficient support, as I had thought it would. I also felt guilty in that, although at times the busy Gareth Griffiths had not looked me in the eye on certain issues, I had misjudged his character. After he left his post a number of letters from me were found in his chaotic office, either unopened, or opened and ignored, which was revealing. I wondered whether he had ever valued my contribution, as he had claimed.

I have been in several minds about how much if at all I should write about my life after retirement. But this and its companion book are meant to provide an account of the whole of my life, not just my working career, and it is now almost 20 years since I hung up my spurs, equivalent to half of my years at the Foreign Office. The foreign policy issues with which I had been involved didn't go away. I continued to keep up with political developments, particularly those affecting my area of expertise, it might be called – Pakistan, Iran and Afghanistan. Certain events, such as the chance meeting with the former Molly Ellis, link with earlier parts of my story.

In the first years of my retirement I was mostly based in London, and took pleasure in playing some part in the local Islington community. I had never had enough time to do this before. I have mentioned that my Canonbury Grove house looked over the New River Walk park. I soon got involved supporting the efforts of a public-spirited American neighbour to clean up the accumulated gunge in the watercourse, droppings of generations of mallards and moorhens, and to keep the water moving by a pump. A series of fundraising events brought the local community together. The council were supportive. I drafted a pocket brochure to help attract 'Friends' (which I found myself doing for a series of other organisations). When the project was completed we had a grand opening by Princess Alexandra, at my suggestion. She charmed everyone as usual, including groups of local urchins who took a little time to grasp that there were other princesses besides Diana. Princess Alexandra planted a tree and watched while fish were put into the water. Thanks to mysteriously good intelligence a heron had appeared the morning before in anticipation! We still see him or one of his kind years later, often so immobile as to be taken for a sculpture. The fish thrive, some grown to a considerable size. It is fun pointing them out, lurking in the summer water, to surprised passers-by.

The opening had been attended by local dignitaries including our MP. I invited the Princess for dinner in my house afterwards. When she accepted I had to have the house painted and new curtains fitted! Guests included Ian Albery from Sadler's Wells and my actress friend Gemma Jones. The owner of a local Islington restaurant, himself a cook, offered to do the meal. It worked out OK, but the food was actually better at a rehearsal I staged a few weeks before. That was one of my most successful dinners, with a good mixture of people: Vidia and Nadira Naipaul, David and Sue Ramsbotham, Susan Howatch and Kay and Charles Saatchi. The latter was less shy than usual. It is of course shameful namedropping to talk about such an event, but on the other hand, thinking back to what my Japanese professor friend had told me about the tea ceremony, a collection of people that are themselves interesting and get on well together, in an attractive environment with good fare, could be said to create a sort of work of art that is unique in time and space.

Just down the road from where I lived was St Stephens church, attended by several of my friends. It was not a particularly distinguished building, constructed in 1839 in the neo-gothic style at a time when more churches were needed for the influx of population into north London. In 1940 incendiaries destroyed the interior. The spire and turrets were later considered unsafe and were partly demolished. I found the blunted spire visually offensive and kept suggesting to those involved with the church that something should be done about it. But I was met with the response, from the personable young vicar and his team, that there were more important priorities, for example the local homeless. Eventually the onset of the millennium induced a change of mood. I was asked to join a committee to see if the £35,000 needed to restore the spire could be found. Fundraising events, including tourist walks in the area, brought the church-going community together. I persuaded Terry Waite, who had helped over British prisoners in Iran, to give a talk, with dinner afterwards. He spoke about coping with loneliness, about which, as an ex-hostage, he was well qualified. His talk was the first of what we hoped would be a series of 'Canonbury lectures' bringing in a wider group of people. I gave a talk myself on 'A Diplomat's Experience of Christianity and other Faiths', later repeated at Ely. People to whom I sent copies were kind, including Runcie and Bishop Stephen Platten, who had accompanied Runcie to Pakistan. I treasure a long and beautifully hand-written letter from the Reverend Charlie Moule, who thought my 'thickly populated' talk 'witty and enthralling'. He asked for a copy to send to friends with the references to himself, which he modestly found embarrassing, cut out. It can't have been long after this that the great man died. A hero departed.

But my main contribution was to go back to Dorothy Sayers. I adapted a chapter of *The Man Born to be King* for the stage, in this case the first chapter about Herod, the wise men and the birth of Jesus, timed for Christmas. I added a few jokes to the text – not approved by the Dorothy Sayers Society, who otherwise admired what we were doing. I spent weeks as director going through the moves with the cast of local people who had mostly no experience of acting. The church was turned into a theatre set. The vicar, a dab hand with saw and hammer, built a structure of arches, at the centre of which Herod's throne replaced the altar. My cousin Susan painted a backdrop for the sort of scene which Herod might have observed from his balcony. The vicar of Trumpington allowed me to cart away sheaths of corn and sacks of seed left over from harvest festival to decorate a shepherd's cottage on one side. The trunk I kept at the end of my bed contained many of the appropriate oriental costumes.

The wife of my youngest nephew, who is a talented milliner, produced a splendid globular crown for Herod, the pattern of which I had seen in the Jewish Museum in Prague. I was proud of the props I found for the wise men's gifts: a flashy mock-gold casket that I had found at the Camden Passage antiques market, a silver urn for frankincense that had been a farewell gift from a Pakistani friend in Karachi and an ancient earthenware pot for the myrrh that I had found in the ruins of Gorgan in Iran. The page who had to carry it was intrigued, and a little nervous, to know that it was almost 1,000 years old.

I took the best part of Herod (of course) as I had done many years before as a child. The essence of Dorothy Sayers' story is that Herod, a remarkable individual who established himself as head of a Jewish kingdom under Roman auspices, defending the edge of the Empire, was determined not to give the Romans any excuse for taking over and was therefore anxious to suppress any local disturbance, such as might be stimulated by stories of the birth of a messiah. Thus massacre of innocents. I enjoyed doing research for the programme notes and became quite an expert on the old king. It may be surprising that the temple he built at Jerusalem was in its day one of the most striking buildings in the whole of the Roman Empire.

The production was only put on for a few nights. (It included music by the church pianist as well as passages on guitar by a friend who was a professional Jewish cantor, appropriate for Herod's court.) It was not perfect but everyone enjoyed themselves. St Stephens' spire was eventually restored and stands proud, surrounded by turrets and topped by an elegant cross. I confess I still get a warm feeling when I see it. I contributed substantially. It was consecrated by the Bishop of Stepney, John Sentamu. He gave a talk about his own experience in Uganda, as part of the lecture series, describing how as a judge he had been on the point of being executed by President Amin for not favouring the latter's family. Saved, if I remember, by a lunch break. I don't think even he would have known how quickly, in his second career, he himself would go on to become, after Stepney, Bishop of Birmingham, and then, after only a few years, a popular and highly regarded Archbishop of York.

Before the scaffolding on the spire was taken down, a few of us were invited to climb to the top where we had a panoramic view, which included the structure of the new Dome on the Thames. That Dome was something with which I tried to become involved. It was another example of a brilliant idea of mine which ran into the sand! I found it exciting to be alive at the time of the run-up to the Millennium. I thought it absolutely right that Britain should mark the occasion with a spectacular building and events. I didn't join those who complained about costs, or who said that the 1 January 2000 was not the right date anyway. I was not concerned about the world's timing machines going on the blink. I supported the concept of a great dome created by one of our most distinguished architects, on a loop in the river Thames accessible via the new Jubilee underground line.

I had a proposal for what should go into it. Having tossed some ideas around with friends I wrote to the minister responsible, Peter Mandelson, in August 1997 suggesting that the Dome should, of course, contain exciting displays about the future, but that we shouldn't neglect the past. After all the Millennium marked a measurement of time originating in the past. It was an appropriate occasion to understand the past in order to plan for the future. I suggested that a spectacular multi-media display should be mounted in the Dome with a vivid, dramatic and scholarly correct depiction of the history of the human race, with the rise and fall of the great civilisations (Toynbee influence), including the birth and spread of the great religions all over the world. I envisaged huge multi-screen maps of the world showing the extent of great empires, against the measurement of time. Actors might appear in costume at certain points. All modern techniques would be used. There might be three two-hour sessions, which could occasionally, like Peter Brook's *Mahabharata* in Paris, be shown in succession. Britain had the scholars and media experts to do this well. It would be educational for children.

Mandelson politely acknowledged my 'interesting ideas' which he passed to Jennie Page, chief executive of the Millennium Company, so that 'it could be fed into the creative process'. In the meantime I had secured support from a variety of specialists in different fields: politicians, churchmen, archaeologists, etc. I quoted this at the end of August when I wrote to Miss Page asking if she had had time to look at my proposals. I pointed out that the project would not only give importance to Christianity (we were marking the birth of Christ) but would be an opportunity to highlight Britain's contribution to history through parliamentary democracy, the Industrial Revolution, and the creation of probably the most extensive empire that the world had ever seen, followed by its mostly peaceful transition to a Commonwealth of independent states. In September I got a reply pointing out that finances were limited. Research had shown that the general public was more interested in the future than the past, which was already well covered in museums!

At this stage if I had been a Letts or a Wakefield I would have hawked my ideas around in a wider circle, including the scientific establishment. Prominence could of course be given to Newton, Darwin and Crick and Watson. A further letter to Mandelson at the beginning of 1998 achieved an apologetic reply later that summer saying that the plans were now well advanced for the Dome content and it was unlikely that my specific proposals could be included. After Mandelson's resignation because of the Hinduja affair (which was unnecessary), Charlie Falconer, a neighbour in Islington and personal friend of Mr Blair, became the new minister responsible for the Dome (his son had been one of the pages of the three kings in the church play). When I wrote to him in January 1999 suggesting that my previous proposals would have fitted in with Britain's claim to be the 'home of time', since clocks were then calibrated from Greenwich, he replied apologetically talking about pressures of space in the Dome.

I report all this because I do think that my ideas might, just might, have made the Dome contents more significant, worthwhile and popular. I still think it a magnificent structure. The opening ceremony was, of course, a disaster. This was mainly because of incompetence in arranging security checks for journalists so that they arrived late, disgruntled and fired up to criticise. Excruciating scenes of the Queen and the Duke being obliged to hold hands in a ring with the Blairs didn't help! The story became mockery and waste.

Unlike many critics I made a point of visiting the Dome myself, and rather enjoyed the experience. I thought that the central dramatic display, including acrobatic ballet on a high trapeze, was brilliant. The separate pavilions around the ring produced by individual companies and organisations were, however, with few exceptions, a disappointment. There would have been plenty of room for the Barrington project! I was surprised that for so many years afterwards no use was found for the Dome, while maintenance was expensive. It needed an American entrepreneur to see its potential and turn it into one of the world's most profitable arenas. It fills a gap, bigger than a theatre and smaller than a stadium, and can now claim to be one of the best comedy, sport and music centres in the world. You will not be surprised from this to learn that I have also been a supporter of the Olympics in London.

When people showed interest in how often I went back to countries where I had served I would point out that now that I was back at home it was a good opportunity to learn more about my own country. Because home postings had usually been demanding I hadn't taken sufficient opportunity to see other parts of Britain. In the course of visiting friends and relations round the country I now saw, for the first time, the inspiring Eden Project in Cornwall, the village of my ancestors near beautiful Tenby in south Wales, the Wordsworth Cottage and Centre in the Lake District and the home of the Brontes near Bradford. I stood at the feet of the magnificent modern sculpture of the Angel of the North, marvelled at the colourful full-length Zurburan portraits of Jacob and Sons in the Bishop of Durham's Palace at Bishop Auckland and the elusive medieval chapel at the heart of Durham Castle. I visited Lindisfarne and the Farne Islands and sections of Hadrian's Wall. I revisited prehistoric stone sites at Stonehenge and more accessible Avebury as well as many country houses and gardens, most well preserved. For the first time I visited the Isle of Wight, including Queen Victoria's favourite Osborne House, with its Indian connections. I was surprised how many Roman villas have now been preserved in England. I walked round the walls of the two cities where this is possible: York and Chester.

Of the country's major cities I only knew London, Edinburgh, Bristol and Leeds. I came to appreciate Newcastle, Glasgow and even maligned Birmingham. The grandeur of Liverpool seemed faded but Manchester was booming. Most of Britain's major cathedrals were familiar to me but there were pleasant surprises such as ancient Rochester in Kent, nestling under the high castle. I knew Bishop Nazir Ali, scholar of Pakistan origin, Britain's first non-white diocesan bishop, on whom I called and with whom I enjoyed subsequently a lively exchange of ideas, including about Persian literature.

Compared with most places in the world travel by car around Britain is easy, with so much to see. I kept a copy of Simon Jenkins' reliable book on *England's Thousand Best Churches* in my car boot, indicating where it is rewarding to stop if you have the time. Treasured discoveries included stained glass (e.g. Fairford in Gloucestershire), wood carving and tomb effigies. The latter are a forgotten part of England's sculptural heritage. Lists of vicars stretching back into medieval times demonstrate the remarkable continuity in our countryside. Several of my friends had become churchwardens to keep their local village church thriving as a focus for the community.

Further afield I had taken the chance during my working life to get to know Greece thoroughly, and Italy. From Japan I had visited Bali and Thailand, even risking an exhilarating parasail experience on Pattaya beach, landing with perfect accuracy. I had enjoyed a cultural holiday in Istanbul with Tetsuko. I had only limited knowledge of Eastern Europe which was now becoming accessible with the end of the Cold War. I began to understand why everyone loved Prague, whose beauty had survived both Nazi and communist occupation. I also loved St Petersburg where I spent hours in the Hermitage museum. A Russian friend living in the city was a specialist in Persian manuscripts whom I had met at seminars in the UK. He and his family made do in minimal accommodation with shared bathrooms, but could not have been more hospitable. It was a refreshing experience to have such frank and sophisticated exchanges with Russians.

I also made a first significant visit to Vienna where I had good friends, but which had somehow escaped me before. I sensed the aura of that great capital city which had lost most of its hinterland but retained so many treasures, including grandiose buildings and magnificent paintings and jewels. Just as one had seen items in Istanbul claiming to go back to the time of the Prophet, in Vienna one was confronted by artefacts from the Holy Roman Empire some claiming to date back to the time of Jesus. I finally made it with a group of good friends to Oberammergau, where the nativity play in the Bavarian Alps takes place only every ten years. I found the earlier scenes with hundreds of people and beasts on the wide stage greeting Jesus more moving than the end. It was disappointing that Pilate, for whom I always had sneaking respect, was portrayed as a Gauleiter – partly, I assumed, to divert responsibility for the death of Christ from the Jewish priesthood. I joined a rewarding boat trip up the west coast of Turkey, including visits to Sardis, Ephesus and Troy. Plenty of echoes of St Paul.

Eventually I decided to fill gaps in my education by tours, usually with a Cambridge link, to three parts of the world that had been unfamiliar to me: the Mediterranean coast of Libya with its amazingly well-preserved Roman and Greek ruins and associated statutory; China, just before the Olympics, where one could only be astounded at the scale of the cities and the modern airports and roads; and Syria. In Libya there were few tourists. One had no impression of local disaffection, partly because there was building going on everywhere. China was exhausting because there was so much to see including the terracotta warriors at Shan. The Great Wall, which we visited at an uncrowded spot, lived up to its reputation. The Chinese we met were self-confident, superstitious and money-orientated, but none had brothers or sisters. We wondered if lonely families in tower blocks might lead to social problems in the future. Syria I visited over Christmas, including a heart-warming visit to a monastery in the dry hills accessible up 150 steps, presided over by a friendly Jesuit father. Damascus had, of course, been the first great imperial Islamic capital but it was easy to forget that the area had also been an important part of the eastern Roman Empire and was full of Roman remains. Arriving over the desert at dusk to see the illuminated ruins of Palmyra was suitably dramatic. Syrians told us that they liked their new President Bashir Assad, since he was a great improvement on his ruthless father and psychopathic elder brother. In view of later political developments I was fortunate to be able to make these visits to Libya and Syria. A bonus on the Libyan trip was the participation of the wise and genial Sir Adrian Cadbury, with his wife, former chairman of the famous chocolate firm. He had been a promoter of ethical corporate governance and a benefactor of Cambridge University. Definitely hero material. The takeover of his family company with loss of its distinctive Quaker ethos later greatly distressed him.

An area of tourism that I came to find particularly attractive was safari holidays in Africa. My nephew Andrew with his wife and family were living in South Africa where I enjoyed a spell nearby in a camp in the Kruger, supplemented by a stay in Cape Town hosted by my old Repton and Clare schoolfellow Robin Steward. I had never wanted to visit South Africa during apartheid. I visited several safari sites in Botswana. Best of all was the open countryside of the Masai Mara in Kenya, where I took advice from godson Richard Harney. It was a great experience living in a luxury tent with modern bathroom attached, and excellent food. There was always something interesting to see during the morning and evening expeditions. The direct experience cannot be compared to seeing wildlife on film, however superbly that is now produced. It is extraordinary that wild animals appear to see vehicles as no threat and to ignore the presence of such onlookers. (It is not the same, of course, if you descend to take a photograph!) I remember on one occasion watching a group of cheetahs having just made a kill on an antelope. One by one vultures descended from the sky eyeing them with attentive greed. If they started to get too near the cheetahs would chase them away, like the old game of grandmother's footsteps. Eventually the big cats had had their fill and vultures plunged in, with a couple of storks. Then we noticed, from behind our vehicle, a hyena galloping towards the scene tearing into the middle of the fray and running off with a large part of the carcass. One never knew what to expect.

There was attractive and interesting wildlife to be found also in the Seychelles, beautiful islands in the centre of the Indian Ocean, and above all in the Galapagos in the Pacific. My tour there started with a few days in Quito, the capital of Ecuador, full of old Spanish churches. While waiting for the flight on to the islands, our group couldn't fail to be amused at an advertisement for local 'Icarus Airways', which didn't sound very promising given the fate of that classical character! Once on the Galapagos we stayed in a hotel and went out on daily sea trips. The islands were not beautiful in themselves but the way the local wildlife seemed completely impervious to human presence was amazing. The stars were the albatrosses, the giant tortoises and blue-footed boobies, a form of gannet so fast and aerodynamic when diving in the sea for fish, but on land almost comical in their courtship dances at one's very feet. After visiting the islands it is easy to acquire the habit of talking to wild creatures as if they are companions.

As I started to unpack from that holiday and turned on the television I saw the first aircraft crashing into the twin towers in New York.

14

WINDING DOWN

My reactions to 9/11 and the views I tried to express in the media and other public fora are the only part of my activities after retirement described elsewhere. I was strongly opposed to the invasion of Iraq and apprehensive about our presence in Afghanistan which I thought should be soon ended.

As time went on, however, my personal high-level contacts in 'the establishment', through which I might get views heard at the Palace, Number 10, Lambeth and among the senior civil service, inevitably disappeared. Except for those involved in the quasi-academic societies with which I was involved I saw my former diplomatic colleagues mainly at funerals, and the parties afterwards. Good health was a lottery. I would entertain friends, especially foreign friends, at the Athenaeum, where the food had become better and they liked the traditional atmosphere. Otherwise I would see my long-standing barber Stephen, a source of good conversation and gossip, more often than many of my friends, especially those who lived at the other side of London, say at Richmond or Chiswick. I still enjoyed London, including its theatres and museums. But I began to spend more and more time in Cambridge where social life was more proximate and convenient.

I was lucky in retirement at Cambridge to have agreeable and supportive neighbours, who soon drafted me to be chairman of the local Banhams Close Residents' Association. It was not an onerous job. They included a distinguished novelist, an academic mathematician and a senior engineer, world expert on the structure of Gothic cathedrals. A couple of residents who did not quite fit in were succeeded to our relief by a team who were helpful about everything, including a husband of practical bent who was generously ready to fix minor household problems.

I was also fortunate in the current Fellows of Clare. Contrary to some misconceptions, I found academics very much interested in the world's problems, not living in ivory towers. I was initially in demand for talks about Islam, Afghanistan and Pakistan and had no difficulty in convincing people of my own views, for example on the invasion of Iraq. An accessible source of authority on Islam was the series of books by my Pakistani friend Akbar Ahmed, whose wife was from the Swat ruling family. He had been political officer and anthropologist in Pakistan, academic in Cambridge and (a risky move) Pakistan High Commissioner in London. He has ended as a successful pundit at the American University in Washington DC, a valuable spokesman for better understanding of moderate Islam, and for Abrahamic interfaith cooperation.

Cambridge was full of elderly people with interesting pasts and young ones with promising futures. I came to know a succession of students at Clare who were bright and open-minded, coming from a variety of backgrounds. The Dilettante Society helped. One of the contributions I was able to make was, perhaps, to organise a series of parties in my little house overlooking the river to which I invited both students and professors. I included children and even grandchildren of old friends, when I found out that they were at Cambridge. Most students were, of course, a couple of years younger than I and most of my colleagues had been in the 1950s, since we had had to do National Service. Many young people were grateful for the chance to mix with older members of the university. The same applied in reverse. Senior members would tell me how delighted they had been to talk to students in an informal setting.

It was not an exaggeration to say that among academics in Cambridge were people of the utmost international distinction. One came into contact with a sprinkling of Nobel prizewinners. One Clare Fellow, Tim Hunt, gave a talk at a College alumni gathering on 'How to win a Nobel Prize', with a charming light touch. Modesty usually accompanied distinction. A typical example was a scholar whom I had sat next to at a lunch in Trinity and was introduced to me as Sir Andrew Huxley. He was a Nobel prizewinner, half-brother of Julian and Aldous, a former master of Trinity and president of the Royal Society and member of the Order of Merit, but you could not imagine a more unassuming individual. He came to one of my parties and entranced a number of undergraduates there.

I was interested in talking to Sir Andrew about the Huxley family, since true to my interest, some might call it obsession, with family trees, manifested in Pakistan, Afghanistan and Japan, I began to realise that the interconnecting intellectual aristocracy of Cambridge was unique. The city was smaller than Oxford, therefore a more compact community. I suspect that the intermarriage that took place between the main academic families was because the wives and daughters were educated, ahead of their time, leading to compatible unions. I soon began to collect information about the various branches of the Darwin family and the Keynes (three current Fellows of Trinity were from that family). Also the Trevelyans, Huxleys, the Wedgwoods and so on. They were all linked together. (I discovered such nuggets as the fact that the grandmother of my old ambassador in Tehran Sir Geoffrey Harrison had been the daughter of Josiah Wedgwood and niece of Charles Darwin.) My former ambassador when I was in the United Nations mission, Sir John Thomson, had a brother with whom I had a session, with this brother's wife, to discuss family trees. In each case both their father and grandfather had been Nobel prizewinners! The former provost of Kings, Noel Annan, who had a huge range of academic contacts, had written about Cambridge family connections in his book *The Dons* published in 1999. I hope one day to produce a chart that will link all the names at a glance. Another dilettante hobby.

Visitors loved coming to Cambridge, including family and old friends. There was a good opportunity to invite guests to the two feasts that were organised in Clare every year. Friends from abroad who made the trip to Cambridge were given the Barrington tour which included, besides Clare College and its garden, Kings Chapel and Trinity Great Court. Sometimes there would also be a trip to Ely. I liked to remind visitors of the distinction between Cambridge and Oxford, which was that the Oxford man walks down the street as if he owns it, whereas the Cambridge man walks down as if he doesn't care who owns it! I pointed out that in Cambridge we split atoms whereas in Oxford they split hairs! Unfair, of course, but it is noteworthy that two of the seminal scientific advances of the twentieth century occurred in Cambridge: Rutherford splitting the atom and Crick and Watson discovering the secret of DNA.

Visitors with particular interests would find appropriate expertise in Cambridge. The university was the centre of the British Antarctic

Survey, as well as the Scott Polar Institute, so that my friend Roger Mear, who had walked to the South Pole, would find congenial spirits. Since Birdlife International was based in Cambridge there was someone to meet for Julian Pettifer, then president of the Royal Society for the Protection of Birds. There were plenty of people knowledgeable about animal behaviour. At one time there was a young Fellow at Clare whom I was delighted to discover was a world expert on pterodactyls!

It is only in a place like Cambridge that one can number astronomers and astrophysicists among your circle of friends. As it happened two were Fellows of Clare. I was fortunate enough also to meet the Astronomer Royal, Lord Martin Rees, master of Trinity, one of those men of outstanding intellectual calibre who have no airs. You do not feel ashamed in asking him the simplest of questions. Being invited to his Lodge was the Cambridge equivalent of going to Buckingham Palace. It helped a little that I could introduce Rees to a man of practical experience of space, Michael Foale, British astronaut, whose parents were neighbours of mine. It was fascinating talking to Michael, hero of the Mir spacecraft, on what it was actually like to see our little world from high up in space, the only thing of colour in a drab dark sky. Since he speaks good Russian Michael was in 2012 responsible for NASA's main liaison with the Russian space programme.

Professor Donald Lynden-Bell invited me to talk at a dinner of the Royal Institute of Astronomy Club. I quoted there Walt Whitman's poem which I have always loved: 'When I heard the learned astronomer ...,' juxtaposing academic erudition with the mysterious majesty of the heavens. I cheekily reminded those present about the White Queen in *Alice Through the Looking-Glass*, who maintained that it was perfectly possible, if you tried hard enough, to believe in impossible things (like dark matter!). She used to practise several times each day before breakfast!

I enjoyed the company of Jeffrey and Mary Archer in Cambridge and the crowded summer parties in the garden of their Granchester home. Mary played a major role in fundraising and governance for Addenbrooke's Hospital, which is a city in itself. Lord Archer, who has enjoyed a rollercoaster life, doesn't take himself too seriously. He knows how to tell a good story. The unadorned books he wrote about life in prison shed a revealing light about the British underclass. At one point he planned to write a book about Mallory and was happy when I arranged a meeting over lunch with my civil service contemporary Bill

Norton, whose father had been in command of the Everest expedition during which Mallory died. Despite Bill's apprehension they got on well since Archer had clearly done a lot of homework. One of Mallory's team had been for a time Visiting Fellow at Clare College and some of the senior Fellows had known him. Mountaineering linked again with Roger Mear and the climbers I had met in Pakistan, with Jan Morris, and also with a Clare contemporary Dr Peter Steele, authority on high-altitude medicine and biographer of the Himalayan mountaineer Shipton.

As well as Persian poetry I continued to enjoy poetry in my own language and found that I could remember a good deal of it by heart. When the papers of Siegfried Sassoon were purchased by the Cambridge University Library, partly thanks to a donation from Clare College to which I contributed, I took a lead in suggesting that the College should organise a seminar about Sassoon and his poetry. This took place in the new lecture room linked to Memorial Court. I produced a family tree of the Sassoons, much assisted by a Sassoon friend. They had been a Jewish family from Baghdad who had settled in Bombay, making money there in shipping. Then they moved to London where some of the sons of the patriarch became part of the Prince of Wales' (later King Edward VII) social circle. It helped that I had met Siegfried when I was a student at Clare, though I discovered that a contemporary Nicholas Herbert, now Lord Hemingford, had known him quite well at that time. At the seminar Nicholas gave a fascinating personal account of what it was like to be with the old man, including the strain on nerves when motoring. Evidently Siegfried would drive at the same pace no matter whether going straight ahead, or around corners, or through towns and villages! I contacted the main three biographers of Sassoon, one of whom came and spoke at the seminar, as well as the poet's only granddaughter who made a rare and welcome appearance. Someone had the excellent idea of asking a talented undergraduate to read some of Sassoon's poetry. Clare Fellow Dr Richard Gooder chaired the seminar, providing appropriate academic authority. I have been dilatory in following up but I still hope that a continuing link can be established, because of Sassoon, between Clare and World War I poetry studies.

Everything in Cambridge takes place in surroundings of great beauty, despite the absence of hills. Even mounds are rare. Spring is a spectacular season. A sea of little blue flowers appears by the back gate of Trinity, soon followed by riots of daffodils, crocuses, aconites and tulips along the Backs by the river. The parks are well maintained and often colourful. Each college has its own special garden, some difficult to discover. Clare's is particularly fine, especially in July, perfect for the party I gave there to mark my 70th birthday. The main herbaceous walk is glorious at that time with banks of blue and yellow flowers in different tones, building up on each side to delphiniums and Rudbeckia daisies at the back.

My own little house offers an ever-changing scene, with the river in the foreground and Midsummer Common beyond. There is usually something going on to see out of the window as I take my siesta: walkers with dogs and children, joggers and cyclists. Occasionally brown Red Poll bullocks graze on the Common. Once one of these beasts slipped into the river and couldn't get out. It finally escaped with difficulty on our side, mooing in distress at its companions over the water. Those of us who saw the situation quickly organised a series of human signposts to persuade the errant animal to go around the streets behind our houses and over the footbridge. The joy of the prodigal's return, with much grunting and brushing of noses was a delight.

In term-time elegant boats of eight or four or less, rowing in unison, slide up and down the river. During the races, the Bumps, which take place further down the Cam, they return home either elated, covered with bits of greenery, or slumped forward and despondent. Swans, in their dazzling white beauty, are regular companions. They are at their best in the evenings when sometimes you see a couple progressing proudly up the river with their four or five large cygnet infants in 'V' formation behind. Mallards are common, moorhens rare. I shall not forget one special occasion when my neighbour Jill Paton Walsh suggested that I go up one floor and look out of the window. There, perched on a metal rail only a few yards from my house, was a brilliantly coloured little kingfisher. For 15 minutes I couldn't take my eyes away as it looked sharply right and left and on several occasions dipped into the river, coming up with a little fish that it swallowed. I even wrote an indifferent sonnet about it! I had seen three different sorts of kingfisher in Islamabad, and pied kingfishers on the Nile, but to spot an exquisite bird at midday, right in front of my house, was a treat. I like to think it was a sign of good fortune.

I used to joke that one of the reasons that I had largely moved to Cambridge was that the statistics for expectation of life were better there than in London! The idea actually makes sense, living where the pace of life is slower. I had hardly been ill during my working life, so much so that I fear that I was somewhat intolerant of colleagues with ailments. I have now got to the sorry stage where, when meeting old male friends, we immediately start exchanging news about our respective infirmities. When someone asked the comic pianist Victor Borge what he felt about growing old, he replied 'It is much better than the alternative'! Everyone continues to say that I look well, which precludes me asking for too much sympathy.

I enjoy food and have never been prepared to starve myself to death just to live longer. In fact I have become rather too clever at cooking food that I enjoy. I have always been able to cope with less sleep than others, rather like Margaret Thatcher. But I now sleep for short periods only. The question is then whether there is so much going on in my mind that I can get to sleep again after a trip to the bathroom. I remember my monk friend in Kyoto, Kobori San, suggesting to me that if I should find it difficult to empty my mind of dross as required in the aim of meditation leading perhaps to enlightenment, a good tactic is to concentrate simply on one's breathing since that has to go on. Not easy. In any case I always have a pencil and paper ready to jot down things I remember need doing. Sometimes the first line of a difficult letter comes to me in the night. I often recite poetry to myself. Recently I have been perfecting the soliloquies of Hamlet, a role I am sorry I never had the chance to play.

Sleeping in short bouts has meant that I dream a lot and remember my dreams. I often see familiar faces in incongruous settings. Occasionally the transpositions depicted are so odd that I chuckle with laughter in my pillow after I wake. Who really knows what goes on in our head when we dream? I don't believe scientists have begun to tackle the problem, since there is no financial incentive. There are so many unanswered questions about dreams, as about the mind more generally. Meanwhile most of us put up with senior moments, dignified as 'mild cognitive impairment', which can be serious when, at a social gathering, a well-known name drops completely out of consciousness.

I will draw this rather morbid passage to an end by recounting a happy story. In August 2006 I participated in an enjoyable weekend of celebrations at Trinity College Oxford to mark the 70th birthday of

Michael Thomas, son of my old Repton headmaster. I had enjoyed the hospitality of Michael and his late wife Jane (who died too young) several times at Worcester. At dinner in the college hall I found myself sitting next to a young man working at the College of Arms. It was Robert Noel, the Lancaster Herald. I told him that when I had been awarded my knighthood in 1990 I had been approached by one of his colleagues telling me I was now eligible to be granted a Coat of Arms (at a price). After a few exchanges I had never pursued this. Noel asked why I didn't think again and come and see him in London.

At the time I was exploring Cambridge family trees and looking into my own Barrington antecedents. It would be worth talking to Noel about these matters also. In his office he quizzed me on my own background and interests. Eventually I decided to start the process of acquiring Arms, taking me back to stories of Robin Hood that I had so enjoyed as a child. It would be self-indulgent, but why not? I could afford it. A book plate would be useful for the volumes I planned to leave to certain institutions. My father would have been pleased. What clinched it was when Noel told me that Arms could be granted specifically designating me as son of my father, so that his other descendants, my sister and her sons, could also benefit. My nephews would be able to use my shield quartered with what they might inherit on their father's side.

Over the next six months I had a fascinating series of oral and written exchanges with Robert Noel. Some of his initial proposals I thought unsuitable. Some of my ideas were ruled out. For instance a suggested change in the form of the helmet met the response that this was only (as an example) for marquesses! There were limits on the number of links that could be registered, so some were very discreet. The design incorporated chevrons appearing in the arms of my grander Barrington ancestors of Hatfield forest. Also in Lady Clare's shield. A cross with a tapered tail linked with Belmont and Repton. Four ermine spots represented myself and my three nephews against a background appropriate for the patron saint of metals, my father's business. There were associations with two churches: Trumpington and St Stephens Canonbury. There were obscure indications relating to Egypt, Japan, Afghanistan and the Commonwealth.

I thought carefully about choosing a motto. I wanted something in simple English, not a cryptic phrase in Latin or French. 'With kindness to wisdom and peace' emerged from a solo brain-storming session. It covered what I had aimed for in life as well as what underlies good diplomatic practice. For a crest over the helm the College of Arms artist followed closely my own draft of a kneeling wise man clutching a large book, marked by a crescent, which might indicate Islam or even Persian poetry. He is reaching out to a tower, a type known as a Quetta tower, marked with the cross, on which is perched a dove with an olive branch. That covered wisdom and peace with the aspiration of closer understanding between Islam and Christianity.

Kindness was more difficult. Noel suggested that the cinquefoil symbol of the purple hellebore, commonly known as the winter rose, was associated with welcome, Advent and therefore kindness. Advent linked with St Nicholas. An unexpected bonus appeared when I made a special trip to Paris with Victoria Schofield to view the fabulous Bactrian gold, discovered in northern Afghanistan in 1978 and dating back to the first century AD. I was delighted to see that several pieces carried the cinquefoil flower design, usually turquoise on gold. Kindness, was, of course, appropriate for the professions of my three nephews: a clergyman (care of souls), a vet (care of animals) and a schoolmaster (care of children).

I confess it was exciting when the exquisitely hand-painted and calligraphed parchment scroll, with seals attached, arrived in a long red box. I show it shyly to special friends. Many British people have or could have Arms, but most decent people don't talk about them! Or write about them! There is a special Michael and George chapel inside St Paul's Cathedral on the right as you enter by the main door. When I asked if I could now attach my name and Arms to one of the chapel stalls I was soon brought down to earth. There was a queue! Currently there are about five Knight Commanders of the Order who would have to die before they could offer a place to me! Of course I have no wish to hasten their demise. Of course not!

I am not frightened of death. It is comforting to think that my essence or 'soul' might survive my body in some form. I was once attracted to one of Gurdjieff's theories, that we survive as long as some people on earth still remember us. Good excuse for writing a book. (I have friends who are Gurdjieffites.) In any case I felt it might be a pity if some of my experiences were not recorded in some fashion, particularly since I can boast of no progeny. It is often true that you have more influence on younger friends and associates than you realise. I hope that in my case it will be thought of as positive. Perhaps I may leave some footprints in the sands of time. There is still more I should do to help other people, with money or, even more important, time.

There is no use hiding the fact that at 79 I now savour the beauty of each spring and wonder how many more I shall be able to enjoy. I even think in terms of those wretched management theory targets. For a time I wanted to survive the millennium. Then it was my three score years and ten. (The following passage in psalm 90 is not very encouraging!) I focused subsequently on Prince William's royal wedding which I much enjoyed, where his radiant bride and her family were such a good advertisement for the British middle class. Then there was the Jubilee and the Olympics, both highly successful, making British people feel proud of themselves. After watching the night of three golds for Britain I caught Olympicitis. Credit must be given for the planning and organisation to the ineffable Sebastian Lord Coe, and also to Mr Blair for helping swing the selection of London. It will be tempting fate to get too excited about my 80th birthday but it would be a good excuse for a great party! Or two!

If I am spared at the end, after finishing this book and one or two other tasks, I should love to become a recluse and concentrate on trying to paint. I should need to have a supply of 'Killer' Sudokus to keep my brain active. At least I know that members of my family are prospering, including my eight grandnephews and nieces whose company I so much enjoy. The same is true of most of my close friends and godchildren. Repton and Clare thrive, as does Cambridge University. I am not sure that I can say the same about the Foreign Office which needs to rediscover its expertise and self-confidence and to recoup some of its authority. Would that British governments could refrain from attacking the civil service generally, of which we should be proud. A better informed debate is needed about Britain's relationship with our European neighbours. It goes without saying that I think it important that the UK should remain an active member of the European Union, for political as well as economic reasons. Britain should continue to play a leading role in helping to solve world problems and avert conflict. This is more important for a trading nation than distributing aid, telling other people how to run their own countries, or sending troops when things get out of hand. And if we are to send troops, better to protect our own people in the Falklands than venturing in foreign quagmires in the cause of a Western view of human rights.

I still wish that I had been able to persuade influential people to resolve the Kashmir problem, which would itself contribute to a better future for Afghanistan. The United Nations should be more involved, and more effective generally. I also wish that in countries like Pakistan, Afghanistan and Iran, for which I have affection, sincere moderate Muslims would assert themselves in the face of power-hungry extremists. Wise, enlightened international leaders are in short supply, not only in the subcontinent. Western leaders need to understand better the mindsets of other peoples. My generation has avoided world war but we are leaving behind an uncertain and often violent planet, with the particular current danger of a conflagration involving Islam.

It's a planet we should cherish. The Taliban should not be forgiven for the destruction of the giant buddhas of Bamiyan. I hope that the world's rulers will protect and conserve all the monuments and cultural artefacts that are part of mankind's history. I am not ashamed of my efforts in this cause. Stories about those who secretly saved the Afghan gold and some of the Timbuktu manuscripts lifted the spirits. For good measure I wish that modern Britain could be better reconciled to and proud of the good things in our past, and certainly that the United Kingdom should include the Scots. They have been responsible for many British achievements overseas and I know our friends abroad will think less of us all if there is separation. I also hope that the Anglican Church can solve its disputes and stay united. But hey! These things are now out of my control and no longer my responsibility! Roll on the canvases and paints!

In one of my father's last letters I found this passage: 'I read a good many autobiographies these days and must say that most of them give a very unsatisfactory feeling about their authors. Either they say nothing spicy or indiscreet and sound dull or they give the impression that the writer is too full of himself and makes the reader feel unsympathetic. You know what I mean?' Wise man.

APPENDIX:
PICCADILLY SERMON

TEXT OF SERMON GIVEN AT
ST JAMES'S CHURCH, PICCADILLY
AT 11 A.M. ON SUNDAY,
17 NOVEMBER 1996
BY
SIR NICHOLAS BARRINGTON KCMG, CVO

I am neither qualified nor worthy to preach to, or instruct, this congregation – least of all to pontificate. But the powers-that-be, which means Donald, whom I have known for 40 years (the Revd Donald Reeves, Rector of St James's), thought it might be of interest for me to say something of my own personal beliefs, and value system, after a lifetime travelling round the world in the diplomatic service.

I shall try to be frank. You may know the story of the man in a balloon lost in a fog 100 feet up in the air. Seeing a man down below, he asked, 'Where am I?' The answer was: 'You are in a balloon 100 feet up in the air.' 'Excuse me,' he said 'are you a diplomat?' 'How amazing,' was the response, 'how did you know?' 'Because what you said was accurate, but completely useless!' In fact I was more frank than most as a diplomat. And now I am retired and entirely my own master.

A good diplomat should, of course, learn as much as possible about the history, culture and religion of the country where he serves, as well as its politics and economics. And living abroad gives one an objective view of one's own country. Often one appreciates it more.

I am proud to be British; of the society we have made here, and our achievements overseas. I am also proud to be European – though this seems strangely unfashionable in some quarters nowadays. I knew Jean Monnet, who is one of my heroes. Building co-operation among European nations who nearly destroyed themselves and others in two world wars is a very positive development in my view. Another hero, whom I met originally in Afghanistan, was the historian Arnold Toynbee. He encouraged me to think of world history on a grand scale: the rise and fall of civilisations. I take delight, as he did, in the rich diversity of cultures throughout our world, past and present. I have enjoyed sparks of immediate rapport and friendship with people of different age, sex, race, language, nationality and religion round the world. I am proud also, therefore, of being a citizen of the world.

In his last book, *Mankind and Mother Earth*, Toynbee reminded us what a tiny finite space and time-scale had provided the arena for human development. What he calls the 'Biosphere' is a very thin film round this minor planet of ours, where gravity and atmosphere allow humans to live or fly or dig a small way into the earth.

The life of this beautiful old church and this city is insignificant, of course, in the total of existence on earth as we know it. It was over 60 million years ago that dinosaurs roamed here. It took millions of years for humanoid apes to develop fire, tools, language. Recorded history in the alluvial valleys of the great rivers started about 5,000 years ago. I served in Egypt: the pyramids, whose grandeur has hardly been surpassed, were built much longer before Christ then we are after Christ. The study of world history leads to appropriate humility.

Spatially we are a minute fleck in a universe, whose limits, if they exist at all, are so vast as to be difficult to conceive. The latest galaxies discovered, and they often discover new ones, are over ten billions of light years away. Other habitable biospheres with intelligent beings may exist, but it could take humans breeding several generations inside fast rockets to reach them, and it seems unlikely this will happen. Scientists have done much to discover the microcomposition of matter (electrons, quarks, photons, gluons, etc. – I have read my Stephen Hawking – I have also heard him lecture: what a triumph of willpower and intelligence over physical disability!), although there are areas of which they still know very little – such as the brain, and the source of that other world of dreams, for example. But even the greatest astronomers and astrophysicists admit how little they really know of the origin and scale of the universe. We may never know. Hawking claims that a big bang took place 10,000 million years ago. But how accurate can that mathematical calculation be? And who started the big bang?

If space is almost unending, where is God? It was John Robinson, Dean of Clare College, Cambridge, when I was an undergraduate there, who suggested that God was unlikely to be the white-bearded patriarch sitting in the clouds, depicted so vividly by Michelangelo. The three-storey concept of Heaven up there and Hell in the bowels of the earth could be discarded. Wisely. I remember a teacher at school telling us how terrified he had been as a small boy when told that if he was good, when he died he would go up to Heaven, and sit on a cloud, and play a harp, for EVER!

But if God is not up there, or out there, where is He? or She? or It? Robinson wrote of God as 'depth', as 'ground of our being', as 'love': 'the reality undergirding and penetrating through creation'. Not easy concepts. According to a letter in *The Times*, an American Unitarian, fed up with discussion about changing references to God as male in the Bible, said he used to preface his prayers: 'To whom it may concern'!

I am sure there are things we humans will never be able to grasp, including the real nature of God. I have often used the metaphor of the five blind men and the elephant, which may be familiar to you: one felt the leg and thought it was a tree, another the tusk and thought it was a spear, another the tail and thought it was a rope, etc. They each had a portion of the truth but none could conceive of the remarkable whole that is an elephant. I think this a fair image for the great world religions, perhaps even scientific disciplines and other human perceptions, all reaching for the truth through different paths. Each may have validity, though I would argue, as a Christian, that ours is the closest vision. Full understanding will remain impossible for ordinary mortals. As the Qur'an says, 'We have been given to know very little' (Surah 17). Bertrand Russell once said that 'the trouble with the world is that the stupid are cocksure and the intelligent are full of doubt'. Omar Khayyam, renowned as the greatest all-round scientist and scholar of his age in eleventh-century Iran, argued that we know only for sure that we live and will die. If God is good why does he make us, as a potter makes a pot, and then smash us to pieces? Why indeed does a good God allow such suffering in the world? Is the Creator perhaps dead?

What helped convince me to the contrary was the positive achievements and attributes of mankind, and the sublime moral heights of which humans are capable. I have been particularly swayed by the products of man's creativity: The bust of Nefertiti in Berlin, the proportions of the Parthenon, our inspiring Gothic cathedrals, the Sistine Chapel, Zen gardens in Kyoto, the magic of the Taj Mahal (which I have seen from every angle at all hours of the day), even the mountainous walls of steel and glass in New York's 6th Avenue. And of course the literature, the music, the lives of great thinkers and saints, the Bible and the whole witness of the Christian Church. I don't believe all this happened by chance. I know it didn't start by itself. Some outside intelligence is involved.

Mr Dawkins, author of *The Selfish Gene*, on the other hand, claims that Darwinism provides the answer to all existence, and that science and religion are incompatible. 'The universe we observe,' he wrote, 'has precisely the properties we should expect if there is, at bottom, no design, no purpose, no evil and no good, nothing but blind pitiless indifference.' I don't agree. I do not believe that the love, kindness, appreciation of truth and beauty shown by man are just part of his animal inheritance. We are not a mechanical universe on autopilot. It is rationally more likely, in my view, that there is some outside creator and observer. It is arrogant and wrong to say that things that can't be explained by science don't exist.

For myself, therefore, I have become first and foremost a theist. I believe in a God who we cannot fully comprehend but who cares about us, a God who is aware of my personality and yes, will allow it to survive death in some form. Admittedly that part is gut belief, rather than any rational balance of probabilities. I believe in a God one can talk to. Do you remember St Teresa of Avila who was nearly drowned by a flood, and exclaimed to God, 'If this is how you treat your friends, no wonder you have so few of them!'? I suppose that saints have the right to speak frankly!

I consider that those who do believe in a God, and in spiritual values, have something very important in common. I feel more in tune with them in many ways – be they Arabs or Tibetans or whatever – than with members of my own background and culture who do not believe. I call myself a Christian, advocating ecumenism while most comfortable personally as a middle-of-the-road Anglican. But I have respect for other religions. One of the men I have most admired in my life was a Zen Buddhist monk in Kyoto who had achieved such balance in his character and harmony with his surroundings that he emanated positive goodness (and humour) as if he were the source of some physical vibes. You may have had similar experiences in the presence of certain people. It was interesting that he agreed it was important to help people, but even more to keep spiritual truth and values pure and preserved for future generations. He taught me not to worry about the past (it's over), nor the future (if something needs to be done, do it), but to concentrate on doing as well as possible the activity of the moment.

Of course the contemplative mystic approach traverses many areas of belief. It is little known how much tolerance and love is displayed by those in the Islamic mystic tradition, the Sufis. One such holy man put a notice above his door: 'Anyone who comes to this house, give him bread to eat whatever his faith. If Almighty God has given him a soul, he deserves at least some bread from me.' I have served in several Muslim countries. Stereotypes are very misleading. Extremists certainly exist, some violent. Usually their actions do not flow from Islam itself but from resentment towards the West. But there are millions of devout Muslims who are not only upright and humane, but respectful of Christianity. They revere Jesus, who is one of their prophets, though they think that he did not die on the cross but was spirited away. Most Muslims take their religion very seriously. Compare how many, of all social groups, take no food or drink during daylight hours for the whole of the month of Ramadan, with the number of Christians who make any sort of sacrifice during Lent. Or any sacrifices at all, come to that.

The media, I'm afraid, helps distort our view of Islam by inviting extremists to be its spokesmen (to create, as they might argue, good controversial television). We should hear more from moderate representatives like my friend Dr Akbar Ahmed, who writes that Muslims and Christians 'must cease to look at each other with suspicion and intolerance. The differences need not be a basis for misunderstanding, they can be a platform for mutual enrichment.' In my view followers of the major world religions should indeed concentrate more on what they have in common (or can learn from each other) rather than on what divides them. In the current world situation, overshadowed as we are by political and ecological crises, building bridges of understanding with adherents of other religions, particularly with our Muslim neighbours (and compatriots), must be important. I have been trying to do my bit in this respect, working with the Cambridge Divinity Faculty. They are expanding their study of other major world religions, while not diminishing study of Christianity.

Of course for Christians the role of Jesus is crucial. Someone with an advertising mindset put up a notice outside a church that read 'Christ: liar, lunatic or Lord'. There is logic in that, for, given the life he led and the manifest perfection of his moral teaching, Jesus could *not* have been a charlatan or a madman, but was rather therefore what he said he was: 'He who has seen me has seen the Father.' I believe that Jesus' life was a unique phenomenon at a historical time and place: God, showing us what He is like, as far as he can, in the form of a man. Ancient human beliefs about death and rebirth described in *The Golden Bough*, *The King Must Die*, and in the Osiris legend in Egypt, do not detract from the story of God's suffering, in the form of Jesus on the cross, for our sins. Redemption through grace. Those who know about Jesus are fortunate. I don't believe that those who don't know are damned. For me Jesus is God, is Allah, is Buddha, etc. though that may not sound very orthodox.

The essence of Jesus' teaching was of course loving kindness to all people. Thinking about other people and acting accordingly. That ethic corresponds to innate feelings of most of us about what is right, as well as a reasoned assessment of what is most likely to ensure the survival of the human race. I am not just talking of private behaviour. Unless mankind adopts better standards of compassion and consideration for others, violence and greed could lead in the not too distant future to the destruction of human civilisation. It is time for all of us to wake up. I'm not sure we can rely on God to save us if we don't earn his love.

When I was invited to speak at school speech days in Pakistan, where I was Ambassador, I would offer at the end six pieces of advice.

1. Be enthusiastic (have a go, you never know what chance may bring you).
2. Be honest (which includes owning up, and not cheating the Government).
3. Keep fit.
4. Learn as much as you can.
5. Have confidence in yourself.
And
6. Be kind.

That means being generous with your time as well as your money. Often time is more valuable. Giving time to old people and young people, sick people and poor people. Also thinking of the effect on others of what you say and do. Those of you who have seen that excellent film *Emma* will remember how a thoughtless witty remark can be deeply hurtful.

And for me kindness includes the concept of service to the community, including public service. I know commitment to service doesn't fit easily with the new icons of the Market, competition and selfish money-making. It is not sufficiently appreciated, sometimes forgotten.

I joined the Diplomatic Service not to get rich, but to serve my country, and world peace and understanding. Thank heavens there are still many doctors and nurses, teachers, aid-workers, policemen and soldiers, priests, yes and civil servants, who are guided by this unfashionable idea of service. For some years now the Treasury has insisted on all government departments operating 'performance pay', meaning that those who get good reports from their bosses get more money (it encourages people to crawl to those bosses). I made myself unpopular by saying that it was insulting to me to suggest that I would be motivated in this way by money. I had always done the best I could in any job, and would continue to do so. I'm sure it is the same for many of you. Britain owes much to people who have worked (and died) from a sense of service. We only have to think of the pictures of those marching in the Remembrance Day services last Sunday. We shall discourage such people at our peril. 'For what shall it profit a man...'

Of course one may say that it is easy not to be obsessed with money when one is retired, like me, and without family responsibilities. 'Virtue is easy,' someone said, 'when sin ceases to become a pleasure.' But I believe that despite the lottery, economic and political theorists misjudge the mood of many people, including young people, when they think that we are all mainly concerned about money. Wealth does not necessarily mean happiness. Everything does not have a price. Moth and rust do corrupt. 'They say that you can't take it with you,' said Robert Morley, 'but to be on the safe side I want to be buried with my credit cards!' The simple adage is, however, more true: 'There are no pockets in shrouds.'

After I gave my talk to one school in Pakistan, some bright small boys came up and asked questions. One said, 'You are a successful man. How do you measure success?' Good question! When I was younger I would have talked about the search after wisdom, which I still have as an objective. T. S. Eliot wrote, 'Where is the knowledge we have lost in information? Where is the wisdom we have lost in knowledge?' With all the written material, television channels and now internet, we have far too much information, in my view, and too little time to distil it and think about it. Even the search for wisdom is valuable. At one level prayer can help. For me it is the heart of any act of worship. We have all so much to learn – from God and from other men. And from ourselves, if we give ourselves time to think. 'We search everwhere for the secret of life,' said the Persian poet. 'But what we seek, far off, is within ourselves.' Learning never stops. Casals was once asked by a student, 'You are 95 years old and the greatest cellist in the world. Why do you still practice for five hours a day?' The answer was: 'I think I am improving.'

The answer that I gave to that schoolboy in Pakistan was that apart from progressing in one's chosen career, a good measure of success was whether you make the most of your abilities, talents and opportunities. They are given by God and should not be wasted.

I suppose that my life now as I grow older (someone once said that we all grow older, but we don't have to get *old*) – as I grow older, my life will be based on three main principles: pursuing learning, the elusive wisdom; using the abilities I have been given (and the opportunities) to best effect; and being kind where I can. It doesn't sound very glorious, but I hope that God, our caring God wherever he is, will accept it as my small contribution to human development – as our biosphere spins in infinite space.

INDEX